# PROTEST AND POLITICAL CONSCIOUSNESS

**Volume 49, Sage Library of Social Research**

# SAGE LIBRARY OF SOCIAL RESEARCH

# PROTEST AND POLITICAL CONSCIOUSNESS

## *ALAN MARSH*

*Preface by* **SAMUEL H. BARNES**

Volume 49
SAGE LIBRARY OF
SOCIAL RESEARCH

 **SAGE PUBLICATIONS**   Beverly Hills   London

*For information address:*

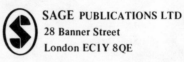

SAGE PUBLICATIONS, INC.
275 South Beverly Drive
Beverly Hills, California 90212

SAGE PUBLICATIONS LTD
28 Banner Street
London EC1Y 8QE

Printed in the United States of America

**Library of Congress Cataloging in Publication Data**

Marsh, Alan.
    Protest and political consciousness.

    (Sage library of social research; v. 49)
    Bibliography: p. 265
    1. Violence—Great Britain. 2. Demonstrations—
Great Britain. 3. Political participation—Great Britain.
4. Political psychology. I. Title.
HN385.2.V5M37      301.5'92'0941      77-8985
ISBN 0-8039-0876-8
ISBN 0-8039-0877-6 pbk.


FIRST PRINTING

# CONTENTS

# PREFACE

*Protest and Political Consciousness* uses the techniques of survey research and the conceptual tools of empirical social science to explore the sources of political protest in Britain. This is an important monograph: it contributes simultaneously to several fields of knowledge; it greatly expands our understanding of protest; it challenges the conventional view that Britain is a deferential polity; it documents the crucial role of psychological variables in mediating between social structure and behavior.

This volume on Britain is the first major published report to emerge from an eight nation collaborative survey research project on the sources of protest in advanced industrial democracies. This project, in which national surveys were carried out in the United States, West Germany, The Netherlands, Austria, Finland, Italy, and Switzerland as well as in Britain, will eventually give rise to a number of cross-national volumes and monographs dealing with individual countries. It is fitting that Dr. Marsh's analysis of Britain is the initial work to be reported, for the British study was the first to go into the field. The development of the survey instrument was the responsibility of the entire group, and pilot studies were carried out in each country. But Marsh took the lead—in the British pilot study—in the validation of the protest questions; and, as principal investigator of the first country in the field, he also contributed greatly to the final form of the survey instrument.

The present monograph introduces most of the themes that arose out of the study as a whole. But this volume also stands alone as a study of political action in Britain. Marsh shows that there is a substantial potential for protest in Britain, and he challenges the view that British political stability results primarily from deference toward leaders on the part of the masses. Since the publication of Walter Bagehot's *The British Constitution* almost a century ago, deference has been a key concept in explaining the smooth functioning of the British political system. The works of Richard Rose, Gabriel Almond, Sidney Verba, Harry Eckstein, and Eric Nordlinger all reflect, in varying degrees, the impact of deference on scholarly thinking about British stability.

The emphasis on deference has lingered despite the objections raised by the work of Alan Silver, Robert McKenzie, David Butler, Donald Stokes, Dennis Kavanaugh, and others. Marsh demonstrates that, though deference is indeed a dominant orientation for a small portion of the population, a very large segment of the British population is willing, under certain conditions, to engage in extremely nondeferential acts of unorthodox political action.

Of course, the operational meanings attached to "deferential" and "unorthodox" are crucial to the study of protest behavior. The measuring instruments introduced in this volume are excellent for their purpose: they rank respondents on a carefully calibrated scale of actions that range from signing petitions to engaging in violent demonstrations, and they rank them according to their approval of the action, whether they have done it, might do it, or would never do it, and how effective they consider the action to be. These protest potential scores are used with measures of conventional participation and repression potential; the latter recognize that support for coercive measures by authorities is highly relevant for political action. Marsh explores relationships between these measures and indicators of social class, ideological sensitivity, political satisfaction, feelings of personal satisfaction and deprivation, trust in government, efficacy, and others.

Perhaps the most interesting of these "other" independent variables is values. Utilizing Inglehart's original materialist/postmaterialist battery plus a more thorough measure of the same dimension developed for the cross-national project, Marsh shows the strong influence of values on individual political behavior and especially on political action. In addition, Marsh has developed measures of *personal* values that complement Inglehart's *public* values; he finds that there are substantial differences in the ways in which personal and public values relate to political action. The British study is the only one in the cross-national project in which the private value scale was administered.

The British study is also unique in that it includes a separate sample of students. Given the important role played by students in recent protest movements, this is an especially felicitous innovation. While British students have not been as visible in protest movements as those of several other countries, Marsh has some important conclusions concerning the sources of student protest. British students indeed score high on protest potential, and he shows the great impact of values, partisanship, dissatisfaction, and field of study on protest potential.

The present volume is also important in expanding the applicability of social psychology to the understanding of contemporary British life. It demonstrates the great value of this subdiscipline for the analysis of complex societal phenomena such as political protest and its antecedents. The present study documents the crucial role that perception plays in intervening between so-called "objective" social characteristics and behavior; it also reveals the necessity for dissatisfaction and feelings of deprivation to be linked with the political system—to be politicized—in order for them to have political consequences. Simplistic theories that relate protest to crude measures of class, income, or ideology simply do not survive even superficial confrontation with good quality data. The role of psychological variables in the linkage process is immense: *Protest and Political Consciousness* identifies, measures, and analyzes these variables in a highly sophisticated manner.

This may be a controversial book, perhaps more so in Britain than in the United States. Some students of British politics will find it difficult to accept Marsh's conclusions concerning the role of deference. Marsh is careful not to speak of the *decline* of deference; he avoids the pitfalls of talking about change with data from a single point in time. We will perhaps never know whether Britain was once more deferential than it is at present. The picture revealed by these data is not that of a people with overwhelming trust in authority or with a limitless devotion to regular procedures in the articulation of grievances. Assuming that Marsh's findings are supported by future research, we will need new and different explanations for the stability of British government. The traditional view of British politics is shaken by this study. Further findings from the cross-national project will indicate whether Britain is unique or whether it in fact fits a pattern of expectations and political action common to other advanced industrial democracies.

*University of Michigan*                                              *Samuel H. Barnes*

# ACKNOWLEDGMENTS

It would be strange for a psychologist to believe that all the good influences upon his work were known and finite and able to be listed in a few paragraphs. Accordingly, to all those whose influence has been processed through what passes for my creative subconscious to reemerge as original work, I tender my thanks and my apologies for any travesties that may have occurred.

Among those who have been my colleagues and associates, I am especially indebted to John Utting, Jim Ring, Samuel H. Barnes, Ronald Inglehart, Max Kaase, and Hans Dieter Klingemann and to all those at the Institute for Social Research, University of Michigan, who were so kind to their interrogative English visitor between 1974 and 1975. Elsewhere, Edward Muller, Paul Sniderman, and Hugh Berrington each gave unstintingly of their time and creative criticism.

Throughout the study, Mark Abrams has, with perfect economy of expression, guided me away from many blind alleys in the maze of analysis and has given me free access to the most profound single assembly of knowledge in the Social Sciences in Britain: his own experience. During the same time, my Ph.D. supervisor at the London School of Economics and Political Science, A. N. 'Bram' Oppenheim, guided my work with a combination of academic skill, intellectual rigor, and concerned good humor that is responsible for much that is of merit in the following pages.

On the practical side, Mary Agar and her remarkable team of interviewers conducted the fieldwork to a very high standard despite a most demanding questionnaire. The student interviews were conducted by Bob Worcester's Market and Opinion Research International. Pat King coped heroically with a coding schedule of quite unreasonable complexity. At various times, Deloris Meek, Joan Bovis, and Valerie Campling turned illegible drafts into typescript with clairvoyant accuracy.

The (British) Social Science Research Council employed me during much of the period of this study and provided me with a year's leave of absence so that I might take advantage of a most generous fellowship provided by the Ford Foundation under their program for West European scholars to visit the United States.

None of the above is in any way responsible for my errors or opinions.

My greatest debt is to my wife, Maureen. It is easy enough to describe how her unsentimental encouragement of my working habits and her skills in the English language have helped, indispensably, this work to a conclusion. But to give in words even adequate thanks for the full extent of her influence would be quite impossible.

*Chapter 1*

# THE STUDY OF UNORTHODOX POLITICAL BEHAVIOR:

## SUBJECT, APPROACH, AND METHOD

## *Introduction*

This study is an investigation into aspects of the social psychology of political participation and behavior in Britain. The study concerns *styles* of political behavior and concentrates upon what is popularly called "protest" behavior or, more formally, "unorthodox political behavior." A complete conceptualization and definition of what is meant by this term is undertaken in the following chapter, but for the moment it may be stated simply that in this study we are interested in what encourages people to depart from, or feel they may depart from, the orthodox pathways of political redress, and choose "direct" methods of expressing their political views and objectives through the use of demonstrations of various kinds, or taking the more specific forms of boycotts, strikes, invasions of property, or even more forceful methods.

The intention is to provide new knowledge and understand in a field of study which is still very ill-defined. At its broadest, it concerns the large-scale social and psychological processes that lie beneath the apparent rise in the use of "direct action" methods of political behavior during the period after 1960 to the present. An immediate question that should be answered here is: "Is this a legitimate field of academic inquiry in the sense that it is a 'real' area of human thought and abstraction or is it merely an artificial label given to a class of behaviors that really has no roots in any coherent set of beliefs and attitudes?" If the latter, then the topic is probably inaccessible to scientific inquiry of the kind implied by a social psychological investigation.

There are many ways of protesting which do seem difficult to classify in a single syndrome of "protest behavior" and some of them are highly ingenious. For example, about twenty Swedish consumer activists calling themselves "The Merry Marauders" protested about the commercialization of Christmas by each dressing as Santa Claus and cheerfully invading a large department store in Stockholm. They removed large quantities of toys and distributed them to children passing by outside and disposed of most of the store's visible stock before the police arrived. Outside a London theater, police held back demonstrators protesting about the detention of two Russian ballet dancers but actually made space for a distinguished young man in a dinner jacket who was handing out what appeared to be programs to the incoming audience. The 'programs' contained a denunciation of the Russian authorities and their artistic management. In Illinois, an unknown activist called "The Fox" quite often invades the offices of corporations he suspects of polluting the local countryside and the Fox river, and leaves a heap of dead fish or other symbol of pollution.

There are many other examples of fringe protest behaviors which carry no amusing irony. The death of Kevin Gately in Red Lion Square in London on June 15, 1975 (probably the first fatality at a demonstration in England in this century) was the culmination of a series of confrontations between two groups—the National Front and the International Marxist Group—who, from quite opposite sides of the political compass are both much given to political unorthodoxy and are clearly impatient with most conventional methods of political action. Few of these kinds of event can be said to form part of everyday political activity and, being outside most people's common experience, protest may be thought an unlikely topic for study among the vast majority of those who never, as it is said, get involved.

But this is not the view taken here. Even impressionistically, it is becoming more and more evident that protest behavior has permeated mass political consciousness and has become a component of most people's views of the political scene and of their ideas concerning the conduct of the political community. Having some attitude towards protest has become part of our political culture; and this is true even if much of that body of opinion is negatively inclined.

Certainly, this development may have been exaggerated by some, and the idea of the 1960s as a distinct Age of Protest may testify merely to the growth of the power of news media to report such events and dramatize their implications. But other accounts and reviews of this period describe the growing pervasiveness of protest in the politics of the 1960s. There is little point in further cataloging the impressive variety of demonstrations, occupations, riots, arson and short periods of apparent anarchy that characterized the political responses of many people throughout the world, especially the young and members of cultural minorities. In fact, the real incidence of behavior is not immediately relevant to this study because here we make no case for the study of protest on the ground that it is some new mass social problem in need of greater understanding. Truly, the excesses of protest are often a problem to the police and the authorities and to others who may suffer personal injury or damage to their property. But to say that protest behavior is intrinsically a "problem" is to take up an ideologically loaded position implying that protest behavior is *deviant* behavior and, therefore, that such departures from the political straight-and-narrow of the liberal democratic, party-representative political system are somehow all undesirable threats to the stability of that system. On the contrary, the argument will be developed below that while actual participation may be uncommon and hence statistically "deviant" in individuals, sympathy for such departures, and their occasional enactment are normal, even necessary parts of the democratic system. This is not to repeat the cliché that all free men have the right to demonstrate, strike, and so on provided they stay within the framework of the law. Again, on the contrary, "The threat of violence," as Nieburg puts it, "and the occasional outbreak of violence that gives the threat credibility, are essential elements in peaceful social change. . . . Individuals and groups exploit the threat as an everyday matter. This induces flexibility and stability in democratic institutions." And there are few demonstrations even in Britain that do not carry the *risk* of some violence.

If our first hypothesis is true and the acceptance, doubtless to varying degrees, of a measure of unorthodoxy in political behavior is a widespread and common component in the political consciousness of most members of the British political community, then this component, this "protest potential" is a variable that is well suited to investigation by social psychological techniques. It is an attitude, an intention, a belief about self. So too, of course, is the intention to vote for the Conservative and Unionist party "if a general election were to be held tomorrow," and such measures do not infallibly prove to have the predictive properties claimed for them. But our purposes are much broader and deeper. We shall see that far from being a random area of unrelated responses, people's beliefs and attitudes about the kinds of behaviors we call protest form a coherent area of thought that is at once both complex and simple and which coalesces psychologically in a way that was previously unsuspected.

## MOVING TOWARD MEASUREMENT

The author's pilot work for this study was published under the title *Explorations in Unorthodox Political Behaviour* because it soon became evident that an area of political consciousness existed in people's minds that had not been described or measured before. It was an uncharted area of political psychology. Certainly, people had been asked their opinions about particular demonstrations, their feelings about supporting strikes and so on, and it was known that support for one kind of militancy was associated with support for another. But the existence in people's minds of a clearly defined "corridor" of participation in progressively more serious or extreme examples of protest behavior might have formerly been dismissed as an exotic abstraction made by a political scientist who was out of touch with the mundane nature of political attitudes in the real world. But it does exist, and moreover it is amenable to investigation through social psychological measurement in the context of social theory. That is to say, it proved possible to locate, describe, and analyze the position of protest potential within the individual's system of beliefs, attitudes, and values.

A detailed description of the instrumentation of protest potential will follow, but, briefly, what happens is that people tend to place examples of protest behavior like demonstrations, boycotts, occupations, and so on, along a single continuum. At one end of this continuum are mild forms of protest like signing petitions and marching peacefully, at the other end are extreme forms like deliberate damage to property and the use of personal violence. Between these extremes are ordered: demonstrations, boycotts, strikes, occupations, and similar activities. The surprising thing is that such widely differing groups as students, young workers, older middle-class and working-class people all ordered the same examples along this continuum in the *same order* and differed one from another only on the extent to which they endorsed, approved, thought to be effective, or actually might do the act of political protest described in each example. They did so, moreover, without being *supplied* with the notion of a continuum by the questionnaire. They assessed each example of protest separately according to several dimensions of attitude and in relation to several different hypothetical political situations. They were little swayed by these distractions. The dimension was constant, merely some would go further than others.

The development of a measuring instrument is one thing, justifying its use in relation to the principal methodological and theoretical problems of the discipline is quite another. The case for protest potential as a real component of political consciousness will strengthen as the analysis unfolds. Meanwhile, the particular orientation of the study from a conceptual and methodological viewpoint should now be considered, starting with an old and difficult puzzle.

## ATTITUDES AND BEHAVIOR

Dispute over the nature of the attitude/behavior relationship has concerned social psychology for some years, and the controversy has drawn the attention of many researchers in this particular field. This controversy would seem central to this study in which it is proposed to build a social psychological explanation of a distinctly behavioral variable.

Political participation has been used as a kind of crucible test by researchers interested in attitude/behavior prediction. When participation of an orthodox kind is used as the dependent variable, quite high degrees of correspondence between attitudes for and against voting, campaigning, etc., and actual behavior are found (eg., Tittle and Hill, 1967). Unorthodox political behavior has produced far more equivocal results. Wicker's rather gloomy review of the problem picks out, among others, Carr and Roberts' finding of poor relationships between attitudes favoring participation in civil rights demonstrations and actual participation by black students. He gives prominence also to the well-known DeFleur and Westie/Linn series of experiments which showed that young female undergraduates who indicate support for civil rights and promise to be photographed with a black person for an NAACP publicity campaign, tend to backslide when confronted with a real opportunity to do so.[1] Wicker concludes: "It is considerably more likely that attitudes will be unrelated or only slightly related to overt behaviours than that attitudes will be closely related to actions."

McPhail (1971) surveyed much of the quantitative literature assembled to explain participation by (mainly) black citizens in civil unrest in North American cities. He found that only 8 percent of the attitude material collected explained a significant proportion of the variance (i.e., more than 9 percent) in the propensity to engage in riot behavior. He concluded that far more realistic measures involving situational factors were necessary if social scientists were ever to achieve greater accuracy in the prediction of behavior. This view is not uncommon, but many researchers in the field have experienced more success than McPhail. Spilerman, for example, concludes from his study of black protest behavior: "An explanation which identifies disorder-proneness as an attribute of the individual seems better able to account for the rioting." In general terms, McClosky too is optimistic: "The survey method does not restrict the political scientist to the study of opinions and attitudes. Used imaginatively, it permits him to learn something about overt political behaviour as well."

All the essential features of this controversy are traceable in (though not actually originating from) Lewin's formulation that behavior is the outcome of predisposition reacting with the environment or "field" of relevant cognitions perceived prior to the emission of behavior $[B = f(P,E)]$. The relative importance of P and E has formed the basis for much later dispute, especially in the well-known controversy concerning the legitimacy of the latent process of attitude formation implied by P. In this debate, Weissberg points out that the failure of even the most sophisticated attitude measurement of P to give accurate behavioral predictions may be due merely to failure to measure E rather than to any conceptual breakdown of the latent attitude process. Often, E stands for error variance rather than environmental constraint.

Our own pilot work took this problem into account and followed a promising line of development indicated by Fishbein's research. He proposes a model for behavioral prediction which accepts, as we do, that real behavioral dispositions are the nearest approximation to significant behavior that we may hope to predict. His results indicate that, provided measures of the respondents conscious behavioral intentions are qualified systematically by (a) his beliefs about the social norms related to that actual behavior (and not some vague class of behaviors), (b) his sense of positive or negative *affect* toward the behavior, and (c) his judgments about the *utility* of such behavior, then real improvements in prediction will occur. Some of the essential features of the writer's pilot model (Marsh, 1974) have survived intact for use in this main study.

But perhaps a genuinely direct relationship between attitude and behavior is neither possible nor even desirable. It is probably naive to expect that if only our questionnaire measures could achieve the right level of sophistication and our statistical techniques were attuned to the right level of complexity, the behavior of any individual in a given social context and known physical surroundings could be calculated accurately from a knowledge of his related attitudes. Certainly, there is room and indeed much use for improvement where specific behavioral outcomes in emotionally charged areas of human activity are important to predict (cf., Fishbein's work in family planning behavior). But what we are as much concerned with here are "the parameters of behavioral license" that may exist among the population regarding the use of protest methods as we are with the likelihood of action by specific individuals. These parameters of license are the boundaries between endorsement and censure that are extended by the general population to protest campaigners (or, as Gamson calls them, "active partisans") that place popular constraints upon the extent of their use of protest methods. It is against an estimate of that threshold of disapproval that active partisans will calculate the point at which they might forfeit public sympathy for their cause through the unpopular extremity of their methods. It is, of course, the same point at which the authorities will be likely to start feeling confident at exercising their (theoretical) monopoly on legitimate violence because they begin to feel the weight of public support at their backs as they move to oppose the protesters. (This is not to say that either party is particularly skilled at this calculation. The "Committee of 100" of the British Campaign for Nuclear Disarmament miscalculated the parameters of license extended to their Ghandhian "direct ation" techniques used during the latter stages of their campaign; and a National Guard commander at Kent State University tragically miscalculated his own license to oppose students protesting the U.S. military incursions into Cambodia.)

In support of this notion of "parameters of license" evidence is available that changes in mass public opinion will result in changes in protest behavior in the same direction. Figure 1.1 is taken from Skolnick's *The Politics of Protest* and shows how increasing disapproval of the war in Vietnam was accompanied by a surge of protest behavior. It may be argued that both public and activists were responding independently to the same increasingly unpleasant accounts of the details of the war. Skolnick gives this possibility due weight but concludes that the slow but steady growth of negative public sentiment was a major factor in launching the protest movement. The activists sensed a powerful body of disquiet, confusion, and a lack of confidence in official explanations for what Skolnick calls "the War with time

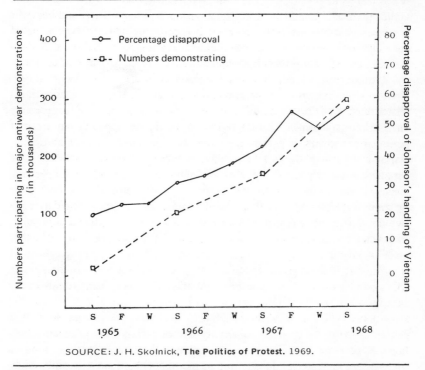

SOURCE: J. H. Skolnick, **The Politics of Protest.** 1969.

Figure 1.1: SIZE OF ANTIWAR DEMONSTRATIONS AND PERCENTAGE OF ANTIWAR SENTIMENT

to think." The American public had no Pearl Harbor to assist an easy identification of the "right" side and found it difficult to identify the "succession of strongmen, juntas and shadow governments" with a democratic ideal in need of defense from communism. Thus they were receptive to counterargument, or at least appeared so to activists who were encouraged to persist.

It would be interesting to know the extent to which this is genuinely a two-way process. W. R. Berkovitz conducted an ingenious experiment into the local impact of protest against the Vietnam war. Samples of spectators and nonspectators of an antiwar protest in a small town in the United States were asked to sign a peace petition and to accept a "peace button" to wear. The "spectator" sample comprised people who were watching or walking past the demonstration; the "nonspectators" were a roughly matched quota sample of people in the same town who had not seen the demonstration at all. Of the total *approached,* more people signed and accepted buttons among the spectator sample than those approached elsewhere. This was not true however, of the total who, having been approached, actually stopped and responded "yes" or "no" to the interviewer's invitation to sign a petition and accept a peace button to wear. Thus, more people deftly avoided the interviewer's approach (interviewers wore peace buttons themselves) when there was no *event* to provide a context for the approach. This indicates that the impact of the demonstration was due more to the attention-getting properties of the event than to its potential to change attitudes.

It would be unwise to dismiss the possibilities of a two-way establishment of parameters of license on the basis of a single experiment. Quite possibly the protest movement had an aggregate effect on public opinion over a longer period. But the linkage that seems most plausible is this: Activists and public respond independently at first to the stimulus for protest conveyed by the media. A few activists respond, probably with scant regard for public opinion. Their response amplifies media coverage of the stimulus and the public responds first by restating their overall parameters of license for the techniques chosen by the activists and then by modifying those parameters somewhat by their perception of the justice of the protest. The enhanced visibility of the movement promotes recruitment but only from sympathizers who already had a high protest potential. The linkage is of course immensely more complex than that described, but this states the main strands of the process.

Eisinger's analysis of racial differences in protest behavior in the United States also suggests a similar socially embedded attitude/behavior linkage. His analysis of community politics in northern U.S. cities indicates that black activists are sensitive to the support of their wider community. Unlike white activists, "Blacks enter protest assured of the broad-based support of their community whereas Whites incur rather higher social and psychological costs and are therefore more likely to be strongly committed." This suggests that the "parameters of protest" of whites are less generous than those provided for blacks and hedge the white activist around with social inhibitions. Blacks are provided with far more permissive models for aggressive political behavior and their legitimate political reference groups have recently embraced the emergent (not to say insurgent) black African nations. In contrast, the relevant models and reference groups for young whites are law-abiding, conciliatory, and consensual: the white congress and state legislature, the white middle-class pressure groups, and so on.

It is being proposed, then, that there exist in the population invisible boundaries of behavioral license that play an important role in regulating the behavior of active partisans in the political arena. Thus, protest potential may be conceived of as a property of both the individual and of the political community. That is to say, personal norms of behavior contribute to community norms as well. It would be unwise to maintain that this attitudinal threshold for behavior is entirely unaffected by the issue at stake or by chance involvements; people do get "swept up" in movements. But again our pilot work indicated that people give more weight to the mode of behavior than the issue in whose cause it is adopted.

Michael Lipsky has spelled out this indirect process in protest movements. Protest *targets* consist, almost invariably, of some agent or institution of authority. The target is influenced, constrained, or actually coerced by expressions and acts of dissent by activists. These expressions and acts are amplified and also modified by the news media and diffused through community reference groups. So too are any responses made by the authorities. This information is compared (by those who think about such things) with the established, long-term norms (parameters) for behavior, and thus emerges an "issue norm" (our term, not Lipsky's), which is communicated back along similar routes to activists. Frequent revisions of issue norms may, in turn, change parameters. It is a very complitcated process and impossible to study through many simultaneous foci. This is why our approach to the problem must be so carefully defined.

So what is more important: to study the individual's propensity to engage in protest or to describe this peculiar species of community norms called "parameter of license"? This study will retain its focus upon the individual. The phrase "a high protest potential" will refer to a readiness of *individuals* to pursue political goals by direct means. If for no other reason, a psychological approach demands such a focus, but it is a deliberately "soft" focus. Our introduction of a partially indirect conceptualization of the attitude behavior relationship serves to emphasize that people do not become mobilized out of a political void. There is a constant interplay between the individual's attitudes and his community's norms.

By way of summary, then, we can pinpoint our approach to the study of protest potential as an example of social psychology applied in the field of political science. Whereas we retain the focus of measurement and analysis upon the *individual* and thus accept the measurement of subjective political consciousness as valid, we conceive of that individual consciousness both a *part* and a *product* of the political community to which he belongs. Thus, the expression of an intention to behave in a certain manner has social and political causes and consequences that must be weighed in the analysis alongside the consequences for individual. In the long run, to try to know *exactly* who might be mobilized in protest behavior is possibly of marginal interest (except perhaps to the authorities) compared with the knowledge of how protest potential becomes concentrated among certain kinds of people who occupy certain social locations and become shaped by critical configurations of social experience and basic psychological dispositions.

## Social Psychology and the Survey Method

The form of measurement appropriate for this kind of study takes the individual as its unit of analysis. The individual's thoughts are obtained about his social condition, his values and ideologies, his feelings about his relationships with other people and with authority, and so on.

The manner of obtaining this information is straightforward enough. We can go out and ask people what they think and feel about protest behavior and about all kinds of other things that we believe may have some bearing on protest. But we do not ask "just anyone" nor do we talk to them in a vague and haphazard fashion. What is required is a sample of the population that, within known tolerances, is representative of the nation and to whom questions may be put in as scientifically controlled a manner as possible. The technique referred to is of course the questionnaire survey and it is the obvious choice for a study of mass political culture.

But is it? Why do we require a survey? Why not wait for the next demonstration in Trafalgar Square and invite a sample of actual protesters back to the laboratory for intensive and, moreover, controlled scrutiny? The nonexperimental nature of survey research has attracted consistent criticism from skeptical social psychologists who favor laboratory procedures, and some hold surveys to be, de facto, unscientific.

Two related criticisms lend support to the view that survey methods are inherently unscientific. The first points out the crucial difference between a "random sample" in survey techniques and the experimental procedure of "randomization," i.e., the assignment of subjects to differing experimental conditions by strictly random methods. Because the researcher can never measure everything, any significant difference between two randomly sampled survey groups or any significant level of association between two variables in a survey analysis can never be absolutely free of correlated errors—i.e., the intervention of unmeasured, intervening variables (see Selvin, 1957). In experimental procedures, however, the initial process of randomization washes out entirely the intrusion of speciously correlated relationships present in the parent population and reflected in the sample. Partly contingent upon this problem, the second point is that variables cannot be explicitly manipulated in surveys but only controlled in post-hoc analysis. This makes the explicit hypothetico-deductive processes of experimental procedure look distinctly soft—even fudged—in the case of surveys.

There is no really convincing refutation of these two criticisms. One may point out, for example, that the lack of opportunity for explicit manipulation of subjects has not handicapped astronomers' claims to scientific status and their explanations of events are 'post-hoc' by unimaginable distances. Or one may explain that chasing correlated errors is actually the procedure through which higher-order survey analysis is conducted. But the point that should really be made is that members of a national random sample have one property that is rarely found among the subjects assembled for an experiment. They are, within calculable tolerances, truly representative of the target population from which they were drawn. It is possible to imagine experimental procedures being conducted upon representative samples, but scarcely feasible, nor even appropriate. Thus survey data go some way toward providing what Katz described as "the naturalistic description of the behaviour of human beings in various social contexts." We have declared an interest in describing, perhaps even explaining to some extent, the "parameters of license" for protest behavior and the location of protest potential in the political community. Only survey data answers these kinds of propositions.

We reach the limits of the explanatory power of survey data when we try to penetrate the actual process of social interchange and behavior wherein the dispositions we measure in a questionnaire are molded toward or away from an attitude-congruent behavioral outcome. As Dowse and Hughes put it,

> the survey tends to treat the individual as the basic social unit. . . . So, in an important sense, the individual is torn out of his social context and the processual, immediate character of much of social life is lost. . . . What is missing, in other words, is information on the processes such as the development of group consensus which helps translate attitude into action.

From good survey data, conjecture along this pathway of explanation is possible. But we cannot see it happen. We will not be present when a group of those our respondents will represent actually decide to protest, and we will not know how they argued their way there. But we will know much about the psycho-social processes that lead certain kinds of people to argue one way or the other. And one cannot do everything.

So, despite some opposition, the questionnaire survey has now an established place in social research. In McClosky's view, it is "the single most important procedure in the 'behavioral' study of politics." This movement has been greatly facilitated by the mathematical strength of sampling theory and the development of statistical techniques and computer facilities that makes possible the use of a very large number of unique responses. Thus Katz's "social context" description may be achieved with some accuracy across a complete range of social conditions by providing the situational background against which the interplay of attitudes and behavior may be examined. However carefully chosen, the subjects of a laboratory experiment cannot provide the same information. It would be sterile to argue that one technique is *inherently* better than the other because each serves a quite different purpose.

And so, attracted by its virtues or at least by its sheer feasibility, large numbers of scholars have been converted to behavioral science through surveys, and this is particularly true in the study of political psychology. "Survey research," in Hyman's words, "seems to rule the realm of political psychology." It is important, though, that some of the more practical deficiencies of survey research in political psychology be briefly acknowledged and discussed to see to what extent such shortcomings may place limits upon what might be achieved in this study.

One aspect of the question of scientific validity, the nonexperimental nature of surveys, has already been raised. Another concerns the remote relationship between the investigator and the manner in which his data are gathered. Can "unscientific" data be put to scientific use? An interviewer going rapidly through a questionnaire with a "C2" housewife who is preparing the family's supper and who is further distracted by three children under five who insist on playing with the show-cards, does not sound much like a scientific event. Nor is it. But when her replies, half-heard by the interviewer above the cheerful din, are coded, processed through the computer, and returned in reams of computer output, suddenly things begin to look very scientific indeed. This impression can be very misleading. Too often, discussions of the statistical properties of survey data give insufficient consideration to the data's humble origins.

Nor is it always possible to improve things after the event. Fothergill and Wilcox's experiments demonstrate, depressingly, that only about 12 percent of interviewing errors can even be detected in the questionnaires. Hyman's NORC studies showed that, beyond a certain point, improved rapport between interviewer and interviewee only encourages the former to make stereotyped assumptions about the latter and place vague and noncommitted responses into categories consistent with the interviewer's assumptions. In this field of inquiry, the possession of strong political views by interviewers could introduce unwelcome bias.

There are three correctives that ease these problems: (1) to employ well-trained interviewers and brief them thoroughly on the use of the questionnaire and have field supervisors check all interviewing schedules on the spot, reinterviewing and checking back if necessary; (2) to have the interviewers record pertinent details of the interview (others present, and the extent of interruption, respondent understanding, and so on); and (3) to have the interviewers themselves answer the questionnaire prior even to briefing, and so provide at least for the possibility of estimating "transmission bias." In this study, each of these was done (see Appendices for details).

In pursuit of this last precaution, some quite fascinating information was obtained. Our interviewers turned out to be a homogenous group of mostly young or middle-aged, middle-class women, who shared an almost monolithic support for the more traditional aspects of Conservative party policy and a firm distaste for any notion remotely left-of-center. If this study should ever attract the criticism that survey effects have biased responses in a politically leftward direction, the interviewing staff must be held blameless.

Problems with the scientific reliability and quality of survey data are intertwined with problems of *substantive* validity and quality. Even if the measurement of people's political opinions and attitudes were as accurate and as "scientific" as taking their body temperature or blood pressure, what would the results really be worth to the accumulation of scientific knowledge? At this level of criticism, the complaint most often heard is that survey data lack any *depth*. Many critics insist that people's responses to questionnaire items are little more than media-conditioned verbal reflexes that reveal nothing of the respondent's real character nor reflect any abiding truth about his social relations. They emphasize instead the value of highly detailed field studies of social relations. This position has attracted an all-embracing label of "ethnomethodology" but is, in fact, taken by scholars having very wide alternative preferences in research style. And it is largely a question of style. Unlike those monogomously wedded to experimental procedures, ethnomethodologists do see scientific validity in talking to ordinary people without manipulating their responses. Indeed, they take this view much further than survey practitioners might and tend to rely upon very detailed depth interviews and minute personal histories to build their insights into the social process under scrutiny. In this way, they hope to avoid the pitfalls of what are often the brusquely constrained category responses of questionnaires. In political psychology, Robert Lane's work is prominent among adherents of the depth interview technique and his work has had considerable influence in establishing the psycho-dynamic interpretation of political thought. But, of course, survey practitioners do not (or at least they should not) make very extravagant claims for the penetration achieved by single questionnaire items. Penetration is not what they are for. Simplicity, obviousness, and accurate (i.e., "reliable") calibration are the virtues of survey questions. Penetration into the social psychological processes that each *series* of questions may be tapping is the task of a combination of statistical skill and scholarly judgment. Depth interviewing maximizes scholarly judgment at the expense of statistical reliability and thus contains all the alternative pitfalls that subjective judgments must imply however learned and informed they may be. Thus, it is more than the repetition of cliché to say that depth studies should provide complementary and not competing opportunities for research. Certainly, no results have come from depth techniques that would support the abandonment of survey techniques.

Yet it would be very foolish to deny that the substantive worth of survey data is deficient in some key respects. Unless the object of a question is very clearly defined, ambiguity will admit a flood of errors. So will sheer unfamiliarity. Even excluding those who Hyman and Sheatsley called the "chronic know-nothings," political stimuli do not exactly seize every respondent's imagination. Questions about matters of state rarely quicken the pulse, and the answers obtained are rarely the product of intense cognitive functioning on the part of the respondent. For example, Converse has demonstrated that a majority of those Americans asked to consider their attitude towards a relatively unfamiliar topic for them—the total nationalization of industry—gave answers in virtually a random manner. Only a minority belonged to that question's own peculiar "issue-public" while the remainder held, if that is the right word, "nonattitudes." In Britain, a polity far more used to hearing about nationalization, nonattitudes also abound. Butler and Stokes have determined that during a single year, 61 percent of the population having views about nationalization modified their opinion in one direction or another.

Other, more concrete, objects elicit more stable attitudes. Political partisanship in the United States, for example, showed a high test/retest correlation of .70, and most change occurred through migration in and out of the independent category rather than switching allegiance between Democrats and Republicans directly. Especially among older people, Butler and Stokes demonstrated similar stabilities for Britain. From a painstaking evaluation of numerous studies, Sears advanced a cautiously optimistic view: "The 'average voter' thus seems to have some clear attitudes towards groups but not much information or many clearly relevant organising principles."

It is not clear whether Sears refers to conscious or unconscious dimensions, but it must be admitted that this notion of "organising principles" of attitude is the stock-in-trade of the social psychologist. In this study, the idea of the underlying structure of attitudes will be put to its customary full use. Yet, the evidence from excellent work by Converse and others is that movements in public attitude that are so easily celebrated by the news media in such handy phrases as "a swing to the right" or a "hardening of leftist militancy" refer to attitudes that reside in a rather low level of cognitive functioning and which exhibit typically human inconsistencies.

The truth is that a good researcher should not expect an efficient statistical performance from survey data concerning political attitudes; a correlation above .60 between two variables will usually indicate that the same question has been asked twice in different forms. This difficult state of affairs is the result of the inefficiency of the data-gathering process multiplied by the inefficiency of people's thinking about politics. The outcome, surprisingly, may still be invaluable and unique data provided certain basic rules of sampling, questionnaire building, and interviewing are observed: that the natural limits of the data are acknowledged at all times; and that these limits are actually incorporated into the analysis. The following account of research will be at pains to reveal these stages of work to the reader's scrutiny so that the quality of the data may be judged thereby.

# NOTE

1. There exists an alternative and, to some, a sexist interpretation to this famous finding. Having been given no notice of the invitation to be photographed, the young women were merely exhibiting a distaste for being photographed unprepared, irrespective of their partner's color.

Chapter 2

# PROTEST IN BRITISH POLITICAL CULTURE

## Understanding Protest in a
## Stable Democracy

The United Kingdom may seem an unlikely site for the study of protest. Whenever a political scientist, particularly if he is also an American, wishes to describe a stable democracy based upon public allegiance, he reaches for the example of British politics as if prompted by a conditioned reflex. Eckstein, for example, regards Britain as the "extreme case of a congruent society" where "individuals are socialized into almost all authority patterns simultaneously," including those of political authority. Britons, therefore, are almost born to political stability. Richard Rose concludes his well-known overview of British political life thus:

> England is outstanding for its durable representative institutions and the allegiance that its citizens give to political authority (p. 399).

And Professor Rose certainly leads us to understand that the first characteristic is contingent upon the second. British institutions work because people respect them.

In Almond and Verba's *Civic Culture* survey, Britain provides the linchpin example of an allegiant democracy. They describe Britain's political stability as the outcome of a curious alchemy. They develop Eckstein's notion of "balanced disparities" to describe how Britain has established an optimal mixture among the polity of a willingness to *participate* in a prescribed manner, i.e., "vote when asked" but little more; of *trust* in the fairness of the system and the essential good faith of those who run it without being entirely uncritical of their actions; of *emotional attachment* to the democratic process as a means of government, and finally, of *consensus*, which is the belief that somehow cleavages within society are partially resolved by the democratic process so that the greatest realizable good is promoted for the greater number.

Almond and Verba try to stress the positive and participatory aspects of the system, but they make it plain that their theory in respect to Britain is an alchemic compound bonded throughout with a single resin: *deference*. Thus, they compare Britain and the United States:

> Both nations achieve a balance of the passive and active roles of the citizen, but whereas in the United States the balance appears to be weighted in the direction of the active, participant role, in Britain it tends somewhat in the direction of the subject, deferential pole (pp. 360-361).

So too Richard Rose: "Leaders in political life are expected to be uncommon men and enjoy deference on that basis."

This chapter will be concerned mainly with establishing the extent to which the British really *are* deferential towards political authority. For this purpose, the idea of *political culture* is crucial.

The study of political culture is the study of the way social attitudes and values shape mass political behaviors. The key feature of the process in Britain is held to be this habit of deference. Leo Amery, fortunately from his point of view, found the British voter "essentially passive." Eckstein summed up the relationship between government and public in Britain by describing a high "correspondence between the leadership's confidence that the public will defer to its wishes and the willingness of the latter to accord that deference," and that "the British expect their rulers to govern more than to represent them." McKenzie and Silver, and Nordlinger found deference to be the key component of working-class support for the Conservative party and possibly also the cause of the timidity of Labour party reformism, which two factors above all have maintained the stability of voting behavior in Britain.

Nordlinger shares Almond and Verba's taste for balance theories and proposes that the balance between deference and directiveness (directive through the proper channels of course) is a more parsimonious explanation of stability than the bulk of the civic culture theory. Although Nordlinger labels his theory "dualistic," what he really describes is a not-very-wide distinction between respectful apathy and respectful participation.

Among political scientists, only Kavanagh has seriously opposed the deference theory, and even he prefaces his views (which are examined below) with the acknowledgment that

> the notion that the British Government is *strong* and the electorate politically docile has, until recently, imposed a stranglehold on interpretations of British politics (p. 336).

Other than Kavanagh's, dissenting opinions have tended to be heard only outside the sphere of the academic study of politics; the most extreme example being Tariq Ali's optimistic title, "The Coming British Revolution."

Thus, political culture theorists hold a majority view that the stability of two-party democracy in Britain rests upon the fact that the average British citizen is deferent towards political authority. He is not cringing, of course, but he combines respect for authority with private dignity and an easygoing complacency that the affairs of the nation are usually in able, well-intended hands.

Such a verdict is both patronizing and wrong and denies the democratic process in Britain the least vitality of its own, as though the power of the electorate were reduced to infrequent and possibly accidental changes in the set of politicians by whom the majority prefer to be told what to do. It is not contested here that deferential attitudes exist in Britain and have certainly been strong in the past. George Orwell describes the horror expressed by the overseer of a hostel for vagrants, who, catching Orwell's Etonian accent among his charges, said that he "did not like to see a gent in trouble" and provided him with some small restoration of his proper station: his own soap and towel. Even after the Second World War, Orwell attached considerable importance to the fact that "Sir" was a word often heard in England.

The habit probably derives in part from the extraordinarily high proportion of working-class people drawn into personal service of the middle classes during the late 19th and early 20th centuries. Every bank clerk could afford a parlor-maid by 1910. In 1900 there were more people working "in service" than in manufacturing industry and in the South East probably most working-class families can claim an older relative who was "in service." But this situation ceased dramatically during the 1930s and 40s and has not been seen since. Whereas social attitudes are certainly durable and are transmitted intergenerationally, it is another matter entirely to hold that this habit of *verbal* deference still holds sway to the extent of being responsible for the stability of two-party democracy.

Nor is the evidence put forward in support of the deference theory especially convincing. Among Nordlinger's working-class Conservatives interviewed in 1964 the "deferentials" were outnumbered better than two to one by "pragmatists"—people who saw in the Conservative party a surer source of the continuation of material prosperity and stable social management than that offered by the Labour party. "Deferentials," in fact, made up only 10 percent of his total (reweighted) sample of working-class voters which also makes it difficult to understand the importance Nordlinger attaches to "acquiescence" as an explanation of stability.

Kavanagh provides an overview of survey evidence which shows clearly, on several separate measures, that the proportion of people giving deferential answers to questions about their attitudes towards political authorities rarely exceeds 20 percent of the total questioned. Kavanagh points out that varieties of the "balanced disparities" theory look suspiciously as though they are trying to have it both ways: People may be politically potent and participatory or they may be passive, they are rarely both. Nor is it ever spelled out by the deference theorists whether this balance is achieved psychologically within individuals or socially and politically within the population between individuals. Kavanagh proposes that the civic culture and related theories have mistaken the proper sequence of events: "Allegiance or support (or deference) is based upon the perceived responsiveness of the system and the elites" (p. 342).

Like everyone else in the modern world, democratic systems of government have to earn the respect they receive. Governments demonstrate their responsiveness, their probity, their competence, and all the other characteristics that modern liberal systems of administration are supposed to have. The public judges to what extent these are present or absent and extends trust, or even deference, on the basis of the extent to which those standards are achieved. Standards may vary, of course, and there sometimes may be confusion between whether it is the *system* that is being appraised or the general competence of the *people who run it* (often implicating civil servants as well as politicians) or merely the ability of those who form the topmost *elites*. This is the distinction that David Easton makes between "diffuse" and "specific" support, and it was the main source of confusion that made political events in the United States during President Richard Nixon's last administration even more traumatic than they needed to be. Reaction against Nixon's lack of probity was quickly transmitted to the political system as well . . . . though not entirely without justification perhaps.

The deference theory derives also from the style of government decision-making in Britain which might best be described as "act first and answer questions in the House afterwards," or, more generously, as "second-stage indirect democracy." The linkage assumed between deference and British governmental style is emphasized by Rosenbaum: "Widespread deference also means that the British do not necessarily gauge the acceptability of governmental policy by the extent to which it results from massive interaction between rulers and ruled" (p. 71). Ministers take decisions and assign their own estimate of public wishes in the matter a certain weight. When the impact of that decision is felt, dissenters (whose numbers may vary as a function of the accuracy of the decision-makers' weighting of public opinion—or their freedom to do so at all) make their views known, preferably through their elected representatives. Referenda and the canvassing of public support play only a minor part in British government. The fact that it "works" is held to be prima facie evidence of deference among the electorate. It may equally be evidence, of course, for complacency, boredom, or ignorance on the part of the electorate, but circular reasoning of this kind does not explain how politics works in the minds of men.

We require a more precise explanation of the means of political redress. One corollary that is contingent upon a deferent electorate will be a very low rate of protest behavior. Since the author is a social psychologist who already has trespassed very far into political science, new research into the true rate and significance of actual protest behavior in Britain will be left to political scientists and historians interested in these matters. Those who have written on the subject report a more widespread use of unorthodox political action than may commonly be supposed.

A group of researchers at Yale University (see Taylor and Hudson 1972) built an aggregate data profile of political events in 136 countries spanning a period of 20 years from 1948 to 1967. Three kinds of unorthodox political event were coded: Protest demonstrations, riots, and armed attacks. The definitions offered for each category are well worth repeating here:

> "A *Protest Demonstration* is a non-violent gathering of people organized for the announced purpose of protesting against a regime, government, or one or more of its leaders; or against its ideology, intended policy, or lack of policy; or against its previous action or intended action" (p. 66).
>
> "A *Riot* is a violent demonstration or disturbance involving a large number of people. 'Violent' implies the use of physical force, which is usually evinced by the destruction of property, the wounding or killing of people by the authorities, the use of riot control equipment and by the rioters use of various weapons" (p. 67).
>
> "An *Armed Attack* is an act of violent political conflict carried out by (or on behalf of) an organised group with the object of weakening or destroying the power exercised by another organised group" (p. 67).

During these twenty years—which (fortunately) stops just short of the violent events in Northern Ireland from 1968 to the present—Britain recorded 132 major political demonstrations which were "perceived as significant at the national level." Sixty-three of these occurred during the 1959-1962 period of campaign for nuclear disarmament (CND) activity. This total of 132 compares with a cross-national median of only 17 such events and elevates Britain to *tenth* place in the rank order of 136 countries, clearly ahead of Italy (109) and Pakistan (108), and just behind Algeria (134), South Korea (136), and South Africa (145). These countries are rarely thought of as equivalent polities to Britain in respect of a scale of domestic political disorder. Even more surprising was Britain's score of 82 "riots"—21 in 1962 alone—still leaving her thirty-sixth in the overall ranking and well above the median value of 34. However, the lack of *severe* violence in Britain is also borne out in the data. A grisly total of more than one million people died in political violence during this time across all nations but only 9 people died in Britain (median = 131) in 45 armed attacks, all of them attributable to what was then residual I.R.A. activity, mostly in 1950. Sadly, the United Kingdom will have remedied her lowly sixty-ninth rank on the severe political violence listings by the time the next World Handbook of Political and Social Indicators is published.

The Handbook also records rates of "Government Sanctions"—mainly the use of censorship, restrictions on freedom of assembly and demonstration, and arrests. Again surprisingly, British governments have been busier in this respect than many others, recording 183 instances of "repressive" activity (median = 95) and are placed forty-fifth in rank-order. One recalls for example some uncharacteristically clumsy attempts in 1962 to harass the Committee of 100 through arrest on conspiracy charges and banning of demonstrations (see B. Cox 1975).

Thus, a simple frequency count does not support the idea of Britain's political stability resting on acquiescence but rather that Britain is well able to compete in a world market for disorderly political behavior. But crude statistics such as these (similar, indeed, to aggregate data that "prove" that American blacks were better off as slaves than as free men) convey nothing of the quality of the events they describe. Historians of a more traditional persuasion have also examined Britain's record of vigorous political dissent and their consensus favors of a similar conclusion.

Cantor's narrative of the twentieth century as the "age of protest" draws heavily upon British experience with protest as distinct from "revolutionary chaos." He regards the suffragette movement as a "prototype for Twentieth Century protest movements" because the movement used coercion and force in support of a *moral* cause. A cause, moreover, in which considerable sectors of the elite in Britain were already feeling morally uncomfortable with their own position. The suffragette pattern of middle-class leadership—strong coercion mostly stopping short of individual physical violence against persons, and strong appeals to justice and morality—is often repeated in British protest movements.

Both Parkin and Driver's analyses of the campaign for nuclear disarmament emphasize these features of "typically British" protest. So too in Hain's account of the highly successful direct action campaign against the visit of South African sportsmen. But it is of significance in itself that a pattern should be set and repeated, and it is itself suggestive that protest is and has been a far more frequent and important part of British political life than is generally acknowledged.

Many writers, especially Critchley and, more recently, Clutterbuck, have been at such pains to stress the *orderliness* of British protest, marked by a near miraculous lack of damage to life and limb, that they somehow overlook the sheer scope of highly unorthodox political behavior. Looking much further back, Harold Priestly draws a common thread of British protest habits from the good people of Redbourn protesting in 1967 for a safe road through that village back to Watt Tyler's "rebellion," which had passed that way six hundred years previously. The fact is that Britain has an extensive historical background of vigorous protest against authority and one which has only lately eschewed violence. Bagehot, who is often quoted as a founder of deference theory, is quoted by Kavanagh for the opposite view: "The natural impulse of the English people is to resist authority" (p. 335). This presumably would also be Hobbes' view since his ideal state made great provision for the discouragement of natural tendencies toward civil unruliness.

The manner in which this "natural impulse" evolved from mob violence and sabotage into its more modern expression in (largely) nonviolent protest is not a central question for this study. But, in passing, doubt must be cast upon Critchley's pious assertions about "unwritten rules" and "playing the game" even though his emphasis upon the value of an unarmed police force is largely correct. The main point to be made is that protest forms an integral part of British political life, and anyone who doubts it is advised to contact the Ministry of the Environment and inquire about the availability of Trafalgar Square for a demonstration; it is usually booked months ahead or it is the subject of yet another official ban. Many of those who often book that site and others are described by Thayer as the British "political fringe," which he characterized in the early 1960s as more vigorous, better organized, and more active in support of an enormous variety of causes than similar groupings anywhere else in the world.

Outside formal organizations, the capacity for informal and often spontaneous "direct action" protest is considerable. Quite prodigious resistance, typically against the siting of new constructions or in protest of the further deterioration of existing amenities, can often build up far more swiftly and effectively than the authorities' capacity to organize a defense of their action (or inaction). Thus, the inhabitants of Cublington protected themselves against an airport, and those of Port Tennant against pollution from the United Carbon factory, and the people of Canvey Island from additional oil refineries.

Another direct action protest movement was undertaken against the Housing Finance Act (the contentiously entitled "Fair Rents Act") during 1972 when large groups of council tenants in more than thirty local authorities withheld rent increases, sometimes with the willing cooperation of their Labour council.

In the case of rent strikes, we have the advantage of one of the very few empirical studies ever undertaken of direct action in Britain. Moorhouse and Chamberlain interviewed samples of rent strikers and nonstrikers in Barking in the London borough of Newham in December 1972 after the act was implemented the previous October. Moorehouse and Chamberlain reasoned that the fact of the rent strike suggested a capacity of the British working class to respond by organizing quite sophisticated acts of defiance against political authority, whereas deference theorists (particularly Clutterbuck) maintained that lower-class people in Britain lack the ideological sophistication necessary for sustained political disobedience. When such acts do occur, they are held to be the outcome of concentrated agitation by extremists. Moorehouse and Chamberlain could find no evidence of agitation but found instead that attitudes towards property ("property" in the precise sense of *rights* to control materials or establishments) among *all* their working-class respondents differed sharply from the normative expectations attached to the deference theory. For example, 37 percent of non-rent strikers and 47 percent of the strikers rejected the normative assertion that "some people say sit-ins by factory workers are wrong under any circumstances because factories do not belong to them." And 42 percent and 53 percent respectively agreed that occupations were justified in the face of redundancy.

In the whole sample, an overwhelming majority (68 percent and 79 percent) approved of homeless families taking over empty houses. Moorhouse and Chamberlain argued that prevailing theories overestimate "the cerebral aspects of revolution-making," and that "it is not necessary for men, certainly not the mass of men, to encompass society intellectually before they set about changing it." They stressed instead that the commonplace acceptance of the rights of ordinary people to take direct action to protect themselves from misfortune and control their own lives (even a little) has a considerable significance in the assessment of a society's capacity for action for radical change—which is basically what we mean here by "protest potential." They concluded: "As well as radical potential, the British lower class also has radical *traditions* and holds radical *attitudes*." This is an especially interesting

statement since lately we have become accustomed to viewing protest movements as middle-class phenomena—a view exemplified by Parkin's survey of
CND participants.

When a formal organization like a trade union taps this potential for
radical action among working-class people, the results are often impressive.
The trade union movement in Britain has always enjoyed a reputation for
moderation, yet, when forced to defend what it regarded as its basic rights
from attempts at regulation by the 1970-1974 Conservative administration,
the union leaders found their "rank and file" support surprisingly resilient.
During this time the movement found that it had more strength in greater
depth than it knew and that the power of political authority to resist that
strength was limited. So too at their "grass roots." Carter quotes the New
Stateman's estimate that in April 1972 some thirty factory occupations were
in progress including those at large factories like Plessey's and Upper Clyde
Shipbuilders. The spontaneity of these acts of resistance by very large groups
of ordinary British workers was more impressive than evidence of left-wing
conspiracy and agitation.

The nationalist movements in Britain have also contributed examples of
the capacity for direct action. The activities of the Welsh nationalists and the
Welsh Language Society (WLS) in removing evidence of English domination
such as roadsigns and pipelines and defying admission in court, spring from an
abiding capacity of the Welsh to express this kind of resentment forcibly.
Evidence that this capacity stems from a local concentration of protest
potential is provided by Madjwick who asked to what extent it was "sometimes justified" to engage in various acts of protest. Although only a minority
openly supported damage and violence (about 15 percent), a third of the
population of Cardiganshire was prepared to block traffic with illegal demonstrations and keep their children from school in protest, and a majority would
be prepared to withhold their local taxes, demonstrate, and strike. Clearly,
the WLS were pushing at the edge of some fairly generous parameters of
license.

The lack of commitment shown by British students toward the European
and American student protest movement might be held as evidence of a
naturally allegiant British attitude among even those who are supposed to
have an inclination for political unorthodoxy. Citrin and Elkin's sophisticated
and well-conceptualized study of political cynicism and dissatisfaction among
British University students in 1968 (of all years) found a "relatively low level
of manifest disaffection." But this may reflect merely the fact that *compared
to French and German students*, British undergraduates had a pleasant life of
study under the benign guidance of concerned faculty. Whereas a majority of
Parisian undergraduates fail the initial examination hurdles erected against
their progress, the vast majority of British students who enroll complete their

degrees. The British government was offering only tepid support for the American military undertakings in Indochina and was certainly not threatening to conscript into war those undergraduates who .failed to get good grades—which was the reality facing those who occupied Berkeley. In short, the British undergraduate in the 1960s was comfortably placed, reasonably assured of advancement, and well removed from the direct ideological and circumstantial pressures faced by the legions of 1968 elsewhere. It is even surprising that so many were persuaded to go to Grosvenor Square on October 27, 1968, and not at all surprising that the event passed off relatively peacefully.

But again we must stress that lack of protest behavior does not necessarily mean lack of protest potential. When commitment and involvement were present, as in the Stop the South Africa Tour campaign, British students were quick to show their capacity for direct action, even in provincial cities. In those universities where serious difficulties occurred over student conditions, especially over student discipline, there have been sustained and occasionally vigorous confrontations with university authorities and the police, which have replicated on a smaller scale events elsewhere. The University of Essex provided the best example, where O'Connor was able to show empirically that a considerable concentration of protest potential had built up among the students, far higher than in comparison samples at St. Andrews and Montpellier Universities.

Probably the most salient factor contributing to the absence of a *mass* student protest movement in Britain has been the absence of a mass of students. There are more full-time registered students in the United States than members of organized labor—nearly 30 percent of under 30s are "at school." In Paris, students form almost a majority of the population of the Quartier Latin. In Britain, university students form only 6-7 percent of their age group, and most complete their studies promptly in three short years. To build a mass movement out of such a group would probably defeat the capacities of several Lenins, let alone one Tariq Ali.

One aspect of British protest behavior that will form no part of this study, except in general discussion, is the events occurring in Northern Ireland and associated incidents in Great Britain. Although it has been done (see Richard Rose, "Governing Without Consensus"), the present writer would not take the responsibility of sending interviewers into the Falls Road area to ask people their views about protest behavior, and since we have forgone information about people's attitudes there, it will not be possible to include that area of political unrest in our general schema—though it must be stressed in passing that those events have left none in doubt as to the sheer potency of protest behavior to initiate political events. Anyway, most of the significant events following the escalation of the civil rights marches of the 1968-1970 period have moved well beyond the largely "nonviolent" scope of this inquiry. As commentators from the United States have been moved to remark—Northern Ireland is "something else."

To sum up this section: We have cast a prejudicial eye upon the conventional wisdom about British political consciousness with respect to support for political authority and the recourse to political unorthodoxy. The evidence advanced in favor of a key attitude of deference among the electorate is found to be weak, and as much evidence seems to exist to indicate the quite different conclusion that protest behavior is important in the formation of British political public opinion. Members of the British electorate are perfectly capable of mobilizing against a target authority through a wide range of protest behaviors and do so quite frequently, unaccompanied by displays of deference and unhindered by feelings of allegiance. Instead we propose that protest behavior, far from being the occasional outbursts of a hopelessly alienated minority (the "rent-a-crowd" theory) is an integral part of British political consciousness and is viewed, under a variety of circumstances, as a legitimate pathway of political redress by widely differing sections of the community. It will be the main task of this inquiry to put numbers to that assertion and thereby to discover the social location and psychological correlates of a neglected field in the study of political behavior. The first steps in accomplishing this are to conceptualize more precisely what is meant by "protest" and then to operationalize this concept of protest behavior in the form of a survey research instrument.

## Defining Protest within General Theory

Like any other emotive word in popular usage, "protest" has been worn almost featureless and is rendered unsuitable as an object for scientific calibration. "Unorthodox political behavior" is more accurate since it immediately implies a distinction between unorthodox and orthodox political behavior. This distinction rests on the presence or absence of normative rules which positively sanction and facilitate the conduct of orthodox politics but which are absent in the case of unorthodox politics. More precisely, there are actual rules and laws that facilitate the conduct of elections and the representation of interests in orthodox party politics, but there are none that encourage the regular occurrence of street protests, demonstrations, boycotts, rent strikes, political strikes, the occupation of administrative premises and so on. There is, however, a great number of laws that restrict or forbid their use.

This key legalistic divide may be found implicit in definitions employed by other researchers. Kaase speaks of "unconventional political behavior (which) can be defined as behavior that does not correspond to the legal and customary regime norms regulating political participation." Likewise, Muller holds "unconventional political behaviour" to be that which "deviates from regime norms," but he correctly excludes essentially private deviations from norms relating to the use of bribery, the theft of materials, or political espionage. Muller also adds a variable dimension in that "unconventional activities can be classified according to whether or not they possess combinations of properties which are more or less stressful to the regime," and he proposes a hierarchy of stress factors in the coalescence of three variables:

(1) the extent of deviation from regime norms
(2) the extent that behavior is organized
(3) the use or non-use of violence.

And we would add:

(4) the numbers mobilized.

Muller's conceptualization is useful in that he suggests a progressive departure from the orthodox pathways of political redress towards the use (alternatively *or* additionally) of unorthodox methods, which need not immediately involve actual law-breaking.

Von Eschen, Kirk, and Pinard coined the appealing phrase "disorderly politics" juxtaposed to "routine politics" to describe the distinction made above between the politics of voting and representation and the politics of protest. Unfortunately perhaps, what they describe as "routine politics" is in many places conducted in a distinctly disorderly manner and their own thesis goes on to demonstrate convincingly that "disorderly politics requires and has an organisational substructure just as does routine politics," and so, despite appearances, is often rather an orderly or even a routine process.

Many researchers often use the terms "direct action" and "civil disobedience" interchangeably with a generalized notion of protest behavior when these terms really describe rather specialized forms of protest. Discussion of these terms has a strong appeal for political philosophers and social theorists interested in the many facets of man's relationship with the state, and no attempt will be made here to interrupt their debate with new observations since little of it is directly relevant. It must be acknowledged though, that as the "stress-upon-regime" factor increases, so those pursuing an unorthodox pathway of redress for a political grievance will be led into behavior that actually transgresses laws and not merely those who breach what are supposed to be wider normative expectations of good behavior. Thus, "civil disobedience" can be an important factor in unorthodox political behavior but there is an important qualification, well expressed by Cohen, who is content to accept that "deliberate unlawful protest is a rough definition of civil disobedience," but adds that "most protest, however vehement, is not civil disobedience because civil disobedience necessarily involves some *deliberate* infraction of the law" (p. 41).

This stress upon the deliberate defiance of the law, often for the sake of moral principle, is shared by many other writers on the subject (cf., Carter, Van Den Haag, or Bondurant) and qualifies our dependence upon a legalistic dividing line. We must stress, in turn, that illegality does not begin where legality ceases and that whereas much civil disobedience is indeed a breach of a specific law aimed to draw attention to injustice inherent in the law itself, much else involves the breach of law to dramatize a protest against some other injustice for which redress is sought. Whether or not such breach is deliberate can often be determined only by empirical observation of specific examples.

Macfarlane makes a good case for the use of the term "political disobedience" to describe protest. He too adheres to a legally oriented definition but also stresses motives:

> "Political disobedience embraces the performance of any act prohibited by the state or the law, or as the non-performance of any act required by the State or the law, with the purpose of securing changes in the actions, policies, or laws of the State" (p. 13).

It is probably unnecessary to stress that protest has to be *about* something to be protest. People do not march to Trafalgar Square carrying blank placards nor do they occupy Rhodesia House from idle curiosity about its interior decor. But the extent to which people realistically expect to "secure changes in the actions, policies, or laws of the State" is another variable quantity we must consider.

## Developing a Measure of Protest Potential

The pilot work for this study (see Marsh 1974) which was mentioned in Chapter One, isolated some key examples of protest behavior that seemed to traverse the psychological distance between orthodox and unorthodox political behavior in progressive stages. These examples are set down in Figure 2.1 in a kind of conceptual diagram which relates the examples, and the dimension they form, to the concepts discussed above.

A new example of "painting slogans on walls" was added to the dimension for the present study because it was estimated to form part of the first threshold overlap between orthodox and unorthodox political behavior, together with "petitions," and lawful demonstrations. These three techniques may be used in pursuit of both forms of behavior, though demonstration is much more usually an unorthodox technique. The second threshold is illustrated by "boycotts" which marks a fairly unequivocal entry into political unorthodoxy and the first steps of "direct action." "Unofficial strikes" and

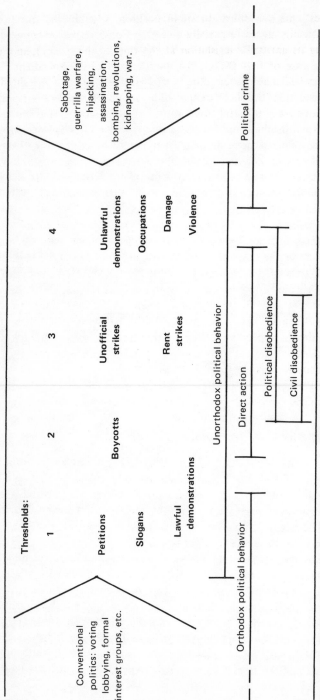

Figure 2.1: CONCEPTUAL DIAGRAM OF THE DIMENSIONALITY OF UNORTHODOX POLITICAL BEHAVIOR

"rent strikes" mark a third threshold position, wherein the question of conscious illegality arises (especially since the Conservative government was still pursuing its antistrike legislation at the time of the survey); and, especially in the case of rent strikes, the question of "civil disobedience" and "political disobedience" enters. The crucial area between this threshold and the fourth and final threshold of the deliberate use of violence for political ends is indicated by unlawful demonstrations, occupations, and damage to property. "Civil disobedience" usually stops short of damage and violence and is often modeled upon Gandhi's Satyagraha movement which always eschewed all acts of violence. "Political disobedience" may involve violence but rarely more sophisticated forms of violent resistance (guerrilla war etc.), which are in the province of "political crime," first conceptualized in 1924 by Calton-Hall and recently reemployed by Rose in exactly the same context of Northern Ireland.

Our pretest work also indicated that people use three key concepts to think about these examples of political behavior. These are: (1) a generalized sense of approval or disapproval: a dimension of positive-to-negative *affect*; (2) a *cognitive* dimension focused upon the extent to which such behavior may be effective; and (3) a *behavioral* dimension, i.e., the extent to which people may or may not participate in such behavior. That these three dimensions should appear to reflect the traditional social psychological formulation into affective, cognitive and behavioral components is purely fortuitous but nonetheless gratifying.

This, then, is the schema for operationalizing the concept of unorthodox political behavior into a survey instrument designed to measure national parameters of protest potential. We may now turn to the results obtained by its use.

## Estimating the Parameters of License for Protest in Britain

### THE SURVEY: *Sampling*

A multistage national probability sample of *households* was drawn using the electoral register as a sampling frame. One hundred and twenty parliamentary constituencies were randomly selected with probability proportional to size, at the first stage, having first been stratified by region, an urban/rural factor and by the proportion of the vote achieved by the Labour party in the 1970 general election. Two wards were then randomly sampled within urban constituencies and one ward in rural constituencies. Seventeen names and addresses of their households were then selected at random within each ward in rural constituencies, and nine and eight addresses in each of the pairs of wards in urban constituencies. The exceptions to this rule were twenty-six constituencies wherein the proportion of households, according to the 1966 sample census, whose head pursued a professional or managerial occupation exceeded 20 percent, i.e., what are popularly known as 'solid' middle-class areas. This was done to inflate the number of respondents who had middle-class backgrounds, especially those who were young and well educated. The theoretical reasons for so doing will become clear later. Finally, a respondent was selected from each household according to the method prescribed by Kish (see Appendix for full details).

From the national sample of 2,318 a total of 1,785 useable interviews were obtained during the period from October 1, 1973 to February 7, 1974 (the date the first 1974 general election was announced), which represents a response rate of 77 percent. More than three-quarters of the interviews were obtained before December 24.

## THE PRINCIPAL DEPENDENT VARIABLE: PROTEST POTENTIAL

Each of the ten stimulus examples of unorthodox political behavior were printed on separate cards, as illustrated in Appendix One. Intuitively, we reasoned that the specificity of the stimulus object would have an important influence on the reliability of the behavioral intentions that people felt regarding them. There are aspects of Fishbein's work that support this approach, and recent research by Weigel et al. (1974) has confirmed empirically that specific invitations to described examples of environmental activism had more of a behavioral impact than generalized exhortations. Thus, our examples of protest behavior were made as unequivocal and simple as possible.

Respondents then indicated whether they failed to recognize any item, and unrecognized items were removed from the set. The rate of recognition was very high; only "boycotts" attracted a noticeable number of puzzled responses, about 7 percent in fact. Three additional scale cards were introduced. Upon these respondents successively placed the item cards to indicate first whether they approved strongly, approved, disapproved, or disapproved strongly of each behavior "in a general way"; secondly, whether they thought each behavior very effective, somewhat effective, not very effective, or not at all effective; and thirdly, which of the behaviors they had engaged in, "during the past ten years"; or, if not, would engage in, might engage in, or would never engage in.

This technique may appear unhelpfully brusque or too impersonal to elicit accurately people's real feelings about the stimuli presented. In fact, the opposite is probably true. To have the interviewer plough through thirty verbal repetitions of the same type of question (especially in rerandomized order) would be both boring and confusing to the respondent. The use of the cards, however, gave the respondents time to muse, shuffle the cards around in their hands, and think about their attitudes without interruption or the worry of expressing themselves properly to the stranger sitting opposite. The interviewers confirmed that the technique "worked well," often despite their own initial doubts about its value. The results obtained are given in Table 2.1.

Comparing these results with the conceptual diagram derived from our pretest work, we find general confirmation of a dimension of unorthodoxy passing through a series of thresholds away from conventional politics towards violence. As may be expected, petitions are a widely accepted technique but the clear majority support given to lawful demonstrations was more surprising. Only slightly less than majority support was extended to the use of boycotts, even though this item is tainted with the sometimes vigorous opposition to South African sports events. Rent strikes draw support from between a third and a quarter of the population though some doubt is cast upon their comparative effectiveness. The previous collapse of resistance to the 1972 Housing Finance Act may have devalued the effectiveness of this tactic in many people's minds. A similar proportion are prepared to support unofficial strikes *though apparently in the face of their own disapproval* probably because they and many others acknowledge their effectiveness.

The approach toward "threshold four" is clearly signaled by the minority support given to the use of occupations of buildings or factories and the use

**Table 2.1: Attitudes Towards Unorthodox Political Behavior (in percentages)**

|  | Signing Petitions | Lawful Demonstrations | Boycotts | Rent Strikes | Unofficial Strikes | Occupying Buildings | Blocking Traffic | Painting Slogans on Walls | Damaging Property | Personal Violence |
|---|---|---|---|---|---|---|---|---|---|---|
| Strong approval | 26 | 14 | 6 | 4 | 2 | 2 | 2 | — | 1 | — |
| Approval | 60 | 55 | 31 | 20 | 14 | 13 | 13 | 1 | 1 | 2 |
| Disapproval | 10 | 23 | 44 | 51 | 48 | 43 | 46 | 32 | 22 | 12 |
| Strong disapproval | 3 | 8 | 17 | 25 | 36 | 41 | 40 | 67 | 77 | 86 |
| | | | | | | | | | | |
| Very effective | 15 | 10 | 7 | 6 | 9 | 5 | 5 | 2 | 4 | 4 |
| Somewhat effective | 58 | 50 | 41 | 21 | 33 | 24 | 26 | 4 | 6 | 7 |
| Not very effective | 22 | 28 | 38 | 40 | 34 | 32 | 32 | 23 | 18 | 18 |
| Not at all effective | 5 | 11 | 14 | 33 | 24 | 39 | 37 | 71 | 72 | 71 |
| | | | | | | | | | | |
| Have done | 23 | 6 | 6 | 2 | 5 | 1 | 1 | — | 1 | — |
| Would do | 33 | 26 | 19 | 10 | 7 | 6 | 7 | — | 1 | 1 |
| Might do | 22 | 25 | 25 | 21 | 16 | 13 | 15 | 2 | 2 | 4 |
| Never do | 23 | 43 | 51 | 67 | 72 | 80 | 76 | 97 | 96 | 95 |

of illegal street demonstrations to block traffic (between 15 percent and 25 percent), though again estimates of their effectiveness tend to be higher. The arrival at "threshold four" is marked equally clearly by the almost total rejection of the use of violence or damage to property as a legitimate political resource.

If additional proof were even needed, these results support Macfarlane's assertion that

> what we are normally confronted with in constitutional democracies is action directed not at the overthrow of the social system or the government but of particular government policies. In so far as this requires widespread public support and approval for one's aims, it places a low premium upon violence" (p. 20).

One very surprising result was the universal condemnation of "painting slogans on walls." Superficially, this activity seems harmless enough, sometimes even amusing, and was placed in Figure 2.1 among those items now confirmed as acceptable to the majority because "fly-posting" and sloganizing is a common feature of political campaigns in both the orthodox and unorthodox spheres. The only reasonable conclusion is that most people regard the activity as a defacement of visual surroundings and thereby a public nuisance, and that many others may associate political daubings with graffiti other than the strictly political. Activists, on the other hand, will regard slogan-painting as immature, irresponsible, and ineffective. Whatever the precise reason, this item will be excluded from future consideration in this analysis.

Further insight into the attitudinal structure of protest potential emerges from a comparison between the three dimensions tested. Generally speaking, they are well aligned, especially the approval and behavioral dimensions, and the three most acceptable and three least acceptable items retain the same rank-order within each dimension. The only noticeable departures are rent strikes, which are thought relatively acceptable by a large minority but also relatively ineffective, and unofficial strikes, which are regarded with considerable disapproval by most people, but at the same time (ruefully perhaps) rather effective and, more surprisingly, attract positive behavioral responses from 28 percent of the total population.

Further reflection on the interscale comparison suggests a more paradoxical relationship. While it seems reasonable to expect people to be favorably disposed toward and to feel themselves likely to prefer acts they believe are effective, the scale of this relationship is strange. Why should 73 percent of the population believe that "signing a petition" is "somewhat" or even "very effective"? Petitions to parliament or to the town hall from the Chartists onwards, have not been conspicuously successful in bringing about political change and usually form only a kind of ritualized part of a wider campaign, often as a focus for a demonstration. The question wording stressed effectiveness in the context of "when people use them in pressing for *changes*" so their possible effectiveness merely in communication of grievances plays only a minor role in these assessments by respondents. So too at the other end of the scale: Why should 90 percent of our respondents, in a world where political violence has become increasingly an effective instrument for extremist politics, believe that violence is "not very effective" or in the view of most, "not *at all* effective"?

Question order is unlikely to have influenced the ratings. The order of the presentation was not chosen randomly. It is perfectly possible for people to feel free to say that they regard an item as ineffective even when they have just indicated their approval, but it is far more difficult when they have just said they may do it. Therefore the invitation to behavioral commitment was left until last.

Clearer insight into this paradox is found by moving from the aggregate level to the individual level of analysis. The correlations between effectiveness and the two other dimensions range from +.24 in the case of "petitions" up to +.48 for "boycotts." The average interdimensional correlation is +.37 for effectiveness-vs.-approval and +.39 for effectiveness-vs.-behavioral intentions. All three attitudinal dimensions are related (approval and behavior more so than these two with effectiveness) but not exactly coinciding. Even so, it would be reasonable to expect even greater independence of the cognitive, externalized judgment of effectiveness as opposed to the more subjective and closely related feelings of approval and behavioral intentions.

At the positive and negative extremes of the dimensions (i.e., "petitions" and "violence"), what is probably happening is this: Our pilot work indicated that the protest dimension was essentially characterized by a powerful "corridor" of positive-to-negative affect. People feel strongly about these matters and, consequently, when asked to introduce an objective assessment alongside their subjective feelings about the same stimulus objects, their judgment becomes suspect. This effect was convincingly demonstrated by Blumenthal et al., who found that relatively nonviolent acts such as demonstrations were considered "violent" by those who *disapproved* of them, and violent acts like "police beating students" were considered "nonviolent" by those who *approved* of such acts. Pretest work for this study found a positive correlation of .45 between approval/disapproval and peacefulness/violence ratings of protest. So there exists a strong tendency for objective ratings—like effectiveness—to be aligned with the subjective ratings simply on the basis of positive and negative polarity. If it is "good," it is probably "effective" because "effective" is a positive value. This argument cannot be pushed too far because some of the relationships for the core items are obviously sensible; for example: unofficial strikes *are* regarded by many as a kind of "necessary evil."

The assertion that protest behaviors form a single psychopolitical dimension must now be put to a more severe test of unidimensional scaling. This test has two useful functions, first, to provide an estimate of the extent of unidimensionality (how "narrow" is the "corridor"), and secondly, to provide a single numerical index which may be employed as a measure of "protest potential." The technical details of this process would disrupt the progress of this text to an unhelpful extent so the statistical record of scale construction for this and subsequent similar undertakings have been confined to the Appendix.

Working concurrently with our pretest study, other researchers arrived quite independently at a similar approach to the measurement of unorthodox political behavior. Most similar is Edward Muller's work in Waterloo, Iowa, in which he presented very similar stimuli to respondents, but he sketched each "threshold-point" on the scale in some detail. For example, his "type III" threshold was described as follows: "Trying to stop the government from functioning by engaging in sit-ins, mass demonstrations, takeovers of buildings, and things like that (1972, p. 929).

Muller's scale traversed the distance from legal demonstrations to civil war ("arming oneself in preparation for battles with government authorities such as the police or National Guard") and conformed to a unidimensional structure for both "approval" and "behavioral intentions," and these two dimensions he found sufficiently closely related to merit their inclusion in a combined scale.

O'Conner's study at the Universities of Essex, St. Andrews, and Montpellier also derived a unidimensional, cumulative structure from a ten-item scale of the extent to which students had attended a rally, petitioned, demonstrated, (on campus, in town, or in London), contributed to protest movement funds, had been arrested for civil disobedience, committed violence, and so on.

The basic question underlying the presentation of these protest stimuli is: "Think about protest. Generally speaking, *how far are you prepared to go*?" If these items genuinely traverse a single dimension from positive-to-negative, from the commonplace to the extreme, then we ought to obtain a response from most people of: "thus far, and no further." This is exactly the principle underlying Guttman scaling techniques. In a unidimensional scale that is also cumulative there ought to be a very high probability that someone who, for example, returns a total of four positive approval scores ought, on the basis of the rank order shown in Table 2.1, approve of rent strikes and the three more popular items and disapprove of all the remaining less popular items. The extent to which this is likely is measured by the coefficient of reproducibility, which, in the case of the approval dimension, is .95; for the behavioral dimension .94; but for the effectiveness dimension only .89; whereas .90 is considered a minimum acceptable result, and then only if the most and least "popular" items do not have unduly skewed marginal distributions. This particular coefficient enjoys an indifferent reputation among statistics of reliability (see White and Saltz 1957) and the skewed marginality of the more extreme items makes even the two apparently reliable scales a little suspect.

Careful inspection of the data revealed that the *internal* structure of the effectiveness dimension contained subtle but important deviations from a true cumulative pattern, the most significant of which suggested that those people who regarded occupations, traffic blocks, and violence as *effective* tended to regard petitions and lawful demonstrations as *ineffective,* thus accumulating an unacceptably high number of "errors" in the response-patterns. That a certain contempt for the effectiveness of "moderation" should form part of the attitude of "militants" would surprise no popular commentator on the subject.

It was decided to leave aside the effectiveness dimension for separate reference at appropriate stages of the analysis (see Chapter 3) and instead to create a protest potential score by merging the approval and behavioral dimensions.

With very little practice, it is possible to derive scores from a large number of contributory items which support a particular view as to what the *aggregate* outcome might be. In this case, we have established the argument that the tendency toward protest will be "high"—higher anyway than thought likely by most theorists. Consequently, we shall be at pains to *minimize* the possibility that *positive* protest scores will accumulate unless there is demonstrable proof that positive scores are appropriate.

The first stage of this minimization procedure was to eliminate from consideration all those who did not recognize or expressed no opinion on more than two items in *either* the approval or the behavioral dimension. This eliminated 5 percent of the respondents. The remaining missing data codes were recoded to *negative* responses. Then, for each item, a positive response was recorded for each respondent who indicated that he or she *had* participated in the activity described in the last ten years or *would* definitely do so. A positive response was also recorded for those who said they *might* participate but *only if they also said they approved of this kind of activity.* Nearly everyone who fell in the first category also approved the activity, but the numbers of those saying they "might do" was halved by the use of the approval qualification.

The details of the scaling procedure and the principal components analysis associated with it (see Appendix) indicated that the scale could be improved by grouping the two items concerned with strikes and rent strikes into a single threshold point on the scale and likewise the two items concerning occupations and traffic blocks. The items concerning damage and violence, though neatly defining the end of the scale, had already served their purpose even at this early stage of the analysis. So little variance was added by their inclusion (only 35 respondents gave positive responses to either item) that they may be safely put aside as quite outside the positive vectors of British political consciousness.

When the positive responses are examined before cumulative scaling procedures are applied, we obtain the results given in Figure 2.2. The results accurately summarize the data in Table 2.1. To examine the earlier point concerning the possibly misleading effects of cumulative scaling, we compared the upper and lower limits of the cumulative function of the scale with the "corrected" version. The three scales indicate dissimilar conclusions. The highest point on the scale behaves particularly erratically and fully half the

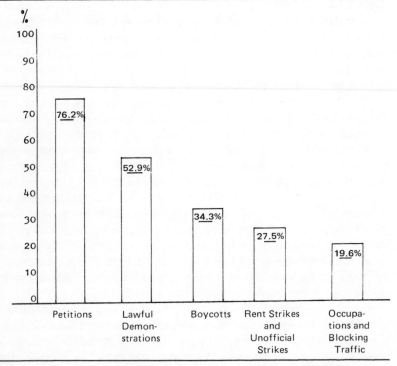

Figure 2.2: POSITIVE RESPONSES TO THRESHOLD POINTS OF PROTEST

Table 2.2: Distribution of Guttman-Scale Scores of Protest Potential

| No Protest | Petitions | Lawful Demon-strations | Boycotts | Rent Strikes/ Strikes | Occupations Blocking Traffic |
|---|---|---|---|---|---|
| 22.1% | 21.4% | 20.2% | 14.8% | 9.9% | 11.6% |

("Don't know" to more than 2 items: 5%)

Unweighted (n) = 1,671
Weighted (n) = 1,388

"errors" in the scale are caused by people who give positive responses to the most extreme position but not to more "moderate" examples. The obvious temptation (from the point of view of discrediting the deference theory) to leave their highest response as a face-value score was resisted, and instead a standard Guttman-scaling procedure, which corrects error cases to a median value between the two adjacent positive responses, was used. By using this technique we arrived at a corrected position given in Table 2.2.

If it were ever meaningful to ask the question, "How militant is Britain?", Table 2.2 would provide the closest estimate available. Forty-three percent of the population will have nothing more to do with protest than to sign a petition and half of these doubt they would do even that. But 35 percent would go further and engage in lawful demonstrations, and many of them would even operate boycotts against some protest target. The remaining 22 percent would clearly enter the third threshold zone of illegal demonstrations, half of them would stop at unofficial strikes and withholding their dues from the local authority or the inland revenue in protest. But the remainder would go "all the way" and take their politics into the street through the use of blockades and occupations. The conservative manner in which these estimates were constructed encourages the belief that this 22 percent really are committed to the legitimacy of nonlegal protest. Relative to our basic hypothesis, these results offer far more support for the argument that protest is an integrated feature of political consciousness in Britain than to the established position that the British have an exaggerated respect for political authority. Less than half the population shun protest while more than one fifth (an estimate representing some 7 million adults) accept the full gamut of aggressive protest against the authorities, legal and illegal. Twenty-two percent may be a minority; but it is not a very small one.

How seriously should these responses be taken? To probe further into the cognitive content of attitudes towards unorthodox political behavior, respondents were asked: "Are there *ever* times when it is justified to break the law to protest about something you feel may be very unjust or harmful?" Fully 56 percent thought there were such times, 36 percent thought there were not, and 8 percent reserved their opinion. This result alone does extensive damage to the view that people in Britain incline towards a passive view of political authority. These results may be compared with those obtained by Rose and Mossawir who asked a similar national sample in 1966 if there might ever be circumstances wherein it was justified to break the law. A smaller proportion, 46 percent, said there were but cited a rather vague humanitarian scenario in justification, and only 27 percent thought a breach of law justified by individual conscience.

The lack of explicit political referent in their respondents' replies gave support to Rose and Mossawir's contention that "strong evidence" exists "of their (the British public's) willingness to comply with basic political laws". Our evidence brings this contention into doubt. When asked to apply a *political* frame of reference, people actually give greater license than when asked to apply a more general and therefore probably "criminal" frame of reference. This apparent contradiction derives largely from the contextual difference. Rose and Mossawir mistakenly derived a political conclusion from nonpolitical attitudes. If one requires information about a political attitude, one must ask, as we did, a political question.

So what had our sample in mind? Those who admitted the possibility of justified lawbreaking were asked, "What times are these?" Table 2.3 shows that the scenarios attached by respondents to *political* lawbreaking are largely sensible and realistic. Figures are given for the sample as a whole and separately for those scoring low, medium, and high on the protest potential scale. Overall, there is a slight tendency for legitimization to be concentrated upon the protection of basic civil liberties, and this is especially true of people high on protest potential. But taken together, the coding categories dealing with the protection of basic living standards and the furtherance of industrial action in a wage dispute suggest the preeminence of economic considerations and here the difference between protesters and nonprotesters is less obvious. Other smaller categories emerge of a less specific nature: the protection of the environment and improvement of facilities, and legitimization in terms of conflict with unreasonable, unresponsive, or even repressive authorities, and here there is only very slight tendency for protesters to predominate. There is, however, a clear tendency for a much higher proportion of protesters to endorse lawbreaking in a political interest (81 percent against 49 percent of nonprotesters) and to be a little more articulate in their justifications—only 15 percent are unable to describe possible scenarios compared with 27 percent of the nonprotesters. The responses of those in the middle of the scale more closely resemble protesters than nonprotesters. These results provide excellent construct validity for the protest potential scale and indicate that the relatively high levels of protest potential described are neither a scaling artifact nor idiosyncratic bravado.

## Table 2.3: Protest Potential and the Justification of Illegal Protest

*"Is it ever justified to break the law to protest about something that is very unjust or harmful::*

*No, never: 36%; don't know: 8%; yes: 56%.*

| | Distribution of Those Saying "Yes" by Protest Potential (in percentages) | | |
| --- | --- | --- | --- |
| | Low 34 | Medium 38 | High 29 |
| Percentage saying "Yes" but unable to specify an example | 27 | 20 | 15 |

Percentage of *remainder* giving following *reasons* justifying lawbreaking:

| | Low | Medium | High |
| --- | --- | --- | --- |
| To resist threats to living standards, combat excessive rent, rate, tax or (especially) price increases—includes most extreme examples, e.g., "steal if starving" | 21 | 18 | 16 |
| To further industrial action, strikes, etc. (especially) if faced with official instransigence, and to oppose Industrial Relations Act, protect workers rights (e.g., free collective bargaining) | 12 | 17 | 18 |
| To protect civil liberties; matters of conscience; to challenge an authoritarian or illegitimate regime (e.g., dictatorship, coup, junta, "another Hitler," etc.) and to resist the threat of unjust laws which infringe on basic civil, religious, or minority rights | 14 | 26 | 25 |
| To force improvements in neighborhood facilities or resist a threat the the "environment," e.g., school crossing protest, stop juggernauts, new airport, etc. | 5 | 7 | 10 |
| As a generalized means of furthering a legitimate cause, especially when authorities have been unresponsive to conventional pressures | 11 | 12 | 11 |
| In response to more extreme provocation by authorities; wrongful accusation; official persecutions, police harrassment; etc. | 16 | 14 | 12 |
| To protect property right; resist dispossession or eviction; (especially) squatting, etc. | 13 | 12 | 12 |
| In response to attack on own person or family | 5 | 3 | 4 |
| "Vigilante principle," i.e., taking the law into one's own hands to resist or attack subversive elements in society or to support authority (e.g., police) attempts to resist them. "Sorting out troublemakers" (e.g., strikers, I.R.A., students, squatters, immigrants) | 9 | 4 | 5 |
| Other, idiosyncratic response | 8 | 5 | 7 |
| Percentage giving two or three responses | 11 | 17 | 20 |

Taking a wider view of these results, it is striking that so few respondents mentioned any of the real life scenarios that have provided the subject matter of protest movements in recent times. Very few specifically mentioned support for the liberation of the peoples of Indochina, the abandonment of nuclear weapons, or the overthrow of the capitalist system, nor for that matter did they mention the restoration of capital punishment, the repatriation of immigrants, or the repeal of the Abortion Act. Respondents stating specific issues were so few that they did not warrant a separate coding category. The responses given were far more behavior-specific than issue-specific which confirms our earlier finding that unorthodox political behavior is judged within a mature cognitive framework concerned with the general legitimacy of various modes of political behavior, independently of issues and campaigns.

On reflection, it is remarkable that the items in the protest scale *should* scale along a single dimension since they tend to be deployed in rather different issue contexts. Why did respondents not reply, "Ah well, that depends on what it is in aid of?" That people's responses *in principle* can satisfy quite stringent analysis criteria of unidimensionality is indicative of an abiding psychopolitical dimension within British political consciousness which has gone unnoticed in previous research.

The following chapter will explore the wider psychopolitical structure of attitudes towards unorthodox political behavior and, in that wider context, describe the social location of protest potential.

*Chapter 3*


**PROTEST, ORTHODOXY AND REPRESSION:**

**THE GENERAL STRUCTURE OF ATTITUDES TOWARDS**

**PARTICIPATION AND THE SOCIAL LOCATION OF ACTIVISM**


## A Wider Concept of Protest

Throughout the conceptualization and description of attitudes towards un-orthodox political behavior presented in the preceding chapter, some care was taken *not* to present the concept of "protest" as some kind of opposite to orthodox political behavior. Theoretical positions on this matter have now matured to a point where they align with political reality. Active partisans will signal their discontent and demands for redress for political grievances through a mixture of political methods. For example, a demonstration may conclude in a lobby of Parliament, or an unofficial strike may occur to prevoke the intervention of officials. This point is not immediately obvious because the puzzled reaction to the outbursts of students and blacks in the 1960s encouraged a striving after cognitive simplicity among many commentators. Numerous writers (see especially Lipset's work) tended to ascribe the growth of protest movements to a breakdown of inflexible orthodox politics in the face of alternative methods arising directly from increasing popular contempt for establishment politics. The point has been only recently grasped that these alternatives need not be mutually exclusive.

This impression of mutual exclusivity has arisen because orthodox politicians and authorities are so often the target of protest. But one of Turner's conditions for defining "credible protest" draws attention to the subtle differences between protest "designed to proke ameliorative action by some target group" by *persuasion or by coercion,* i.e., by the arousal of sympathy or fear or, better still, an optimum combination of both. However alienated and extreme a protest may appear, if it retains the aim of enlisting the *help* of existing authorities, the activists involved cannot have rejected the relevance of conventional politics for the cure of their grievance. Indeed, much protest arises not because a disadvantaged group has rejected conventional politics, but because conventional politicians have rejected or excluded them. This was certainly true of the black protest movement in the United States, whose study led James Q. Wilson to conceptualize protest as a "problem of power-lessness." Protest creates a bargaining force for relatively disenfranchised groups where none existed previously. This bargaining force is of a limited kind because it offers only a negative inducement, i.e., the prospect of their desisting from protest should positive inducements be forthcoming from the protest target. A negative inducement of this kind can be seen as less crudely coercive if the protest goal is highly specific and "endowed with a moral or sacrosanct quality which makes compromise difficult." A dignified sit-in at a lunch counter in Mississippi to demand equal service for blacks as well as for whites is just such a goal.

Eisinger, who had the advantage over Wilson of watching black protest run its full course from prayful dignity to arson and looting, retains Wilson's notion of "negative inducement" but no longer sees it as especially limited. Protest is mass action designed to maximize meager political resources while minimizing costs and is therefore a "cost-benefit calculation." He agrees also with Nieburg that protest "relies on an implicit threat of violence" and stresses that "as long as protesters do not manipulate the threat of violence openly they enjoy a slim legality, even legitimacy," and he concludes:

> Protest is then a device by which groups of people manipulate the fear of violence and disorder while at the same time they protect themselves from paying the potentially extreme costs of acknowledging such a strategy.

While it may appear that Eisinger is imputing at least a degree in political science to every protester, he is correct in stressing that protesters use protest to augment their political leverage over an unresponsive system, not to install an alternative system of social administration. While revolutionaries may use protest to try to ferment prerevolutionary conditions, revolutionaries have proved only rarely to be the instigators and almost never the beneficiaries of protest movements.

Wilson, writing in 1961, underlined his material bargaining theory with what was then a reasonable statement: "Protest actions involving such tactics as mass meetings, picketing and boycotts and strikes rarely find enthusiastic participants among upper-middle and higher status individuals."

By 1968, other theorists in the United States had to accommodate the uncomfortable fact that the most privileged group in the country—indeed the most privileged of that group—(see Keniston or Flacks) had not merely joined the black struggle but had reduced to an embattled confusion many universities—institutions of the very system that was designed to ensure their own future privileges. Reviewing Wilson's influential article, Lipsky agreed that: "Protest represents an important aspect of minority and lower income group politics," but hastened to add: "Groups which seek psychological gratification from politics but cannot or do not expect material political rewards may be attracted to militant protest leaders."

Possibly more than a million reproductions of Che Guevara's portrait upon student walls will testify the truth of that statement. It would be difficult to deny that protest behavior can have its own intrinsic gratification. For example, Driver dryly describes the contraction of the mass appeal of CND as a process whereby "demonstrations were gradually left more and more to those who actually enjoyed them." Despite this, the essentially instrumental character of protest remains uppermost—certainly so in Britain—and gives rise to the hypothesis that some kind of *positive* relationship will exist between protest potential and the preparedness to engage in orthodox political behavior.

Given the obvious importance for political theory this hypothesis holds, it is very surprising that so little evidence has accumulated, but what evidence does exist is all positive. Aberbach and Walker found that unconventional *and* conventional political behavior among blacks was contingent upon distrust of political authorities, and that remedy was sought through both kinds of activity. A current study in the San Francisco Bay area by the Survey Research Center at Berkeley found a very similar effect and also found a positive correlation between their conventional participation and protest participation indices of 0.394. Even more impressive is Muller's results from a study of German farmers, workers, and intellectuals, which indicated a gamma correlation coefficient of .705 between his scale measures of protest potential (adopted almost completely from Marsh 1974, which he relabels "aggressive political behavior") and a conventional political behavior index. Muller describes the relationship in detail:

> Those who show no participation in conventional activity are virtually certain not to participate in aggressive activity; those who participate in conventional activity are unlikely to participate in aggressive activity;

but practically all of those who participate in aggressive activity also participate in conventional activity.

Results from this study are very similar. Respondents were asked to indicate the extent of their participation in orthodox politics using an Anglicised version of the ISR participation scale. They indicated how often they read political views in the newspapers, discussed politics with friends, tried to convince friends to vote as they did, contributed to political efforts to solve community problems, attended a political meeting, contacted officials or spent time working for a party or candidate. Respondents were given a positive score if they reported they did these things "often" or "sometimes" and a negative score for "seldom" or "never." A Guttman scaling procedure similar to that described for the protest potential scale (see Appendix for details) was applied and found to yield a reliable scale (coefficient of reproducibility = .92). The distribution of orthodox political activism is given in Table 3.1, and we obtain no impression of fervent participation in the workings of representative democracy. Twenty-three percent will not even read the political section of the newspapers and a cumulative total of 69 percent will do no more than talk about it; the remaining third do get involved in varying degrees, but only 8 percent have ever had anything to do with an election campaign.

The predicted positive relationship between protest potential and orthodox participation emerges. There is a product-moment correlation of +.27 between the two scales, which actually improves to .32 when the effect of age of respondent is partialed out. This is respectably close to the San Francisco result. When the interrelationship is studied in detail, we see that we do not have Muller's "corner correlation" but a linear relationship which admits many exceptions. Not *all* our protesters enjoin orthodox behavior (about 40 percent of those "high," and 35 percent of those "medium" on the

**Table 3.1: Distribution of Orthodox (or Conventional) Political Activism**

| | Respondent "Often" or "Sometimes" | | |
|---|---|---|---|
| Does Nothing | Reads Politics | Discusses Politics | Works for Community |
| 25% | 18% | 26% | 7% |
| Contacts Politicians | Persuades Friends How to Vote | Attends Party Political Meetings | Works for a Political Candidate |
| 6% | 6% | 5% | 8% |

(n) = 1,720/1,443 (w)

scale, in fact) but there is a general trend that political activism is associated with *both* orthodox and unorthodox political behavior. This strongly contradicts the conventional wisdom that protesters are usually a politically alienated minority. In Britain, at least, there is a fair chance that they will be the same people who knock on doors during elections.

An even simpler test of the possible political alienation of potential protesters is to determine whether or not they bother to vote in national or local elections. This question is complicated by the effects of age. Whereas there is a very slight tendency for nonvoters to have a higher protest potential (supporting the alienation hypothesis), in the national case (the election of June 1970), we see that among the reasons given for nonvoting there is a contrast between those who were then simply too young (43 percent high on the protest scale) and those who were (and probably still are) infirm (6 percent). Those who reject parties ("none of them do any good," "they're as bad as each other") have only an average protest potential and those who just "don't care"—the *real* political alienates—have a much *lower* protest potential. This pattern is confirmed, though less markedly in the case of those who abstain from voting in their local council elections. While the evidence is a little inconclusive, there is certainly no support in these data for the hypothesis, first proposed by Kornhauser, that protesters are political isolates. His second hypothesis—that they are *social* isolates—will be examined in the second half of this chapter. Meanwhile, there is another question to examine. If not conventional politics, what is the conceptual and empirical "opposite" of protest potential, and why should the question be asked?

The relevance of the question stems from our mass social psychological concern with "parameters of license." It is not enough to know to what extent people will countenance and participate in protest, we need also to know to what extent support exists for government measures to control political unorthodoxy. What are the parameters of license for *super*-orthodox political behavior or *"repression potential"*? To what extent are people who do not support protest in general (or a protest in particular) likely to call down the power of the state upon the heads of those challenging the regime? This question is by no means as clear-cut as it seems. Antifascist forces in the 1930s in Britain were caught upon the horns of this particular dilemma when a debate raged as to whether Oswald Mosley's British Union of Fascists should be curbed by Government action banning demonstrations. Benewick describes how distaste for their aggressive political methods (and for the similar methods they drew forth from antifascists) was matched by equal distaste for totalitarian constraints upon the right to free political expression, which may be equally used even upon those demonstrating in favor of the status quo or some democratic reform. The dilemma has recently reemerged concerning the "draconian measures" (as they were described by Roy

Jenkins, the Home Secretary who introduced them in the House of Commons) to curb the activities of the Provisional Irish Republican Army in 1973.

The term super-orthodox political behavior is coined here because it may be felt that "repression" (even more so than "protest") is an emotive and unreliable term; a term, moreover, that might be considered extravagant. Even Mr. Peter Hain, the leader of Young Liberal direct action compaigns, whose acquaintance with the lawful consequences of direct action is considerable, is prepared to concede that "whilst the British police are probably the most reasonable and tolerant in the world, my experience of demonstrations has shown them to be very far from perfect." Cox's analysis of British civil liberties with respect to the right of assembly shows that the authorities have often taken aggressive and prejudicial action against certain protest groups who posed no obvious (certainly no violent) threat to the state. On occasion, such actions have amounted to repression like the extravagant and gratuitous use of police force at demonstrations (e.g., Thurloe Square in 1936 or Trafalgar Square in 1962) or malicious prosecution (e.g., the Karam ruling in 1972 that "conspiracy to trespass" was a serious offense) and surprisingly frequent use of troops to control strikes and total bans on demonstrations under the Public Order Act (e.g., 1947-1950 in London). This kind of action may legitimately be described as "repression"—whether it is also "oppression" is a matter outside the scope of this investigation.

This concept of super-orthodox political behavior or "repression potential" was operationalized in the questionnaire by four questions which asked respondents to indicate to what extent they *approved* of

(a) the courts giving severe sentences to protesters who disregard the police;
(b) the police using force against demonstrators;
(c) the government using troops to break strikes; and
(d) the government passing laws to forbid all public protest demonstrations.

Respondents were also asked to estimate the effectiveness of these actions. Table 3.2 gives the results of these questions, and it will be seen at once that there exists widespread approval for intervention by the police to control demonstrations and to use the courts to punish those who disregard the police backed by an equally widespread conviction that these actions are effective. Less than majority consent exists for the use of troops to break strikes (though a large majority concedes the hypothetical effectiveness of such action), and while a large minority (25 percent) would support a government ban upon demonstrations, most people would regard such action as ineffective. For each of the four items there is a positive correlation

## Table 3.2: Distribution of Super-Orthodox Political Attitudes (in percentages)

|  | Approve Strongly | Approve | Disapprove | Disapprove Strongly | Very Effective | Somewhat Effective | Not Very Effective | Not at all Effective |
|---|---|---|---|---|---|---|---|---|
| The Courts giving severe sentences to protestors who disregard the police | 24 | 56 | 18 | 2 | 26 | 45 | 24 | 5 |
| The police using force against demonstrators | 15 | 58 | 22 | 3 | 24 | 54 | 19 | 4 |
| The Government using troops to break strikes | 7 | 39 | 32 | 20 | 22 | 38 | 23 | 16 |
| The Government passing laws to forbid all public protest demonstrations | 4 | 21 | 52 | 22 | 10 | 25 | 39 | 26 |

between the approval and the effectiveness ratings of .36; .40; .41; and .51 respectively as listed above. This indicates that approval may well be partly contingent upon estimates of effectiveness. This will be taken up again below.

Guttman-scale analysis was applied to both dimensions and a very reliable scale emerged for the approval dimension (rep. = .95), (see Appendix), indicating with precision "how far the Government should go." The effectiveness dimension did not conform to the cumulative model, indicating that some people supported more extreme methods and thought them effective possibly because they thought milder constraints ineffective, while others thought milder constraints effective (and therefore "adequate") and saw more extreme methods possibly as counterproductive. Table 3.3 shows the overall scale distribution of support for super-orthodox political behavior.

In contrast to our results from the protest potential scale, these estimates of repression potential seem to rehabilitate the "deference theory" of British

## Table 3.3: Distribution of "Repression Potential"

| | Respondent approves of:  (= 100%) | | | |
|---|---|---|---|---|
| No Counter-action | Courts Punishing Demonstrations | Police Using Force | Troops vs. Strikes | Government bans all Demonstrations |
| 11.6% | 14.8% | 29.2% | 26.5% | 17.9% |

"Don't know" to more than one item = 7%

Unweighted (n) = 1,660
Weighted (n)   = 1,386

political culture. But the extent to which this may be true depends upon a rather subjective interpretation of the data. Superficially, it gives the government and the police almost a free hand to move against demonstrations as they see fit. Yet there is nothing particularly "deferent" about reaffirming that political disobedients should accept the lawful consequences of their actions. Indeed, Cohen insists that civil disobedience is morally, even logically, invalid if punishment is not accepted. Punishment is *part* of the protest. Nor is the prospect of the police using force a particularly "draconian" spectacle in Britain, except on those occasions when the police feel seriously threatened, it is usually limited to "pushing and shoving" and is often almost good-natured.[1] Even "the use of troops" item may well have been endowed with a greater level of approval than it might otherwise have been given since troops were standing by during the interview period to intervene in the miners' strike to service hospitals with electricity. This may have masked our question's emphasis on *"breaking"* strikes. Only 18 percent would go "all the way" and endorse a complete set of super-orthodox actions which may be contrasted with 22 percent who would participate in the illegal protest items on the protest potential scale.

Even if we accept, as probably we should, that there is no logical contradiction between the majority who will countenance demonstrations and a similar majority who approve of strict police and legal constraints upon them, there is still an interesting test to be made between these two measures. Blumenthal et al., in their study of social and political violence in America, used a very similar distinction between "violence for social change" and "violence for social control" and had factor scales for measuring both. No relationship at all (i.e., a near zero correlation) was found between the two scales. People placed themselves high or low on either scale apparently at random, even though each scale appeared valid in its own right. There just were large numbers of American men who approved of violence for both reasons.

Our own results do not replicate the American study. As expected, there is a *negative* relationship between unorthodox and super-orthodox political methods: $r = -0.33$, which holds at $r = -0.28$ even when the effect of age is partialed out.[2] The clearest discontinuities are those between people who deny the government's right to curb protest and who themselves support protest strongly (42 percent "high" on protest potential); those who believe in "moderate" police action, and who may or may not support protest; and those who support vigorous antiprotest action, and who shun protest altogether. Those who are "low" on both scales are not really in a contradictory position, they are voting for a quiet life, while those who are in an apparently contradictory position (i.e., "high" on both scales) are simply very rare (n=76). The value of a detailed psychological approach may be seen clearly in this analysis. What may have appeared an aberration appears under closer inspection to be a valid relationship: Most people appear to believe that protest is allowable provided it does not get out of hand and that lawbreaking, however understandable, should not go unpunished. To ensure this, support is expressed for moderate police action backed by the authority of the courts.

In this context, it is interesting to examine together people's beliefs concerning the effectiveness of both protest and repression. As we have seen, those who express positive behavioral dispositions toward examples of protest behavior, tend also to believe, item for item, that their use is an effective means of "pressing for changes." So too, those who would endorse the government's use of repressive acts will be far more likely to believe their use effective than those who believe the government should not take such action. Despite this close relationship, neither of those cognitively based effectiveness dimensions quite conforms to the unidimensional and cumulative model that is found for the affective dimensions of approval and behavioral intention. Sooner than lament this finding as some technical deficiency, it seems possible that this difference in attitude structure may have something to tell us.

The scaling model to which the two sets of effectiveness scores do conform is the additive Likert scale. The items are evenly correlated and tap a strong common factor (see Appendix). Using the full range of scores (one to four) two effectiveness scales were constructed by adding the relevant items.

The reasoning that connects the belief in the effectiveness of an act (its "perceived utility" in theoretically precise terminology) to the performance of the same act, rests in the widest sense upon learning theory. Specifically, the argument is derived from those aspects of learning theory that stress the power of positive reward ("reinforcement") to increase the likelihood of a repetition of the rewarded act in the future. This tendency will generalize to other examples of the class of behaviors to which the rewarded act may belong and will do so according to a lawfully decremental response-generalization curve. These are the two cardinal principles of operant conditioning theory. Thus, if activists come to believe (and it need not be true) that participation in, say, a sit-in demonstration in government offices has proved to have a high utility in pressing political demands, then more behavior of this kind will be emitted by them in the future provided there is no marked decrement in related sources of motivation. Also, the high perceived utility of this act will generalize to similar acts like street blockades, factory occupations, picketing, or even boycotts and make their occurrence more likely. Although the sterner elements of the behaviorist school would not find it admissible, we feel reasonably confident that in human beings vicarious reward learning is a reality. As, say, one group of students wrest concessions from their university's disciplinary board by forceful means, so others will be persuaded of the effectiveness of such acts and be encouraged to do something similar.

Such straightforward Skinnerian hypotheses may seem too obvious to bear spelling-out like this. But the matter becomes much less obvious when attitudes towards repression are brought into the argument. We have confidently predicted that a belief in the effectiveness of protest behavior will have a strong positive impact upon protest potential. Avoiding the appearance of coyness, we can report at once that this is so and that the correlation coefficient is +.49. Now, the items that make up the repression scale are all rather obvious punishments contingent upon protest behavior: They imply physical discomfort, judicial punishment, and the deprivation of civil liberty. Thus a belief in the effectiveness of these things should depress protest potential. It does, but not a great deal; the negative correlation is -.20. Thus we may surmise that a general negative impact of effective social control is dimmed perhaps by the reaction of some activists who regard even effective means of political control as a kind of standing provocation, even an encouragement to protest as evidence of a repressive state. More likely though, is the possibility that many protesters are so convinced of the utility of protest that they take a *wider* view of the "effectiveness" of repression. "Yes," they might say, "they could lock us up or call out the troops" (i.e., short-term effectiveness), "but we should win in the end because such things would arouse public sympathy to our side." As a precedent, the attempts to arrest Committee of 100 members to forestall a demonstration may have done exactly that in 1962.

What is particularly fascinating about this set of relationships is that, although protest potential and repression potential are negatively correlated at -.33, beliefs in their effectiveness are scarcely correlated at all: r = -.09. Thus the respective sources of reward and punishment for protest are independent antecedents of protest potential and are most likely to have a combinatory effect (the multiple correlation of the two variables upon the PP scale is .52).

Shifting the focus to repression potential, we find that the obvious hypothesis that belief in the effectiveness of repression will have a positive impact on RP scores is true: r = +.43. But what effect should a belief in the effectiveness of protest have upon repression potential? A common-sense hypothesis might say that people would not feel inclined to invoke these cruder manifestations of power of the state unless they believed that protest was effective and, hence, a threat. What is common sense, however, is often psychological nonsense. The admission of the effectiveness of protest (in "pressing for changes," remember) would be psychologically punishing to those who support stern measures against protesters. They believe such measures *work*, therefore protest is rendered ineffective. And this is the direction of the relationship: r = -.23.

But we must remind ourselves again that the two effectiveness scores are almost unrelated, so the "therefore" in the preceding sentence is not supported by all the evidence. More likely, then, people who support repression are saying that repression is effective but its negative impact upon the effectiveness of protest is contingent upon the support we, and people like us, give it. Thus, two rather different but equally simple causal models are proposed; partial correlations are given in brackets:

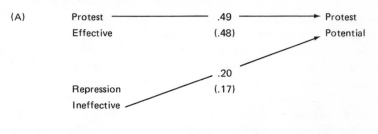

(A) Protest potential is considerably influenced by two independent sources of (principally) reward and (secondarily) of punishment: the effectiveness of protest and the ineffectiveness of repression.

(B) Whereas repression potential is similarly influenced by (principally) reward— 'repression is effective'—it makes far more sense to hold that the belief in the effectiveness of protest is influenced by the support people give to repression, than the other way about.

It is further instructive to examine the relationship between orthodox, unorthodox and super-orthodox politics simultaneously:

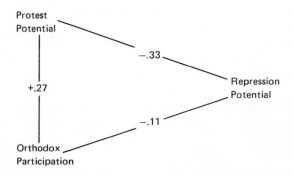

There is a general tendency that what we have called unorthodox and orthodox politics are part of an overlapping universe of "politics for social *change*" while support for super-orthodox political activities is a part of an opposing dimension of "politics for social *control*." This triadic relationship holds constant across five age groups except that older people show a nonsignificant negative relationship between orthodox and super-orthodox scales (due to lack of variance) while the youngest group (16-20 years) shows a similar effect and show a nonsignificant relationship between super-orthodox and unorthodox behavior. Whether this is due to idiosyncratic factors or to intergenerational change is a question for the detailed analysis of the demographic framework in which these measures of political behavior may be located, and this is shortly undertaken below.

Meanwhile, one other test of the relationship between these three dimensions of political behavior is appropriate. This study replicated two questions from the 1960 Almond and Verba "Civic Culture" study in which respondents were asked: "Supposing a new law or regulation were being introduced and you thought it very unjust or harmful, what do you think you could do?" Respondents gave "open-ended" responses to this question both in relation to their local council and to Parliament, and replies to this questionnaire were coded according to the scheme prescribed by Almond and Verba. There appears to have been quite extraordinary stability of attitudes over time. The proportion indicating they would act within the two largest response categories: Those who would contact politicians and support the activities of an ad-hoc protest group, are almost uncannily similar in 1974 as in 1960. There has, however, been some increase in the proportion giving inefficacious replies ("Nothing you can do. . . ." "Don't know. . . ." "It's useless to complain. . . .") and this is especially significant at the *local* level (rising from 23 percent in 1960 to 36 percent in 1973-74). Some of this increase in inefficacy has occurred at the expense of orthodox participation (vote, contact politicians), which may reflect to some extent the effects of the reorganization of local government in 1972-73, which removed many local administrative functions to more remote regional authorities. It also indicates that, in order for the proportions giving efficacious replies to remain superficially similar, many more politically efficacious people are giving multiple responses. Since the proportion of orthodox-type responses has *decreased* somewhat, the proportion of unorthodox replies among the *total of efficacious replies* given must have increased significantly. We see that it has, again particularly in the case of local politics, from 36 percent to 45 percent. So this result is not quite what it first appears: There has been a small but significant decrease in the kind of political efficacy that Almond and Verba called "subject competence" coupled with a similarly small but significant shift towards the inclusion of "unorthodox" political methods in addition to orthodox political action with "marches, demonstrations, and random unspecified protest" emerging as small separate categories. This finding supports our earlier hypothesis that unorthodox political behavior has assumed a greater importance in recent years and has taken its place alongside orthodox politics as a serious set of political alternatives.

Almond and Verba focused upon those responses indicating a solitary act and those indicating participation with others in a group response. We have shifted that focus somewhat to emphasize the distinction between orthodox and unorthodox means of redress. Table 3.4 illustrates the distribution of protest potential, repression potential and orthodox participation separately for those giving "orthodox," "unorthodox," "unspecified," and inefficacious replies to the "subject-competence" questions at the *local* level only. We find a clear and striking pattern:

(a) Those giving *orthodox* replies are slightly higher than average on protest potential, much higher on orthodox participation, and slightly lower on repression potential.
(b) Those giving *unorthodox* replies are much higher than average on the protest scale, higher on orthodox participation, and lower on repression.

This is true mainly of those who specified particular acts of protest and joining protest groups but much less true for those who just mentioned the use of petitions.

(c) Those giving *unspecified* objections are much lower than average on protest potential, a little *higher* than average on orthodox participation and very high on repression potential.
(d) Those giving inefficacious replies are also much lower on protest potential and are similarly very high on repression potential but are very low on orthodox participation.

These results support earlier assertions about the nature of the political behavioral domains tapped by these three measures. There are people who believe in "politics for social change"; some of them incline towards traditional, orthodox methods, while others are increasingly prepared to include the use of unorthodox methods and there are many who may use both. There are other people who believe in "politics for social control," they do not believe in the responsibility or perhaps even the capacity of the individual citizen to respond, even to something they personally feel is unjust. These

**Table 3.4: Types of Participation by Subject Competence (in percentages)**

*To oppose unjust laws, respondent would use:*

| | (n) | By Protest Potential | | | By Orthodox Participation | | | By Repression Potential | | |
|---|---|---|---|---|---|---|---|---|---|---|
| | | Low | Medium | High | Low | Medium | High | Low | Medium | High |
| (a) "Orthodox" Action | | | | | | | | | | |
| 1. Contact politicians | (712) | 30 | 43 | 27 | 26 | 29 | 45 | 31 | 31 | 38 |
| 2. Contact party, vote, use interest group (T.U.s etc.), contact bureaucracy | (122) | 39 | 33 | 28 | 29 | 22 | 49 | 30 | 33 | 37 |
| All respondents (a) | | 32 | 41 | 27 | 27 | 27 | 46 | 30 | 31 | 39 |
| (b) "Unorthodox" Action | | | | | | | | | | |
| 1. Petition | (347) | 32 | 41 | 27 | 35 | 29 | 36 | 29 | 31 | 39 |
| 2. March, boycott, strike, join protest group, use media | (270) | 22 | 41 | 36 | 27 | 28 | 45 | 37 | 30 | 33 |
| All respondents (b) | | 27 | 41 | 32 | 32 | 29 | 39 | 32 | 31 | 37 |
| (c) Unspecified Objectives | (61) | 55 | 31 | 14 | 40 | 22 | 38 | 31 | 16 | 54 |
| (d) "Nothing" | (363) | 56 | 27 | 17 | 59 | 24 | 17 | 21 | 28 | 51 |
| All respondents (a–d) | | 42 | 35 | 23 | 42 | 26 | 32 | 26 | 29 | 45 |

matters are best left to the state, either as an act of positive trust or negative hopelessness. If deference still exists as a force in British politics, it is among this minority that it will be found.

## The Social Location of Protest and Repression

The character of this section will be descriptive rather than analytic. We do not have a *social* theory of political participation to test but an analysis must be set forth that illustrates clearly the "social location" of political behavior, concentrating heavily upon protest potential, that will enable the subsequent psychological analysis to proceed in the surer knowledge of what social characteristics need to be taken into account before conclusions may safely be drawn about more individual or psychological characteristics that may appear to explain protest behavior.

It was stated that no social theory will be tested but there are quite a number of established demographic effects known to have a bearing upon protest behavior and these may be examined in this study without the need for an elaborate theoretical framework. First, commonsense expectations suggest that those most prone to protest will be young. Almost by legend, the young have the energy and the time for the vigorous pursuit of causes and are said to be vulnerable to the ideological sources of motivation associated with protest. Table 3.5 summarizes the main demographic correlates of protest potential and shows first that this expectation is borne out handsomely; there is a negative correlation of r = -.34 between age and protest potential. The relationship is smoothly linear; the older the respondent, the less likely he is to protest. The strong emphasis placed upon the behavioral component of attitudes towards protest may well have strengthened this relationship and it may well be that asking an old-age pensioner how likely it is that he would occupy a building or blockade traffic is a little like asking him—or especially her—how many times a day she vaults her garden fence. It is perhaps surprising even that as many as 37 percent of the retired would seriously contemplate attending a demonstration. In contrast, the highest point on the scale is the *modal* response category for those under 21 years of age.

The strength of this age effect, and the fundamental implications of this social characteristic for this study to some extent determines the empirical and even the theoretical considerations that will concern the remainder of this analysis. When we come to consider what causes protest potential we must also ask: Are we dealing with a life-cycle effect (i.e., something people do when young then abandon) or real intergenerational change, or a mixture of both, and if so to what extent might one interpretation dominate the other?

**Table 3.5: Main Demographic Correlates of Protest Potential (in percentages)**

| | Protest Potential | | | | | |
|---|---|---|---|---|---|---|
| | No Protest | Petitions Only | Demonstrations | Boycotts | Rent Strikes/ Strikes | Occupations/ Blockades |
| *Age* | | | | | | |
| Over 65 | 38 | 25 | 19 | 11 | 4 | 3 |
| 45-64 | 24 | 21 | 23 | 14 | 11 | 8 |
| 30-44 | 15 | 22 | 19 | 17 | 13 | 13 |
| 21-29 | 10 | 18 | 20 | 19 | 14 | 21 |
| 16-20 | 9 | 16 | 21 | 16 | 11 | 28 |
| *Sex* | | | | | | |
| Men | 18 | 17 | 20 | 16 | 13 | 16 |
| Women | 25 | 25 | 20 | 14 | 8 | 8 |
| *Social Class Background* | | | | | | |
| Professional/managerial | 14 | 21 | 24 | 18 | 10 | 14 |
| White collar | 17 | 21 | 24 | 18 | 12 | 9 |
| Skilled manual | 23 | 18 | 19 | 15 | 13 | 12 |
| Unskilled and others | 29 | 25 | 17 | 12 | 8 | 9 |
| *Terminal Educational Age* | | | | | | |
| Under 15 | 32 | 24 | 19 | 11 | 8 | 6 |
| 15 | 16 | 22 | 20 | 17 | 10 | 15 |
| 16-17 | 13 | 19 | 25 | 16 | 12 | 15 |
| Over 18 | 8 | 15 | 23 | 25 | 15 | 14 |
| *Trade Union Membership* | | | | | | |
| Member | 16 | 15 | 19 | 16 | 16 | 17 |
| Nonmember | 24 | 24 | 21 | 14 | 8 | 10 |

| Product-Moment Correlations | Protest Potential | (Partialed on Age) |
|---|---|---|
| Age | .34 | — |
| Sex | .17 | (.19) |
| Social class | .13 | (.12) |
| Education | .20 | (.13) |
| Union membership | .18 | (.18) |

One demographic variable that is genuinely independent of age is sex. Table 3.5 shows that men have a higher protest potential than women and this effect interacts with age to the extent that young women have a *higher* protest potential than even middle-aged men. This is quite a remarkable finding and suggests for example that the growth of the Women's Liberation Movement feeds upon a considerable stock of protest potential among young women.

Another demographic variable largely unaffected by age is geographical region. Wales emerges as the region containing the widest parameters of license favorable to unorthodox politics and confirms, on a countrywide basis, Peter Madjwick's evidence from Cardiganshire of an apparently high protest potential fueling the abiding antiestablishment and nationalist political sentiments characteristic of Wales. That East Anglia should also display a high protest potential is surprising but simply explained: One of our four sampling points in that part of the country turned out to be a hall of residence in the University of East Anglia. Those regions containing the bulk of the population do not in fact vary very much except that London shows the highest levels, as may be expected. Among those regions showing the lowest protest potential are the rural areas of Southwest England, Yorkshire, and the traditional unskilled working-class areas of the Northeast.

Regional variations suggest an underlying effect of social class but the direct relationship between protest potential and social class is elusive. There is a statistically significant but not very great tendency for those whose class background (i.e., the occupation of the head of household) is unskilled working-class to have a lower protest potential than skilled working-class or nonmanual workers, who scarcely differ at all (see Table 3.5). This pattern is repeated when the occupational class of those currently working is examined separately from those who are not head of the household. When the class effect is controlled by age, however, an interesting relationship emerges. Among older respondents the difference between the higher protest potential of the professional middle classes and the skilled working class on the one hand, and the lower protest potential of the white-collar workers and the unskilled workers on the other achieves significant levels (though not great magnitude) but there are absolutely no class differences in protest potential among younger respondents.

Given that occupational class has so little effect, the hypothesis follows that income should be relatively unrelated to protest potential. This is not to be the case. There is a *positive* correlation of $r = 0.29$ between level of income and protest potential—the higher the respondent's income, the *more* likely he is to protest. This relationship diminishes sharply, however, when the effect of the low incomes of the elderly is accounted for. Yet income still remains a better predictor of protest potential than class background.

The fact that income should be a more relevant measure of political action than occupational class may be a reflection of a social process to which

Runciman drew attention. Those elements formally seen to vary systematically with social class—especially income and education—are now starting to "split off" under the impact of the relative success of trade unions bargaining on behalf of skilled workers, and the decline of occupational status of white-collar workers. The kind of belligerence that accompanies successful wage bargaining and encourages also the migration of vigorous, energetic young workers into the high-earning sectors of manual working-class occupations may also be reflected in a taste for aggressive political action.

Education contributes its own effect to protest potential. There is a marked discontinuity between the low protest potential of those who left school at fourteen years of age and those who left later—especially those who left after the age of eighteen and therefore attended college or university. This discontinuity is of course attributable to the 1944 Education Act, which raised the school-leaving age to fifteen. Therefore, most of those leaving school below this age are now over forty-five. This effect persists when the sample is trichotomized at age thirty and age sixty-four. Older college-educated people do emerge as more prone to protest compared even to their moderately well-educated peers. Among younger respondents (under thirty) an intriguing effect emerges: The discontinuity-point simply shifts upwards to age fifteen, along with the school-leaving age. But the differences are not as great as may be expected and are concentrated at the lower end of the scale, i.e., better-educated young people are less likely to eschew protest altogether than are those who left school at fifteen and are somewhat more likely to have a high protest potential especially those attending universities (see Table 3.5). Even they, however, are little match for the thirty members of our sample who are still at school, fully 63 percent of whom have a high protest potential.

Logically perhaps, a discussion should now follow on the special influences of higher education upon protest behavior. To do so now, however, would disrupt this narrative to an unacceptable extent. "Why students protest" has become a subdiscipline of a subdiscipline. This is partly a result of the theoretical difficulties of incorporating the political motivation of students into a general theory of protest behavior. In this study we have taken this separateness seriously and administered the general population questionnaire to a national sample of 289 students. Chapter 8 will be devoted to a comparison of the political attitudes and actions of this student sample with those of the whole community.

Another segment of conventional wisdom in this field of study asserts that a great deal of what has here been called "protest potential" resides among "trade union militants"—the bêtes-noirs of "moderate opinion" and the fountainhead of an unreasonable truculence which must surely be a major element of the disposition measured by the protest scale. Twenty-five percent of our sample admit membership of a trade union and show a significantly higher protest potential than nonmembers. Nor is this effect due to the fact that trade unionists are predominantly male. Young female trade unionists also favor protest more than the majority of their sex who do not belong to unions. Interestingly, this finding is confined to older respondents; though young trade unionists have a somewhat higher protest potential than non-unionists, the difference is not statistically significant. The difference among older respondents is therefore quite striking. Even more interesting is the finding that those among trade unionists who attend union meetings are only a little, and certainly not significantly, more likely to be high on protest potential than those who do not attend. It may be that the reference criteria for attendance used by respondents consisted of merely forming a group around the shop steward when asked to contribute an opinion by a show of hands. But the question stated clearly, "Do you attend branch meetings of your Union?" and only a minority (39 percent) claimed that they ever did attend. The evidence is that they are not a militant minority when compared with other trade unionists nor are they very young. The speculation that industrial unrest is caused by a concentration of young militant trade union-ists, who are motivated by wider aggressive political ideology, and who run union affairs in the face of the apathy of the rank and file draws no support from these data (see Table 3.5). Nor can support be found for speculation that protest potential is concentrated in key groups of unions. Skilled union-ists (e.g., electricians, engineers) have only a marginally higher protest poten-tial than unskilled groups (e.g., GMWU) but not higher than members of white-collar unions like ASTMS, though these people are much rarer in the sample.

Some attempt must be made to estimate the independence of these measures from each other, in the contribution they make to establishing the social location of protest potential and to conduct a comparative analysis with the demographic influences upon the adjacent measures of participa-tion—orthodox and super-orthodox behavior—introduced earlier in this chap-ter. Clearly this analysis promises to become unwieldy and unhelpfully repetitive so precisely detailed descriptive analysis will be sacrificed for the alternative precision and economy afforded by the use of correlation and regression analysis.

At the zero-order level the pattern of results for repression potential mirror those obtained for protest potential with slightly lower values and opposite signs. The emphasis shifts somewhat for orthodox participation in that age assumes much less importance and class and education relatively more influence, but otherwise aligns more with the pattern for protest poten-tial. These results conform to commonsense expectations about conventional political participation rates (cf., Campbell et al., "The American Voter") and suggest confirmation of our earlier assertions that protest and orthodox participation are occupying similar attitudinal universes in opposition to repression potential. Rather more interesting is the fact that the influence of demographic variables operates largely independent of the effect of age not only in the case of predicting protest potential but also for repression potential and orthodox participation. Table 3.6 advances this analysis by use of a standard stepwise multiple regression analysis. Since this technique will overemphasize the result of chance variations in significance levels, the pattern of results given must be interpreted cautiously. For example, in the prediction of protest and repression potentials, social class fails to attain significance because (as was hinted earlier) the main components of social class—income and education—are already contributing their separate influences. Nor is the magnitude of the b-coefficient a particularly reliable estimate of the "importance" of a particular variable. But as a rough guide, the results suggest that age, sex, and union membership are the most powerful predictors of both protest potential *and* repression potential, but the pattern for orthodox participation is rather too weak (only 6 percent of the variance is explained) to be of much help. The emergence of trade unionism as an important variable is particularly interesting. Its influence is exerted in the opposite direction as education and class, since nonunionized workers will be better educated and have higher social status.

When the whole sample is divided simultaneously by age, sex, and trade union membership, the results, as may be expected from the regression analysis, are very striking. Among the under 30s, fully 52 percent of the male trade unionists and 39 percent of the women score high on the protest scale compared with 38 percent and 31 percent respectively among young non-trade unionists. Among older groups (30-64) it is obviously the male trade unionists who show greatest political aggression, still with 37 percent high on the scale.

Weighing the results impressionistically, the parameters of license for unorthodox political behavior seem to widen around two clusterings of demographic characteristics in the population: among the young better-educated middle classes and among young skilled working-class trade unionists, and in the latter case these parameters become especially wide if only male members of the sample are considered. It may appear, therefore, that when Daniel Cohn-Bendit exhorted, "Workers and students, unite!" he knew whereof he spoke. But what he said was true only to a certain extent; there are quite large numbers of potential protesters among older people, surprisingly so in the case of the 45-64 age group. The most important theoretical consideration with respect to the demographic location of protest potential is

Table 3.6: Regression Analysis of Demographic Variables on Participation Indices

|  | (Constant) | Age + | Class + | T.E.A. + | Sex + | Union Membership + | Income + | Region | Multiple Correlation | Variance Explained |
|---|---|---|---|---|---|---|---|---|---|---|
| Protest Potential | (1.72) | .36 | NS | .05 | .41 | .33 | .06 | .07 | .43 | 19% |
| Repression Potential | (3.45) | .19 | NS | .04* | .26 | .37 | NS | .04* | .31 | 10% |
| Orthodox Participation | (3.77) | .20 | .20 | .07 | .05 | NS | .07 | NS | .25 | 6% |

*P < .05 > .01

Otherwise all b coefficients are significant by the 1% level of confidence.

Coefficients are given unstandardized for each equation derived from stepwise multiple regression.

Optimum Equation Predicting Protest Potential

|  | Age + | Sex + | Union Membership + | Education |
|---|---|---|---|---|
| P.P. Score | .31 | .13 | .10 | .08 |

Multiple R = .38          Variance explained = 15%

(Standardized b coefficients, all significant beyond 1% level)

that our findings lend no support at all to the second part of Kornhauser's theory of alienation. Kornhauser's oft-quoted dictum, "People who are atomised readily become mobilised" can find no apparent fit with our data. Those extending greater license of protest behavior are not "fringe people" unable to express themselves through functioning institutions but seem instead relatively well-integrated and more than averagely successful individuals who happen to regard the possibility of protest as a legitimate addition to the social and political options they currently exercise.

There is, however, an even more appropriate test of the atomization theory which was first applied by Parkin in his study of CND supporters. Rather than social isolates, he found that his sample of CNDers were also "joiners" and "doers" on a wide scale. They belonged to all kinds of organizations not at all characteristic of people wandering around on the fringe of the political system voicing random appeals for attention toward a distant and alien authority. But Parkin's sample was taken from a self-consciously middle-class and moralistic group of activists whose humanitarian concerns were certain to spill over into charity work, social endeavours, and orthodox politics. We have the opportunity to examine the group membership network of a general population sample of likely protesters and nonprotesters because our respondents were asked to give full details of what organizations they belonged to.

We found a clear linear increase in protest potential among those who belong to organizations and those who do not, which continues to increase the more organizations the individual reports membership of. Given that so many nonprotesting old people will belong to local associations to assist the elderly, this result dismisses Kornhauser's hypothesis quite conclusively. As one would expect, among specific activities, political memberships attract high protest scores but similarly high scores for members of business associations can only be explained by the presence of young graduate professionals among them, while, even more surprisingly, high scores for members of ex-servicemen's organizations may reflect a very high proportion of trade unionists. The group with the highest score—and a large group at that—are members of athletic clubs. This may be due simply to a majority of these members being male and, naturally, more than half are under thirty. It may also reflect a certain aggressive nature that goes with the pursuit of sport, especially the support of association football clubs. In contrast, though, members of youth clubs do *not* show a high protest potential despite the powerful effect of age in the sample as a whole and even though the great majority are boys. It is an indication that such organizations continue to attract establishment-minded and compliant young people. That members of church, farm, and masonic organizations should show the lowest protest potential *and* exceptionally high repression potentials is no surprise. In the case of working-class "masonic" groups (Buffaloes, Oddfellows, etc.) no trace apparently lingers of Hobsbawn's luddites, swearing secret allegiance to the nineteenth century forerunners of those organizations.

## SUMMARY

This chapter has explored the wider setting of protest potential and found it an important part of a wider distinction between politics for social change and politics for social control. Further evidence has also emerged in favor of the strength of active democratic and participatory sentiments among the British polity and against the preeminence of deference. The parameters of license for protest behavior were found to widen around young educated middle-class people and younger male trade unionists but by no means to the exclusion of other social groups. There is no "closed shop" for unorthodox political behavior, nor is it the exclusive property of the intellectuals. The next chapter will examine protest potential in its party political and ideological context.

# NOTES

1. This is a highly debatable point, of course. Our earlier reference to Cox's analysis and also Humphries' account of police action against minority-group protest would call this into doubt. The point remains true, however, that usually the police will avoid unnecessary force, whereas police in other countries often appear to relish it.

2. Blumental's sample was all-male. A further check on our data shows that the correlation is -0.32 for men and -0.35 for women, an insignificant difference.

*Chapter 4*

# PROTEST AND PARTISANSHIP:

# THE POLITICAL AND IDEOLOGICAL

# LOCATION OF PROTEST

## *The Immediate Political Context*

The previous chapter established the main features of the social location of protest potential and the corresponding location of orthodox and super-orthodox tendencies. We shall now be concerned to shift our point of observation into the domain of orthodox party politics to examine how protest potential lies in relation to the ideological and partisan reference-points of British party politics. It is therefore appropriate to remind the reader of some of the general features of British party politics at the time of the field-work for this survey—October 1973 to January 1974—that may have an important influence upon the results discussed in this chapter.

At this time a Conservative administration under Edward Heath had, as it turned out, nearly completed a term of office started in June 1970 when the Conservative party defeated the Labour party's bid for a third term. During this time, the government had attempted some radical changes in the empha-sis and direction of social and economic development. For the first two years of the administration, a policy was pursued which owed much to free-market doctrines of economic management. Many of these changes were of a fiscal nature, noticeably an increase in the money supply but others carried a more obvious political weight. Two measures in particular are pertinent to this study: The Housing Finance Act and The Industrial Relations Act.

The first of these acts was intended to raise the level of council rents by a series of increments up to those obtaining in the private sectors. Thus council tenants—some 43 percent of all households—were to pay a "commercial rate" for that accommodation, or at least something more closely aligned with private rents for equivalent accommodation. This represented a major departure from the Labour-inspired principle of subsidized accommodation for working-class families. This departure was strongly resisted in many areas and possibly more than fifty rent strikes were undertaken by council tenants (see Moorehouse and Chamberlin 1972) often with the tacit, even overt support of local Labour-controlled councils. Contiguously, though unconnected, vastly more comprehensive rent strikes were undertaken in Northern Ireland in protest against internment, and this provided an effective model for English rent strikers. This movement continued into 1973 but rather sporadically. Also at the time of the survey, many university students were on rent strike in protest against increases in their living costs. Thus many communities throughout Britain were involved in or exposed to this kind of direct action against political authority.

The Industrial Relations Act represented a determined attempt to regulate the authority of trade union organization by abolishing the "closed shop," holding Unions and sometimes individual officials legally responsible for breaches in agreements, providing for ballot procedures to initiate industrial action, and several other measures reducing the unions' freedom of action. In effect, the Act made many kinds of industrial action illegal. Trade unions resisted the passage of this legislation through their Labour party colleagues and by initiating a "Kill the Bill" campaign of mass demonstrations and lobbies of Parliament. Later some unions fought a vigorous campaign of noncooperation with the Industrial Relations Court often incurring heavy financial penalties and even short periods of imprisonment for offenders. This area of what Labour politicians began to describe as "confrontation" took on increased significance when the Government reversed an earlier determination not to limit wage awards by legislation and introduced a series of acts known collectively as "Stages I to III" of an "Anti-inflation package." Strikes by workers in basic industries for wage increases beyond those stipulated by government legislation were lent an increasingly political character by the use of the Industrial Relations Act to resist their effect and regulate their conduct. These particular provisions of the act were seen to be less helpful than intended and reflected back upon the Industrial Relations Court an image more than a little tinged with political partisanship. During the fieldwork period, this series of developments had culminated in a second "confrontation" between the National Union of Mineworkers and their government employers. The Union pressed a pay claim that exceeded the Government's "guidelines" and commenced an overtime ban on November 12, 1973. The government took the opportunity to test its political authority and resisted the demands of the miners, who commenced a total strike on February 9, 1974. The effects of the strike were redoubled by the shortage of fuel oil resulting from the restrictions placed upon oil production by the Organization of Petroleum Exporting Countries during the later stages of the war between Israel and the Egyptian-Syrian alliance in October 1973. In December, the Government imposed very severe restrictions upon the use of power, resulting in a three-day working week for most employed people and issued fuel-rationing coupons. In January, the railway driver's union (A.S.L.E.F.) announced their intention to strike.

The entire period was a remarkable one for British politics and political consciousness was undoubtedly at an unusually high level. This was subsequently reflected in a reversal of the downward trend in postwar voting turnout; 82.3 percent of the electorate voted in the general election on February 28, 1974 compared with 72.3 percent in June 1970. During this time also the sectarian conflict in Northern Ireland had worsened steadily, and this added further to a sense of growing political anomie. The government increasingly found it necessary to make a case for political authority itself, and this case was publicly argued for the first time in modern British politics, certainly since the General Strike of 1926. The question put was: "Who governs Britain?" and the answers obtained were not always very clear. This fact alone may justify this digression into generalized political narrative because the reader is obliged to judge the extent to which this novel feature of political argument (much of it very loud argument) affected the responses examined below.

## Protest and Party Identification

Respondents were asked to name the political party to which they "usually felt closest." Only 13 percent of the total sample felt unable to do so, reaffirming Britain's unusually high rate of "party-identification" (see Rose, "Electoral Behaviour"). Of the remainder, about 40 percent reported their affiliation with the Conservative party, 46 percent for the Labour party, and 14 percent for the Liberals and "others." There was a more even balance between support for the two major parties during the February election which was maintained up to the general election on the 28th of that month in spite of increased defection from both parties toward the Liberal party, who eventually acquired some 18 percent of the votes cast.

All that is known and written about British politics suggests the hypothesis that protest potential will be associated much more with Labour and Liberal sympathies than with Conservative support. Table 4.1 confirms this hypothesis. While significant, the differences in levels of protest potential between supporters of the three parties are not great. Though only 14 percent of Conservatives would seriously consider engaging in illegal forms of protest, this is still a high figure among the supporters of a party whose leaders were *at the time of the survey*, loudly proclaiming the necessity of respect for political authority. Furthermore, less than a majority (47 percent) of Conservatives would abstain from protest and go no further than "petitions," leaving 39 percent who would consider legal forms of unorthodox political behavior. On the other hand, almost as many Labour supporters as Conservatives would abstain from protest (43 percent), though rather more would consider illegal protest (25 percent). The Liberals have the highest protest potential among the "establishment" parties with 28 percent scoring high on the scale but the tiny assortment of Nationalists and Communists (twenty-one respondents in all) score highest with 43 percent. The group with the lowest protest potential, however, are those who fail to identify with a political party at all, or who guard their party identification from inquiry, and the implications of this finding will furnish the starting point of a new discussion below.

The repression potential scale divided party supporters in the opposite direction and did so a little more sharply. Sixty-one percent of Conservatives would use troops against strikers or support a government ban on demonstrations compared with only 31 percent of Labour supporters. Previously in this analysis we have established a consistent trend that the highest levels of protest potential tend to occur contiguously with the lowest levels of repres-

**Table 4.1: Protest Potential by Party Identification (in percentages)**

|  | (n) | No Protest | Petitions Only | Demonstrations | Boycotts | Rent Strikes/ Strikes | Occupations/ Blockades |
|---|---|---|---|---|---|---|---|
| Conservatives | (598) | 22 | 25 | 23 | 16 | 8 | 6 |
| Labour | (627) | 22 | 21 | 18 | 15 | 11 | 12 |
| Liberal | (240) | 16 | 15 | 25 | 17 | 16 | 12 |
| Others | (21) | 10 | 19 | 24 | 5 | 10 | 33 |
| No party | (45) | 33 | 15 | 20 | 10 | 10 | 12 |
| Refuse to answer | (37) | 28 | 32 | 4 | 16 | 8 | 12 |
| Don't know | (126) | 30 | 19 | 18 | 13 | 5 | 16 |

wN = 1,263    $\chi^2$ = 158.1 with 54 d.f.  P = 0.——)  Gamma = .1

sion potential. This is not so among supporters of the Liberal party, who, while having the highest protest potential, have also quite a high level of repression potential (45 percent). This is especially surprising since Liberal views are not normally associated with retributive policies.

Party support is, of course, known to interact with other factors. We examined first the relationship between the P.P. and RP scales and party identification controlled for age. Partisan choice influences protest potential mostly independently of age group membership, but the exceptions to that statement lie in a very unexpected direction: Young Conservative supporters have a protest potential almost as high as young Labour supporters and actually higher than middle-aged Labour or Liberal supporters. More in line with expectation, they do have a rather higher repression potential and thus appear to be a primary source of those holding a "contradictory" position of being high on both scales. It may be fair to assume they are ready to participate in certain kinds of protest they consider justified but are not averse to urging the use of authority power against those protesters of whom they disapprove.

In contrast, the certainty with which older Conservatives eschew protest and endorse repression (71 percent are high on the repression scale) reveals an impressive clarity in the organization of their views. By comparison, even the commitment to protest shown by young Labour and Liberal supporters (only these groups show an unqualified preference for protest over repression) looks tentative.

Youth and partisan choice, therefore, interact positively to maximize protest potential on the "young centre-to-left" of the party political continuum. Is this true within each social class? Table 4.2 shows that it is with two very important exceptions: the older middle-class Labour supporters and young working-class Conservatives, both of whom show unexpectedly high levels of protest potential. Why should this be? Abrams (1974) has demonstrated that middle-class Socialists are politically deviant in two directions: They vote Labour against their apparent class interests by persisting with the partisan choice of their (often working-class) parents yet they share very few of the political values and thoughts of their fellow Labour supporters among the working class. According to Abrams, their higher education permits them to justify their dual political isolation in articulate and ideological terms and to emphasize personal efficacy in political action. Thus they may be far more likely to participate in unorthodox political behavior than are their working-class peers among Labour supporters. In fact they maintain a protest potential actually higher than many much younger than themselves.

The other interesting feature of Table 4.2 is the division among the young Conservatives. Whereas middle-class Conservatives under thirty are the only young group to resemble most older respondents in holding back in greater

Table 4.2: Protest Potential by Party, Age, and Social Class of Head of Household (in percentages)

| Social Class | (n) | 16—29 | | | 30—64 | | | 65+ | | |
|---|---|---|---|---|---|---|---|---|---|---|
| | | Low | Med | High | Low | Med | High | Low | Med | High |
| *Conservative* | | | | | | | | | | |
| middle class | (307) | 29 | 40 | 31 | 42 | 46 | 12 | 53 | 42 | 5 |
| working class | (254) | 25 | 36 | 39 | 37 | 42 | 21 | 73 | 24 | 2 |
| *Labour* | | | | | | | | | | |
| middle class | (102) | 20 | 36 | 44 | 19 | 33 | 48 | 47 | 32 | 21 |
| working class | (473) | 29 | 35 | 36 | 42 | 35 | 23 | 67 | 24 | 9 |
| *Liberal* | | | | | | | | | | |
| middle class | (124) | 19 | 47 | 34 | 24 | 48 | 28 | 29 | 47 | 24 |
| working class | (100) | 15 | 35 | 50 | 43 | 34 | 23 | 42 | 42 | 15 |

numbers from more vigorous forms of protest, working-class young Conservatives reveal a protest potential even higher than young working-class Labour supporters. What seemed to start, therefore, as a rather straightforward analysis describing the socio-political location of protest potential as a property of youthful left-inclined people is complicated by the addition to the ranks of the "protest-prone" of young working-class Conservatives and older middle-class Labour supporters, two groups with very little in common, socially or politically. Except, of course, that they are *both* politically "deviant" groups, each projecting their political loyalties across the grain of their class identification. The behavior of the middle-class Labour supporters is highly predictable in the light of Parkin's analysis of CND supporters—exactly the kind of "principled" issue that would characterize the protest motivation of the middle-class radical. (The expectation of "middle-class radicalism" was one factor prompting our oversampling of middle-class areas.) The behavior of the young working-class Tories, on the other hand, is less expected. Nordlinger's data[1] would certainly lead us to expect Conservatives under the age of thirty to be somewhat less "deferential" than their elders but he does not prepare us for such a clear demonstration of aggressive intentions. That their own party should have chosen, at the time of the survey, to prepare an election campaign which had as its main purpose the reaffirmation of political authority itself indicates that surprise at this result would not be confined to academic circles. Working-class young Tories and even many of their middle-class copartisans, are clearly set at an uncomfortable distance from their political leaders, on styles of action anyway. Equally interesting is the class division among young Liberal supporters. Whereas we are accustomed to thinking of "typical" middle-class young Liberal protest activity (anti-Apartheid, antijuggernaut, antipollution, and so on) it is young Liberals from working-class homes who show much greater protest potential than their middle-class copartisans.

Two hypotheses about the relationship between party choice and protest are suggested by these findings:

(1) The relationship is mediated by "class consciousness"
(2) The relationship is mediated by an individual sense of distance from political parties in general and from the political party of habitual allegiance in particular.

These hypotheses will be examined in turn.

## Protest, Parties, and "Class-Consciousness"

Centers established the case for the separate predictive properties of the social class to which an individual assigns himself as distinct from the class to which a sociologist assigns him on grounds of the nature of his employment or the employment of the head of his household. Butler and Stokes have found the measure of considerable use in explaining the presence of middle-class Labour support and working-class Tories: They "identify" with the class "represented" by the party for whom they vote. Table 4.3 shows the extent of cross-class identification and that, allowing for the less finely calibrated class coding of our sample, the proportion of middle-class people identifying with the working class and vice versa has remained remarkably constant over eleven years, possibly excepting an apparent increase of "middle-class" identification among unskilled workers. This is probably accounted for by our inclusion of the economically inactive among this group. The proportion of major party supporters voting Labour in each group has also remained remarkably constant. Identification with the middle-class increases the tendency to support the Conservatives among working-class people, and identification with the working class increases Labour sympathies among middle-class people. Given the slight overall preference for Labour and Liberal among protesters, this suggests the hypothesis that "radicalism"—hence also protest potential—will be increased among Labour supporters whose class identity is congruent with political sympathies and further depressed among class-congruent Tories. None of this is so. In the case of Conservatives, we find that the aggressive political response among young working-class Tories is actually amplified, i.e., young Tories who *think* of themselves as working-class tend to be a more concentrated group of protesters than those who merely come from working-class households. Among young Liberals and Labour supporters, however, the switch to a subjective measure of class identity causes a migration of protest

Table 4.3: Class Self-Image by Occupation Status of Head of Household in 1963 and 1974 (in percentages)

| Year | Managerial | | Nonmanual | | Manual | |
|------|--------|-------|-------------|-----------------|---------|-----------|
|      | Higher | Lower | Supervisors | Non-Supervisors | Skilled | Unskilled |
| *1963* | | | | | | |
| Middle class | 78 | 65 | 60 | 32 | 17 | 9 |
| Working class | 22 | 35 | 40 | 68 | 83 | 91 |
| *1974* | A | B | | C1 | C2 | DE |
| Middle class | 79 | 67 | | 49 | 26 | 20 |
| Working class | 21 | 33 | | 51 | 74 | 80 |

SOURCE: D. Butler and D. Stokes, **Political Change in Britain.** 1971, p. 58.

potential away from the working-class towards the middle-class. This is probably a reflection of young radicals in working-class households who, receiving higher education, might expect a "middle-class" future. The Labour supporters in this last category will naturally replace the protest-prone middle-aged Socialists noted earlier.

A more sharply defined hypothesis suggests that congruence between objective and subjective social class and not between subjective class and party identification is the more appropriate measure. Again our hypothesis is clearly disconfirmed: The group emerging with significantly the highest protest potential (irrespective of age) are the middle-class Labour supporters who know and affirm their own class status, much higher than those middle-class Labour supporters who identify themselves as working-class. Similarly, working-class Conservatives do not show depressed levels of protest potential if they identify with the party-congruent choice of a middle-class self-image. The lowest protest potential among Conservatives and of any group, is shown by the working-class Tories who admit to working-class status. Possibly in this cell we have located Nordlinger's deferentials who in this sample comprise 10 percent of those who identify with a party and a class: exactly the same proportion found in Nordlinger's sample. They certainly exhibit deferent attitudes towards political action: a lack of commitment to protest and a high repression potential (a mean of 3.7 on the five-point repression scale). Yet it is still difficult to imagine this group being able to project a sufficient influence to be the primary source of political stability in England.

An alternative hypothesis may be derived from an appreciation of Runci-man's work and of the results obtained from the Goldthorpe and Lockwood affluent worker studies. These studies, among many other things, suggested that continued embourgeoisification of employed manual workers from an early high material base continually drew the sting of radicalism in Britain. From a neo-Marxist viewpoint, the workers have been "bought off." From another view the process has been a rational integration of the capitalist's need to increase markets and the legitimate material ambitions of the workers. Whatever the chosen rhetoric, it follows that an upward identification by the working class towards the middle-class should decrease protest potential. Again the evidence of denies this hypothesis. *Regardless of party*, those working-class people identifying with the middle class are likely to have as high or a higher protest potential than those identifying with the working class.

Of course, we are not using "class consciousness" in the more familiar Marxist sense of the awareness among workers of being a member of an exploited majority, a realization which would be expected to heighten protest potential, indeed to heighten revolutionary potential. Yet the very first cognitive stage of such a realization—the simple identification by workers with their own class fails to raise political aggression even among those who have sufficient class-political consciousness to support their own class-congruent political party, Labour.

## Protest and Psychological Distance from Parties

Chapter Three established that higher levels of protest potential are not associated with an estrangement from orthodox politics but are part of a parallel, dualist attitude towards the use of political action. Protesters vote and are quite prone to involvement in orthodox party politics. But might there not be, *within* a general acceptance of party politics, a reserve about their party loyalties? We hypothesize that those with a high protest potential will be those with weaker-than-average party loyalties among party identifiers and that this will be particularly true of Labour supporters.

Having stated their partisan preference, respondents were asked to indicate their sense of subjective "closeness" to the party of their choice, whether they felt "very close," "fairly close," or "not very close" to their party. Whereas 60 percent of respondents indicated they felt at least "fairly close," to their party, this was much less true of younger respondents (43% of those under 21 felt close to their party) who, as we know, have generally much higher levels of protest potential, which suggests the possibility of an overall linear increase of protest potential as a function of strength of party attachment. The strength of party support overall and the decline of party support among the young is identical among Conservative and Labour supporters but lower overall among Liberal supporters, whose younger members, surprisingly perhaps, seem distinctly unenthusiastic.

Table 4.4 shows that the suggested curvilinear relationship between psychological attachment to party and protest potential is present but is not very strong overall. Those with strong party loyalties have a lower protest potential (14% high on the PP scale) compared with those with weaker loyalties (24%), but so do those with no party loyalties at all. Further divided by age, however, Table 4.4 reveals a striking explanation of the overall effect: Party identifiers over sixty-five have a low protest potential regardless of the strength of that identity and those retired people with no party identity at all reject protest altogether, they are quite outside political action of all kinds. Among those under thirty, a linear relationship exists—protest potential increases with party attachment, but the group very close to a party is so small that the significance of the relationship is slight. It is among those of the majority in the middle-age ranges (30-64) that a clear curvilinear relationship exists: protest potential "peaks" among those "fairly close" to a political party and falls off sharply at each side.

**Table 4.4: Protest Potential by Psychological Distance from Political Party, by Age (in percentages)**

|  | (n) | No Protest | Petitions Only | Demonstrations | Boycotts | Rent Strikes/ Strikes | Occupations/ Blockades |
|---|---|---|---|---|---|---|---|
| Very close to party | (252) | 29 | 26 | 19 | 12 | 6 | 8 |
| Fairly close | (759) | 18 | 21 | 21 | 16 | 12 | 12 |
| Not close | (459) | 21 | 19 | 21 | 16 | 10 | 14 |
| No party | (201) | 30 | 20 | 19 | 12 | 8 | 10 |

$(\chi^2 = 26.4$ with 10 d.f.   P = 0.003)  Gamma = .1

| By Age | (n) | Low | Medium | High |
|---|---|---|---|---|
| *Over 65* |  |  |  |  |
| Very close | (100) | 71 | 22 | 7 |
| Fairly close | (172) | 57 | 35 | 8 |
| Not very close | (75) | 63 | 31 | 6 |
| No party | (27) | 82 | 18 | 0 |
| *30—64* |  |  |  |  |
| Very close | (125) | 45 | 41 | 14 |
| Fairly close | (417) | 36 | 37 | 27 |
| Not very close | (234) | 43 | 35 | 22 |
| No party | (96) | 55 | 30 | 14 |
| *16—29* |  |  |  |  |
| Very close | (25) | 25 | 28 | 47 |
| Fairly close | (168) | 28 | 36 | 37 |
| Not very close | (147) | 21 | 42 | 37 |
| No party | (74) | 30 | 39 | 31 |

So, discounting for a moment those who fail to identify with a political party, protest potential increases inversely with closeness to party. But, among party identifiers, it must be important *which* party is identified with. We find that protest potential increases in linear fashion from all those *very close* to the Conservatives, through those *less close* to the Conservatives, to those *close* to Labour, to those *not close* to Labour having highest levels on the PP scale. We should recognize that most of this effect is due to age: Most of those very close to the Conservatives are older people, and lukewarm Labour supporters are disproportionately young.

To advance this analysis one step further, we must introduce a new measure of party identification which is free of *exclusive* partisan choice. Respondents were given a scale calibrated from 0-100 and asked to indicate the extent to which they *sympathized* with *each* political party; "fifty" indicated a neutral level of sympathy. On this scale, the Labour party was given a mean score of 50.6, the Conservatives 47.4, but the Liberals 52.3. This may indicate that many respondents may have given higher scores to the Liberals having interpreted "sympathy" to mean "feel sorry for"—a traditional sympathy for a game underdog against whom the electoral system clearly discriminates. The negative correlation between the ratings given for the two major parties was a modest -.32, indicating that more than a few Conservative supporters have a measure of sympathy for the Labour party and vice versa. Party-political polarity is never as sharp as may be supposed and this is precisely the measure we were seeking. Interestingly, the sympathy with (and for) the Liberal party is positively correlated with sympathy for *both* major parties, but more so with the Conservatives (.26) than with Labour (.11). This indicates an underlying dimension of overall sympathy for and against all three parties. After a controversial record of Conservative government it is not too surprising that the Liberals should be picking up more support from Conservative sympathizers than Labour.

We examined the correlations of all three participation scores with the party-sympathy scores. As we may expect, sympathy for the Conservatives depresses protest potential (but not all that much), increases repression potential (considerably), and also increases orthodox participation. Sympathy for Labour has the opposite effect upon the PP and RP scores but is not related to orthodox participation one way or the other. Sympathy for the Liberals, however, has only a marginal positive effect upon PP scores. This result masks the earlier-noted effect that Liberal supporters have a high protest potential and tends to confirm that the Liberal party attracts "sympathy" from all around the political compass.

The additional value of this measure over the party identification measures is that we can see the effect of cross-party leanings upon participation from *within* each partisan group. The above analysis was conducted separately for each party and includes, in brackets, correlations where the effect of age has been partialed out.

*Among Conservatives*, higher than average own-party sympathy further depressed levels of protest potential and elevated orthodox participation while the already high levels of repression potential remained unchanged. Conservative sympathy for the Labour party, however, did ameliorate repression potential and orthodox support a little and increased protest potential; sympathy for the Liberals had the same effect.

*Among Labour supporters*, cross-party effects were much less marked. Higher own-party sympathy increased orthodox participation, and a measure of respect for the Conservatives increased repression potential a little, but that is all.

This cross-party analysis was undertaken with a particular interest in the Liberals, who should reveal a duality in their sympathy scores, indicating a "Lib-Lab" or "Lib-Con" orientation which should in turn be reflected in choice of political activism. On the contrary, no cross-party effects were present among Liberals.

Results so far in this Chapter indicate that party choice and the degree of personal commitment accompanying that choice does contribute a partial explanation to understanding protest potential, but also that other influences are at work which are detracting from the orderliness of the weak effects of the Labour-vs.-Conservative dimension. But partisan choice, heavily influenced by family habit, is an imperfect test of political ideology. A more sensitive measure may be obtained by operationalizing the "Left-Right continuum" and an attempt to do so now follows.

## Protest and the Left-Right Continuum

In 1963, Butler and Stokes asked their respondents: "Do you ever think of yourself as being on the Left or the Centre, or the Right in Politics or don't you think of yourself in this way?" The question was not well formulated. The terms "left," "centre," and "right" are used to qualify the question, "Do you ever think of yourself . . . in politics?" and caps this error with an open invitation to ideological noncommittal which was gratefully accepted by the majority of respondents. The quality of the responses of the remaining 25 percent who offered an opinion was such that Butler and Stokes brusquely concluded that the left-right scale is meaningless to most people (pp. 254-261). In 1973, Hans Klingemann presented British and other European respondents with a scale of ten unmarked boxes stretching from the left to the right and without further comment invited respondents to mark their own position on this scale with a pencil. Eighty-two percent of the British respondents accomplished this task, and the data provided very convincing

Table 4.5: The "Left-Right" Scale

| Left | | | | | | | | | | Right |
| 1 | 2 | 3 | 4 | 5 | 6 | 7 | 8 | 9 | 10 | D.K. |
|---|---|---|---|---|---|---|---|---|---|---|
| % 5 | 3 | 7 | 8 | 14 | 18 | 9 | 10 | 4 | 5 | 18 |
| % 6 | 3 | 9 | 9 | 18 | 22 | 11 | 12 | 4 | 6 | — |

$$\overline{x} = 5.7$$

Definitions given to the question: "What do you mean by "left" (and "right") in politics?"

| | Left | | Right | |
| | % of Total | % of Those Using Scale | % of Total | % of Those Using Scale |
|---|---|---|---|---|
| Political Party | 29 | 36 | 34 | 42 |
| General Political Movements | 18 | 23 | 8 | 10 |
| Specific Political Movements | 3 | 3 | 2 | 3 |
| Social Class | 3 | 3 | 3 | 4 |
| Pace of Change | 2 | 2 | 3 | 3 |
| Political Leaders | — | 1 | 1 | 1 |
| Economic Equity | 2 | 2 | 3 | 3 |
| Social Equity | 3 | 4 | 2 | 3 |
| Reversals | 3 | 3 | 3 | 4 |
| Other Response | 11 | 13 | 12 | 15 |
| Used Scale but D.K, meaning | 16 | 20 | 16 | 20 |
| + 18% D.K. | 108%* | 119%* | 105%* | 110%* |

*Some respondents gave more than one definition.

validation indicating that the majority knew quite well what they were doing. The "fit" with party identification and issue orientation was impressively consistent (Klingemann and Inglehart 1975).

In this study, Klingemann's scale was replicated. Respondents were asked: "Many people think of political attitudes as being on the 'Left' or the 'Right'. This is a scale stretching from the Left to the Right. When you think of your own political attitudes, where would you put yourself? Please mark the scale."

In addition, respondents were then asked what precisely they *meant* by "Left" and "Right" in politics. Exactly the same proportion of our respondents (82%) marked our scale as marked Klingemann's with a mean score of 5.7 compared with Klingemann's 5.4. This difference is within sampling error. Table 4.5 shows that the scale has a normal distribution about its mean and includes the evidence of the open-ended question, "What do you mean by Left and Right in politics?" Of those using the scale, 19 percent could offer no definition and 3 percent/4 percent actually reversed the polarity of the dimension attributing "Labour, etc . . ." to the right *and* the "Conservative etc . . ." to the left. The two categories make up 19 percent of the total sample and, added to those who could not place themselves on the scale, indicate that 37 percent of the British population do not identify with the left-right dimension very strongly. A further 14 percent of those giving responses (11% overall) gave rather idiosyncratic answers which are impossible to summarize accurately but generally indicated an ego-centered definition, for example, "Left are people who think like me" or "Right is sensible." This leaves exactly 52 percent of all respondents who gave articulate replies to the question. Of these between 48 percent and 59 percent saw left and right in terms of political parties (depending upon whether left or right was defined) and between 29 percent and 18 percent in terms of "Socialist-vs.-Capitalist."[2] The remainder, about 21 percent, gave very articulate replies indeed, involving clear definitions of class ideology, differences in approach to social and economic equity, and the pace of social change.

It seems safe to conclude therefore that we have successfully operationalized the left-right continuum for an acceptably large proportion of our respondents. Party-identifiers distribute themselves on the left-right scale in predictable fashion. Only 5 percent of Conservatives place themselves left of center and 13 percent of Labour supporters to the right, giving widely differing means of 7.3 and 4.2 respectively. The Liberal party's claim to be a party of the center is handsomely validated: Fully 62 percent of Liberals place themselves in the two center categories—twice the proportion among the other two parties. Basically what we have then is a more finely calibrated Labour-Liberal-Conservative scale which accurately records gradations of ideological overlap between the major-party supporters. Given this fact, the hypothesis follows that protest potential should maximize on the left and repression potential on the right. But what of orthodox political involvement? Angus Campbell (1966) derives from general attitude theory the hypothesis that a curvilinear relationship will exist; that involvement will increase with "extremeness" of partisanship in *both* directions. Sarlvik has successfully developed this V-curve model of conventional activism even in the complex multiparty political system of Sweden. Figure 4.1 plots the proportion of respondents scoring high on the PP, RP, and OP scales.

If we consider for a moment only those respondents scoring in the range of "2" to "10" and ignore those scoring on the "extreme" left "1" position, we have near-perfect confirmation of our threefold hypothesis. Protest potential decreases in linear fashion from a high point of 50 percent on the left, through a center mean of 23 percent, down swiftly to about 11 percent among all those on the right. Repression potential, being a shorter scale (and for other reasons discussed earlier) has a much higher mean of 44 percent

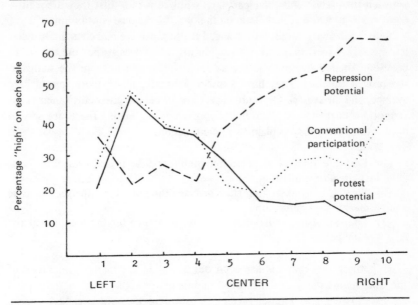

Figure 4.1: BEHAVIOR SCORES BY LEFT-RIGHT SCALE

high. But proportionately the RP scale plots across the left-right dimension providing a precise "mirror" of the PP scale, rising from 20 percent on the left to 66 percent on the right. The V-curve for orthodox involvement is also present, falling from 50 percent high on the left to 20 percent at the center, rising again to 45 percent on the right. Among those on the left, the fit between the plots for protest and orthodox involvement is near perfect—the two measures increase at precisely the same rate. This is an important finding and clearly indicates that there is no increasing *divergence* between orthodox and unorthodox styles of political involvement as a function of increasing "extremity" of left-wing partisanship. Not in the general population at any rate; it is not within the scope of survey research to predict the possible behavior of tiny left-wing groups like the International Marxist Group, the International Socialists, or the Revolutionary Workers Party. More generally speaking, this finding provides an important qualification to our earlier assertions about the positive relationship between orthodox and unorthodox politics as two kinds of politics for social change. This relationship is far more the property of the "left" than of the "right." Those on the right keep the possibility of protest well in the background. What then of our aggressive young Conservatives? Close inspection of the data indicates they are overrepresented among Conservatives placing themselves in the *center* position *and among those who refused to use the scale.* Given the divergence of views between themselves and their party, it is not surprising that they are a little confused as to where they belong on the basic ideological continuum.

Before this analysis may be advanced further into age and class differences, it is necessary to stop ignoring those placing themselves at the "extreme left" position. Their behavior-scale scores are entirely deviant from the trends in the rest of the data. They have a lowish PP score, an RP score approaching average, and an average OP score. There are 79 people involved so their views cannot be dismissed as idiosyncratic or sampling error. There are several hypotheses which may explain this phenomenon:

(1) They are repressive, orthodox Stalinists who regard protest as Trot-skyite adventurism.
(2) They are mistaken, i.e., they reversed the polarity of the scale or gave meaningless definitions.
(3) They are using a different cognitive reference for the location of the scale points.

Hypothesis one may be dismissed out of hand: The mere six members of the Communist party present in our sample have a high protest potential and are careful to place themselves on the center of the left: the "2-4" range. Hypothesis two is not supported by the data. Only seven of the "extreme leftists" reversed the scale, which is a much higher proportion than in the sample overall but does not explain their behavior scores. There was though a stronger-than-average tendency for this group to define left-right in terms of *parties*. To test hypothesis three, the "extreme leftists" were taken out of the sample and examined carefully. They turned out to be a group of older Labour supporters: 66 percent were over 45 and 82 percent voted Labour. These simple facts offer a complex explanation of the phenomenon. Shils has noted that there is a strong tendency for less sophisticated respondents who nonetheless have strong views to use the *extremes* of attitude scales—especially if the scales are finely calibrated. These older Labour supporters have clearly imposed a greater cognitive simplicity upon the left-right dimension than is present elsewhere in the sample. For them, left is Labour and the things that Labour stands for, and, as was partly true in their younger days, that is as far left as one can go.

Looking more closely at the relationship between protest potential and the left-right dimension, the proportion scoring low, medium, or high on the protest potential scale were examined for the whole sample and separately for those aged up to and over thirty. The marginal distributions of the left-right scale indicate the surprising conclusion that young people are not significantly more left-wing than their elders. We see also confirmation of the trend revealed in the party loyalty analysis that leftism has a significantly greater impact upon protest potential among older people.

Table 4.6: Protest Potential by Left-Right Continuum by Age and Social Class

| | 1 | | 2 | 3 | | Difference |
| Age | Left | Center Left | Center | Center Right | Right | Between Points 1 and 3 |
|---|---|---|---|---|---|---|
| *Over 30's* | | | | | | |
| Middle class | 3.8 | 4.0 | 3.2 | 3.0 | 2.5 | 1.5 |
| Working class | 2.9 | 3.2 | 2.8 | 2.7 | 2.4 | 0.5 |
| *Under 30's* | | | | | | |
| Middle class | 4.6 | 4.7 | 3.7 | 3.6 | 3.6 | 1.1 |
| Working class | 4.1 | 4.2 | 3.8 | 4.1 | (3.3)* | 0.1 |

*(n = 8)

Protest potential across the left-right dimension was also plotted for three age groups (16-24, 30-64, 65+) and separately for middle-class and working-class people. These graphs confirmed unequivocally the growing impression in the preceding analysis that leftism has an impact upon protest potential that maximizes powerfully only within the rather narrow socio-political location of older, middle-class radicals. Among the young, ideological disposition is a very poor predictor of protest potential.

The simultaneous impact of the left-right dimension tied to considerations of age and social class is illustrated by Table 4.6. Here the mean protest potential score is recoded for points 1-2, 3-4, 5-6, 7-8, and 9-10 on the LR scale separately for older and younger respondents further dichotomized by social class. The results finely replicate the findings for party choice by age and class: Protest potential declines from high levels on the left to lower levels on the right, and this is much more marked among middle-class respondents, especially if over thirty. Among younger working-class respondents there is no difference at all between the "left" and the "right," they have a high protest potential *regardless* of party choice *and* left-right location. Since a disproportionately large number of the *total* of those scoring high on the PP scale may be found among the working-class young, it seems fair to amplify our earlier conclusion and say that protest potential as a phenomenon is by no means accounted for by the principal dimension of political partisanship of Labour-vs.-Conservative.

## A Wider View of Ideology and Protest

In addition to the three political parties, respondents applied the "sympathy scale" to a wider range of political stimulus objects, which were thought on a priori grounds to be pertinent to protest behavior. Five groups were chosen to represent "protest subjects" or generally radical stimuli: trade unions, colored immigrants, Women's Liberation Movement, student protesters, and revolutionary groups. Other groups represented "protest objects" or generally "establishment" and status quo stimuli: civil servants, company directors and financiers, police, small businessmen, and clergymen.[3]

The relative sympathy scores given to each of these groups and to the political parties indicates the predictable result that most of the status quo groups gain high scores, especially the police, while most of the radical groups are given low ratings, especially student protesters and revolutionaries. Interesting exceptions are trade unions (but whose exclusion from the status quo groups could be questioned), who acquire higher ratings than the Conservative party, and colored immigrants, who in turn are rated higher than company directors. This latter result indicates that the "feel sorry for" interpretation of sympathy may well be operating more on certain groups than on others. Directors do not invite sympathy; they can take care of themselves. Blacks, on the other hand, attract sympathetic attitudes even from those advocating their repatriation "for their own good."

The rank-order of the groups changes as a function of position on the PP scale, yet among those *highest* on the PP scale, the police remains the *most* popular group and the revolutionary groups the *least* popular although the actual ratings respectively decrease and increase in the predictable direction. This fact should be borne in mind in the discussion to follow as it sets British protest potential into a sober perspective. It has not been claimed hitherto that the protest potential scale taps anything resembling the anarcho-socialist dimension of radical politics which the stimulus word "protest" may conjure up in the minds of many people. On the contrary, this finding does much to reemphasize our earlier claim that the "protest potential" tapped by the PP scale is an abiding readiness among many *ordinary* people to seek alternative sources of political redress should circumstances compel them to such action. So far, the analysis of variations in this readiness between differing kinds of ordinary people, although raising the importance of youth and left-wing sympathies has done nothing to detract from this basic finding. Ordinary people in Britain respect the police and sympathize with their difficult job and they do not much like "revolutionaries" even if they are themselves seriously prepared to engage in protest behavior.

Protest potential correlates only modestly with each of the group sympathy scores individually, but does so in directions which conform to the a priori assignment of pro- and antiprotest orientation. Small negative correlations are observable for the police, businessmen (large and small), and clergy, and small positive values for trade unions, immigrants, Women's Liberation, students, and revolutionaries. The conclusion is beginning to crystallize that not a great deal of *total* "ideological" variation is associated with protest participation.

In order to obtain a clearer appreciation of the multiple cross-currents of ideological loyalty and sympathy which are imperfectly reflected in these data, a factor analysis was conducted including the sympathy scores for each group and the three main parties and the scores for the PP, RP, and LR scales. A principal axis solution was obtained and this was rotated orthogonally through varimax criteria. Five factors having an eigenvalue greater than unity

**Table 4.7: Factor Analysis\* of Behavior Scales with Sympathy Scores and Left-Right Scale**

| Items | I | II | III | IV | V | Commu-nalities |
|---|---|---|---|---|---|---|
| | | | FACTORS | | | |
| Protest potential | − | + | + | .606 | + | .44 |
| Repression potential | + | − | − | −.389 | + | .34 |
| Conventional participation | + | − | + | .442 | − | .22 |
| Liberal party | + | − | + | + | .435 | .25 |
| Small businessmen | + | − | − | − | .321 | .20 |
| Women's liberation | + | + | .418 | + | + | .25 |
| Revolutionary groups | − | + | .645 | − | − | .43 |
| Student protestors | + | + | .672 | + | + | .49 |
| Colored immigrants | + | + | .354 | + | + | .23 |
| Labour party | + | .712 | + | + | − | .57 |
| Conservative party | .371 | −.590 | − | − | + | .51 |
| Civil servants | .490 | + | + | + | + | .27 |
| Police | .506 | + | − | − | + | .33 |
| Directors | .538 | + | + | − | − | .39 |
| Clergy | .550 | − | + | − | + | .32 |
| Trade unions | + | .582 | + | + | − | .53 |
| "Right wing" | + | −.584 | − | + | − | .42 |
| | I | II | III | IV | V | |
| | "Pro-establishment" | "Labour vs. Tory" | "Radicalism" | "Political Action" | "Liberalism" | |
| % of total variance | 18 | 14 | 9 | 7 | 6 (=54%) | |
| % of common variance | 42 | 29 | 14 | 9 | 6 (=100%) | |

\*Principal axis solution, rotated to varimax criterion.

emerged in the principal axis solution, which together accounted for 54 percent of the total variance. After rotation, a configuration of item loadings for each factor was reached, which achieved an unusually clear description of the structures implicit in the data (see Table 4.7).

The first factor, not uncommonly in this kind of analysis, is a "consensual" factor, i.e., something that most people tend to agree about. On this factor load people's basic sympathy for the police, civil servants, and the clergy. Two correlated items having less aggregate popularity: company directors and the Conservative party also load on this factor (though the Tories load lightest), suggesting that this "consensual" factor is a "proestablishment" factor. That sympathy with the representatives and agents of the status quo should emerge first from such an analysis (even though accounting for only 18% of the total variance) must be counted as a blow against the recurring theme of this study, that the deference theory is an inappropriate description of British political culture. There is no doubt that deference remains a feature of the political landscape and it juts out of the topology achieved by this analysis with an obviousness that must embarrass the theoretical line taken here.[4]

It would not appear intellectually honest to explain away this result in technical terms. But there is an explanation, and it is a technical one. Briefly, what happens is that sympathy (or lack of hostility) toward the three core items—clergy, police, and civil servants—occurs right around the political compass and transcends every ideological cleavage. Having thus formed the only basis for a consensual factor, the rotational procedure constrains two items which are ideologically loaded (Tories and directors) to load highly upon that factor because their positive correlations with each of the three core items exceed the negative loadings they have on the other ideologically polarized factors. This is certainly true of the "company directors" item. The Conservative party loads much higher on the second factor in a negative direction, together with rightward polarity of the LR scale. On this factor, of course, the Labour party and the trade unions load positively to form the conventional, Labour-vs.-Tory axis of British political life. The significance of this finding lies in its rather stark obviousness, i.e., the items of the first, proestablishment factor do not load on it except for the Tory party. It would be much too glib to then conclude that deference is not tied to political partisanship and is "therefore" not ideologically relevant. The impression of orthogonality is imposed by the whole technique and the dual loading of the Tory party (the *only* dual loading in the whole analysis) is a clear warning against this. It is probably more plausible (but no more conclusive) to argue that the proestablishment items are liberated to form the first consensual factor because so many people of the Labour left declared their sympathy for them and "therefore" deference may encourage political stability.

The third factor to be defined by the analysis is a "proradicalism" factor on which load the Women's Liberation Movement, revolutionary groups, student protesters, and, to a lesser extent, colored immigrants. But what of protest and repression? Surely they should respectively load positively and negatively on this radicalism factor? Not at all; they form instead a fourth "political behavior" factor. This is a very encouraging finding in terms of the preceding analysis which suggested all along that, despite the overall tendency for protest to be associated with leftism, the commitment to action was not tied at all strongly to the political or ideological value system. Even so, one has the immediate suspicion that this is merely an artifact of the obvious triad of correlations between the three behavior scales clinging together like a triangular raft amid the sea of rather low correlations generated among the sympathy scores and which is ideologically neutralized by the conventional political behavior scale. When scores on the conventional participation scale are removed from analysis, the protest and regression scales ought to fly to their respective ideological polarities on the radicalism factor and perhaps also on the Labour-vs.-Tory factor. But this does not happen at all. When the CP scale is removed from the analysis, very little changes and the protest and repression scale remain as an independent fourth factor.

To be more certain of this really very surprising finding, the analysis was repeated once more with the number of factors to be extracted artificially constrained to three and the analysis further "tuned" by inserting the initial multiple correlations into the diagonal instead of the more usually assumed unity. Thus the analysis was forced to include protest and repression with the other items. It does so, but with a huge display of reluctance. The Protest scale does not load at all on the Labour-vs.-Tory dimension, nor on the proestablishment factor, and loads only lightly on the proradicalism factor. The repression scale does load negatively on this factor but retains near-loadings in the other two factors. The communalities of the two behavior scales became very low (especially protest) indicating that their presence in the analysis contributes only little to the explanation of the shared variance of all the items. In the unconstrained solution they were higher (of course) but were also as high as most other items.

It may be noted in passing that two other items have very low communalities: the Liberals and small businessmen. Referring back to the original analysis (Table 4.7), we find that these two items also formed their own (fifth) factor. That the association between Liberal sympathies and small businessmen should be thus detected is an impressive testimony to the sensitivity of this kind of analysis.

So what does this very complex analysis mean? The answer, of course, is that factor analysis does not "mean" anything. It is a highly artificial way of describing as certainties the most general *tendencies* in the data. But these tendencies confirm trends that we have established already by more straight-forward analysis. Deferential feelings still exist in the political community if "deference" is the way one should describe sympathy for the agents of social control. But it exists in general, consensual feelings that have only limited political or ideological implications. Significantly, the main Labour-vs.-Tory axis remains unentangled with the radicalism dimension and the focus of our study, the protest potential scale, clearly demonstrates one very important property—that it is not exclusively a leftist predisposition but has become an additional and real alternative for political action for ordinary people of many political persuasions. Put more precisely, we can state that the behavioral component of protest is of greater significance than its affective polarity.

In a final attempt to obtain an explanatory (rather than a descriptive) edge from these data, the preceding analysis was conducted separately for respondents over and under thirty years of age. The result obtained for each age group is essentially very similar. Labour-vs.-Tory dimensions emerge among young people, but less strongly than among older people, and the "establishment cluster" emerges for each group. The most important difference is that in the constrained solution, the "protest dimension" achieves a marginal dominance among the young (i.e., it is the first factor), and the PP and RP scores load far more certainly upon that dimension. Protest had crystallized among young people's ideological cognitions to a greater extent than among older people and at the expense of the traditional left-right, Labour-Tory, axis of politics. Yet the most remarkable aspect of this analysis remains the continuity of structure between older and younger people rather than the differences. This suggests a conclusion that the much higher overall *levels* of protest potential among young people coexist within very much the same ideological structure. The weight of literature (cf., Marcuse, Tourainne, Kenniston) which suggests that there has been substantial restructuring of the radical-conservative dimension among younger people in Western society has left little impression upon our respondents. If "New Left-ism" had made any serious inroads into popular consciousness among young people in Britain the "establishment" groups, which are all recognizably the bête-noirs of the New Left, would have been included as negative elements in the protest dimension. The principal conclusion must be that whereas the overall demographic location of protest potential is partly qualified by ideological sympathies with left-wing politics, this qualification is less significant among young people who are still the group showing high protest potential. This means that the sharp intergenerational increase in the *quantity* of protest potential is not a function of *qualitative* ideological differences in the definitional structure of political sympathies. There is not even a really significant shift to the "left" among young people even though more of them are prepared to vote Labour than their elders. In 1964 Phillip Abrams and Alan Little were able to write that "Britain has achieved something approaching perfect political socialisation." Our data indicate that the ideological continuities between young and old still support such a conclusion on a partisan level, but that young people have a very different level of behavioral response. And it is this behavioral component that counts for most. Actions, it seems, speak louder even than rhetoric.

## Ideological Resentment and Righteous Indignation

Thus far we have sought an explanation of different levels of protest in our informants' formal responses to fixed ideological stimuli. The assumption that those objects carry positive or negative loadings linked to low or high protest potential has proved only partly justified. Since protest potential is here conceived of as a means of redress, what relevant stimulus groups can respondents themselves provide which may be dynamically linked to protest independently of left or right self-placement? Earlier, we attempted a distinction between ideological stimulus groups who were protest objects, and those who may be protest subjects. The term "protest objects" suggests groups on whose behalf redress may be sought. Consequently respondents were asked whether they believed there to exist any "overprivileged groups . . . people getting really more rewards than they deserve or have an unduly privileged position in our society" and also any "underprivileged groups: people getting a poor deal from society, not really getting the rewards or even the basic rights they deserve." With these two questions we tap reference group sources of two kinds of *righteous indignation*. It is this sentiment which is held by Lupsha to be causal factor in violent protest behavior in the United States. He says:

> Indignation seems particularly appropriate for explaining violence as its logic locates it in that intersection of the psychological and the ethical where ideas of rightness and legitimacy originate.

There are certainly ample quantities of indignation in Britain from which to test for kinds and objects of indignation linked to protest. Eighty percent of the population regard some other group as "overprivileged" but the denial of inequality does not of itself indicate very much lower levels of protest potential; what surely matters is the target of resentment. Sixteen percent of the responses focus upon politicians, but, in line with what we already know about the relationship between orthodox politicians and unorthodox politics, this view is not especially associated with protest. Neither is the resentment (11%) focused upon nouveau riches groups like sportsmen or entertainers.

The remainder of the codeable responses divide almost equally into two clear groups; those who name bourgeois targets of resentment: royalty and aristocracy, the "idle rich," speculators and financiers, and professional and managerial groups; and those who name "proletarian" groups by whom they feel threatened or toward whom they feel resentful: "welfare spongers," "greedy workers" (car workers, dockers, miners, etc.), colored immigrants, and students. Among the responses given by those high on the PP scale, 68 percent focus upon bourgeois targets and only 20 percent upon "threatening proletarians"; among those low on the protest scale these proportions are 46 percent and 41 percent respectively. Although these figures indicate an expected "leftist" antibourgeois trend in the sources of indignation felt by protesters, we should not be surprised at the numbers of nonprotesters who resent the rich. More significantly however, it should be noted that still a large number of protesters felt indignant about the recipients of welfare and the apparent success of trade union bargaining power. This is not what may popularly be expected of "protesters" and perhaps indicates the influence of young working-class Tories and Liberals.

Unlike those who deny the existence of overprivilege, the denial of underprivilege in society is associated with lower levels of protest potential (10%-vs.-24%). Eighty-five percent of people believe, as Priestly's couple put it: "There is always someone worse off than yourself" and the majority name "old people" as those who bear the greatest burden of deprivation. The chronically ill and women, as one respondent put it, "left alone to cope," also attract much sympathy from protesters and nonprotesters alike but protesters are marginally more likely to name, in addition, ill-paid professionals (e.g., "young doctors"), workers in dangerous jobs ("miners," "fishermen"), and the poor and working classes.

Support is therefore available for Lupsha's hypothesis—certain kinds of indignation are linked to protest potential. Concentrating for a moment upon one of the more obvious effects—the choice of bourgeois targets for the accusation of overprivilege, those who name royalty, the rich, etc. have of course a higher protest potential than those who name "welfare spongers" and "greedy workers," but those who name at least one group from *both* categories have the *highest* protest potential, thus revealing a generally belligerent *disposition* which is independent of the ideological direction of the general flow of indignation. Some of this effect is supplied by the influence of those Labour supporters who score "high" on the protest scale by virtue of their support for unofficial strikes but who detect overprivilege in many quarters. It is intersting that it is only among younger Labour supporters that a clear majority claim to detect overprivilege among bourgeois groups alone. Liberal sentiment, for example, is surprisingly vehement against "greedy workers," even among the many younger Liberals with a high protest potential.

There is, then, no escape from the conclusion that political leaning in the party and ideological sense furnishes only a partial explanation of protest potential. The protest potential of the left and the repressive tendency of those of the right are clearly reported in the data but our scales are biting much deeper into other areas of thought and attitude that have no direct connection with the more superficial meanings of "politics."

# NOTES

1. *The Working-Class Tories*, p. 18.

2. This imbalance is due, of course, to numbers of Conservatives who defined the "right" as "Conservative, Tory, etc." but the "left" as "Socialists," which is the traditional term of abuse reserved by politically conscious Tories for the Labour party.

3. To check for possible order-of-presentation effects, the order of the list of groups was inverted for a random half of the respondents. There were no statistically significant differences in the ratings given to each group by those giving their ratings in one order or the other.

4. There is no doubt either about the clarity of the description achieved. Only the Conservative party loads on more than one factor, every other item is singular to one factor and no item is omitted, i.e., the description is "complete." This is the kind of result one associates with *quartimax* rotation (i.e., maximizing *item* loading, rather than factor loading as in varimax solutions). A *quartimax* rotation was obtained. The factor loadings were entirely similar, differing only at the second or third decimal place.

*Chapter 5*

# THE NONPARTISAN BASIS OF POLITICAL ACTION

An apparent disadvantage of the survey technique in political psychology is that certain kinds of people continually filter themselves out of active consideration by declaring ignorance or uninterest in the questions asked. Typically such a respondent will suggest to the interviewer that she would be better advised to seek the views of a more knowledgeable person, someone who may know the "right" answers, or else often shrugs his or her shoulders and uses phrases like "I never bother with this kind of thing." Such a respondent is often elderly (or rather young) and often poorly educated, but it would be quite wrong to conclude that all our "don't knows" are unintelligent people, or more importantly, that only those with adequate educational training or actual experience in politics can comprehend the basic political concepts probed in this survey. Indeed, some care has been taken in the design of this survey to operationalize basic concepts in a basic fashion and to steer away from the more usual approach involving the use of issue-oriented questions. We did not, for example, seek to create a left-right ideological dimension from a series of *issue* questions about abortion, divorce, royalty, immigration, capital punishment, nationalization, and so on (cf., Eysenck, Wilson and Patterson) but preferred instead to ask a simple and direct question and then probe carefully the meaning of the answers given.

The fact is that "Don't know" is only the first point on an upward *continuum* of political interest and political conceptualization, which is itself a measure of the connectedness of the respondent's normal world of daily thought and the world of politics. How many people can be said to really experience a clear level of cognitive connectedness between their everyday life and the world of politics? The American political psychologist Philip Converse suggests that only about 10 percent of the population have complex "belief systems" that deserve the name of ideology, and it is only among those usually rather well-educated or involved people that theories of political ideology and motivation really hang together. It is an unsettling fact that the extent to which modern theories of political behavior align with empirical evidence increases as a direct function of the similarity between the researcher and his subjects. That is to say, strongly correlated sets of data (high levels of constraint, as Converse puts it) emerge most readily from young, well-educated, white, middle-class professionals.

We saw in the previous chapter that only a little more than half of our respondents had a good grasp of the left-right dimension, and only a quarter articulated the concept at all ideologically. This is better than 10 percent, but it means that when a British political commentator suggests that, for example, the 1970 general election result reflected a previously undetected "shift to the right" among the electorate, he is very likely, according to Converse's interpretation of these kinds of data, to be talking nonsense. Or at best he is uttering a tautology since, for the majority of those who care to think about it, the 'right' is defined as the Tory party anyway. While essentially correct, this probably overstates the case. If people are attracted in increased numbers to the policy utterances of the party that most of them agree represents the "right," then some kind of "shift to the right" may be plausibly said to have occurred. The point is that the shift *in people's minds* probably occurred at rather a commonplace level of cerebral functioning. And why should it not? Half of social psychology is built on the strongly supported assumption that people strive after cognitive simplicity and will avoid the stress of mental complexity when no obvious reward for dealing with complexity is evident. Paradoxically it is this natural and understandable tendency that makes political psychology difficult.

But this problem must be faced, and we do so in this chapter with a certain advantage over many previous researchers in the field. Having adhered to *basic* political concepts in an attempt to explain clearly defined predispositions to *behave* in certain ways, we have avoided many of the problems of sorting out what Converse laments as the largely inaccessible issue universe of the political belief system. This concern to keep it simple irritated some of our more sophisticated respondents, but their impatience may perversely be taken as encouragement that the survey instruments used in this study meant something to the bulk of the population. For example, the principal focus of the study, the protest potential scale, has exactly this property. Each element of the scale demands no more than that a concrete stimulus object (strikes, petitions, etc.) be evaluated on a single dimension ("approve" or "would do"). This approach worked very well. But if we had appealed directly to the underlying attitude dimension of feelings towards political authority, which we believe are tapped by the scale, and asked an apparently direct question like: "To what extent are you likely to endorse those who would contest political authority?" we should almost certainly have "discovered" that protest was the exclusive property of the young intellectual left. As it is, we have a measure that placed protest potential as a property of all kinds of ordinary people as well as the predicted "leftist" influence and this much wider spread of variance in the population leaves the causality of protest open to *nonpartisan* explanations. By "nonpartisan" we mean those influences upon protest behavior that are not directly dependent upon the ideological value system of party and interest-group politics.

Four nonpartisan measures will be examined in this chapter: political interest, levels of political conceptualization, political efficacy, and political trust. All of these deal in varying ways with the problem of connectedness between the individual and politics, yet none have a polarity that is a priori linked to ideological polarities. In the sphere of party politics, we have seen already that a voluntary detachment from parties (the "psychological distance" measure) carried its own implications for political action. So a sensible place to open this inquiry is to ask respondents quite simply: "How interested would you say you are in politics?" Table 5.1 shows that, for the sample as a whole, protest potential is not closely linked with degrees of political interest. Those few people (10%) who declare a strong interest in politics have only a slightly higher protest potential than those of the great majority (68%) who admit only modest or low levels of interest, although those who declare that they have not the slightest interest (22%) do show lower levels of protest potential.

This result is unsurprising and suggests the influence of greater political curiosity among younger people. This, however, is not the case; young people have *less* interest in politics than their elders. Those young people who *do*

Table 5.1: Protest Potential and Political Interest (in percentages)

| Interested | (%) | No Protest | Petitions Only | Demon- strations | Boy- cotts | Rent Strikes/ Strikes | Occupations Blockades |
|---|---|---|---|---|---|---|---|
| Very | (10) | 16 | 21 | 22 | 15 | 11 | 15 (=100%) |
| Somewhat | (36) | 16 | 20 | 20 | 18 | 13 | 13 |
| Not very | (32) | 21 | 22 | 21 | 15 | 10 | 12 |
| Not at all | (22) | 36 | 24 | 18 | 10 | 5 | 7 |
| | (100%) | | | | | | |

have a great interest in politics also show the highest levels of protest potential, but we find that young people generally are *less* interested in politics than older people though again the age difference is so great that young people with no interest in politics have a protest potential almost as high as that of older people (30-64 age group) who are very interested in politics.

This result is probably linked to the nature of the stimulus object, "politics." Whereas political interest is positively correlated with protest potential at .20, and with repression potential at -.13, it is correlated with orthodox participation at .48 and with "closeness to political party" at .29. Thus "politics" to most people probably *means* orthodox party politics, and many people, especially young people, may have only modest levels of involvement in orthodox politics. In these results we see again that protest potential lies in the same area of politics-for-change as does orthodox political behavior, but is set at a discrete distance from orthodox politics. Therefore, all we can say is that, independently of age, increased generalized political interest may increase protest potential and depress repression potential, but is really much more likely to increase orthodox participation.

## Political Conceptualization [1]

In the previous chapter, reference was made to the definitions offered by people using the left-right scale of the meaning of the terms left and right. Careful appraisal of these definitions revealed a distinct hierarchy of concepts employed by respondents to describe left and right, and this hierarchical value may itself be used as an independent measure of the *level of political conceptualization* possessed by individual respondents. Each respondent was given a score from 1 to 5 according to this schema:

(1) Unable (or unwilling) to use L R scale.
(2) Used scale but able to give no more than an idiosyncratic definition and usually no definition at all.
(3) Defined LR in terms of "Labour" and "Conservative" or leading politicians of those parties (Wilson-versus-Heath).
(4) Definition in terms of broad socio-political movements, e.g., "socialist" and "capitalist" or specific social-political movements, e.g., "Anarchist, Syndicalist, Trade Union, Labour" and "Nationalism, Racism, Fascism."
(5) Sophisticated, articulate definition in terms of:
    (a) pace of change (revolutionary, progressive vs. reactionary, conformist)
    (b) class conflict (workers, poor, lower classes vs. Bourgeois, aristocracy etc.)

    (c)  economic equity (state control vs. laissez-faire)

    (d)  social equity (equalitarianism vs. preservation of social hierarchy)

A priori, there are several weaknesses that might be evident in this schema. A number of otherwise politically sophisticated respondents may have scored "1" having refused to use the LR scale because it represents for them an outmoded political dimension which they regard themselves as now outside. Some Conservatives scored higher than they might otherwise because of their vaguely contemptuous use of the word "Socialist" to describe the Labour party. Others may have offered "Labour vs. Conservative" as an easy short-hand description of a dimension which they, in fact, conceived of in quite complex terms if really pressed to do so. But generally the measure seems a sound one.

Conceptual sophistication is not found uniformly across the LR scale and it was noted in Chapter Four that the "extreme" left-wingers were "low conceptualizers" and thus were not in the least extreme. This is also true of those who opted for the middle position (many of them Liberal supporters). Conceptualization actually tends to maximize among those who chose the mid-left *and* mid-right positions on the scale. The measure is positively correlated with terminal educational age (r=.24) but is by no means strongly dependent on education. Despite considerable advances in the scope and quality of education, young people are not significantly better-informed about the nature of 'left' and 'right' than are older people and are only marginally better informed than the retired. Scoring each respondent according to the *highest* conceptual level he reached, we obtain this national distribution and compare it with Butler and Stokes' 1963 estimates:

| | 1<br>Zero Conceptu-<br>alization | 2<br>Very<br>Low | 3<br>Parties and<br>Politicians | 4<br>Political<br>Movements | 5<br>Sophisticated<br>Response |
|---|---|---|---|---|---|
| | 17% | 30% | 25% | 20% | 9% |
| Analogous Butler<br>and Stokes results | (60) | (20) | ( ← 18 → ) | | (2) |

This confirms that real conceptual sophistication is quite as rare as Converse alleges but is accompanied by the presence of a larger number of people who have a perfectly adequate grasp of the political realities of an ideological continuum. Those who are genuinely at a loss are a very large minority (47%) but one which compares favorably with Butler and Stokes' estimate of over 80 percent. We can only account for this difference, as noted earlier, by the strange wording of the Nuffield Survey question. There is no evidence to support the alternative hypothesis of change over time.

Table 5.2: Protest Potential by Conceptualization of the Left-Right Dimension (in percentages)

| Left-Right Means | (%) | No Pro-test | Peti-tions Only | Demon-strations | Boy-cotts | Rent Strikes/ Strikes | Occupations/ Blockades |
|---|---|---|---|---|---|---|---|
| (0) Nothing | (17) | 31 | 22 | 18 | 10 | 8 | 11 (=100%) |
| (1) Very little | (30) | 28 | 23 | 20 | 12 | 7 | 10 |
| (2) Political parties | (25) | 23 | 24 | 19 | 15 | 11 | 8 |
| (3) General move-ments | (20) | 9 | 19 | 22 | 21 | 13 | 15 |
| (4) Sophisticated | (9) | 11 | 11 | 24 | 19 | 13 | 21 |

Moorehouse and Chamberlain were quoted earlier as stressing that it is not necessary for men to encompass the world intellectually before they set out to change it. If this were necessary, they maintain, most of the world's revolutionary movements would have been still-born among small bands of men who occupy their time "quoting Lenin quoting Kautsky." But if intellectual comprehension of political and ideological reality is not a necessary (nor even a sufficient) basis for political mobilization, *it may well help*. Having constructed a measure of conceptual sophistication vis-à-vis a major ideological axis among our respondents' political cognitions, we are now in a position to establish just *how much* this kind of comprehension facilitates political activity. Table 5.2 divides the protest potential scale by each level of conceptual sophistication and demonstrates very clearly that those revealing a high level of conceptualization do have a higher protest potential, especially those offering the most sophisticated responses but, substantiating Moorehouse and Chamberlain, there is not a correspondingly marked diminution in protest potential among those having the lowest levels of conceptualization. Thus ideological sophistication is not a necessary component of the will to change the world through direct political action but, as we suspected, it can certainly be a help.

As was the case with expressed political interest, conceptual sophistication correlates more certainly with orthodox political behavior (.27) than with protest (.22) or repression potential (-.17). But correlation analysis of these kinds of data rarely yield very impressive results because what we are studying is the tendency for relative minorities in the population to move toward the more extreme end of scales of behavioral intent and these scales have somewhat skewed distributions. Thus the important comparative measure is the relative proportion of those scoring high on the scale. When we examine high scorers on the three behavior scales across five levels of conceptual sophistication, we find protest potential unchanged across the three lower levels but rising steeply through levels four and five. Repression potential *drops* steeply toward the highest level of conceptualization while orthodox behavior rises smoothly right across the scale. Thus, among those having the highest level of political comprehension, we find people who are easily mobilized in orthodox or unorthodox political behavior and also people (not necessarily the same people of course) who reject recourse to repressive authority measures. But they are *not* all "intellectual left-wingers." Sixty-two percent of these conceptually sophisticated respondents place themselves in the center or right positions of the LR scale. We shall have reason to return to the relationship between ideology, protest, and nonpartisan influence later in the chapter.

When the foregoing analysis is repeated separately for each behavior scale further divided by age group membership, the familiar age effect upon the protest potential scale separates the scores for young, middle-aged, and old completely. High conceptualization has the largest effect on the middle-aged and very little effect on the oldest group except to inhibit membership of the low-protest group. Orthodox behavior on the other hand is much less dependent upon age and conceptualization increases orthodox political activity uniformly for each age group. This result makes a good deal of sense. Old people are rarely disposed to demonstrate, but, as every constituency party organiser (Labour or Tory) will testify, they often form the backbone of an election campaign workforce.

The results for the repression scale are particularly interesting since higher levels of conceptualization depress repression potential severely for *all* age groups. Thus, politically sophisticated old people in common with their peers have a low protest potential; but, unlike many other older people, they have a very low repression potential and also an especially high orthodox potential. They seem to be people who retain a traditional yet civilized idea that politics is a matter for the politicians and those who elect them and not for street demonstrators or the police or the courts. From one point of view, they might well fit the description of the classic bourgeois liberal whose ideology rests upon the optimistic view of mankind that when provided with a nonrepressive political environment, people will behave in a responsible, self-restrained manner.

Since it has been established that the political parties are very much the most important stimuli in the cognigive field of most people's political thought, a second attempt was made to establish a measure of conceptual sophistication using the parties and not the left-right scale as the relevant stimuli. This is the method Converse based his own research upon. Respondents were asked to give their views about the two main parties in this manner: "What do you like about the Labour party?" and "What do you dislike . . . ." and these questions were then repeated for the Conservative party. The answers to these four questions were coded separately according to a very complex schema. This schema was then systematically recoded to produce a six-level measure of political conceptualization in the following manner:

(1) *No conceptualization:* i.e., "don't know" to all four questions.
(2) *Intrinsic values* only: Largest groups among this category are those who answered "everything" and "nothing" to the "like" and "dislike" questions (more usually vice versa) and those who said, "I just like/dislike them," "They are my party," or "I was brought up Labour/Conservative," and so on.
(3) *Politician and party characteristics:* At this level respondents express likes and dislikes in terms of leaders (Wilson-Heath) or some collective attribute of the party like "They have good ideas" or "They're always squabbling among themselves."
(4) *Group interests:* Typically: "They look after the working man," or "They maintain middle-class privilege," or other reference to groups in society that have a special identification with the party.
(5) *Specific issues:* Here the respondent articulates a response to some policy characteristic of the party: "They intend to nationalize everything," "They set up the health service," "They preserve free enterprise," "They will maintain the grammar schools."
(6) *Ideological content:* These expressions can be elusive and are most difficult to code. Reference to political creeds was included. "Too Socialist/Communist/Marxist revolutionary" etc., but most ideological responses referred to an axis of social and economic equity concerned with the maintenance of privilege and/or distribution of wealth in society. Many of these responses were not very articulate, cf., "They want better sharing out of things," but were clearly organized as support of (or opposition to) social equity and, as such, reflected a fundamental ideological axis in British politics.

The following distribution of party conceptualization was obtained:

| (1) No Conceptualisation | (2) Intrinsic Values | (3) Politicians | (4) Group Interests | (5) Issues and Policies | (6) Ideologues and Near-ideologues |
|---|---|---|---|---|---|
| 16% | 7% | 11% | 15% | 29% | 22% |

It may be that this scale was scored generously; respondents were given four chances to mention a higher-order concept in their evaluation of the parties and the recoding process took the highest level achieved over the array of responses. In this way the coding system seized upon the least glint of conceptual sophistication shown by the respondent. Coding for this study was also less stringent about the recognition of higher-order concepts than previous examples of the technique, particularly Converse's system. Yet, it does seem that conceptual sophistication is more widespread in the British polity than has formerly been thought. The results correlate well with the scale obtained for the "definition of LR" scale (r=.39) and is also relatively more free of the influence of formal education (r=.15) because the coding instructions concentrated carefully upon the nature of the *concepts* used rather than the level of verbal dexterity exhibited by the respondent. Again there is no tendency for young people to show more sophistication than older respondents. The tendency for both mid-left and mid-right wingers to have a higher conceptualization than the extreme and the center is again evident. Yet, independently of age and ideology, level of conceptualization is a modest predictor of protest potential. Table 5.3 shows that those with no conceptualization have a low PP score; there is little increase in protest potential through levels two to five ("intrinsic values," "politicians," "groups," to "issues") but a clear result that ideologues are more protest-prone than others. This is especially true of young ideologues, only 10 percent of whom would eschew protest entirely, and 58 percent of whom would engage in illegal forms of protest. So again it is evident that the ability to encompass the political world accelerates the will to be mobilized in protest activity and even more so in orthodox activities(r=.32).

But the evidence remains that a majority of potential protesters have only rather commonplace notions about what constitutes the good and bad points of the major parties and some not even that. Ideologues constitute 22 percent

Table 5.3: Protest Potential by Level of Political Conceptualization (in percentages)

| LPC | (%) | No Pro-test | Peti-tions Only | Demon-strations | Boy-cotts | Rent Strikes/ Strikes | Occupations/ Blockades |
|---|---|---|---|---|---|---|---|
| (1) None | (16) | 34 | 20 | 17 | 16 | 6 | 8 (=100%) |
| (2) Intrinsic value | (7) | 37 | 22 | 17 | 5 | 5 | 13 |
| (3) Politicians and party char-acteristics | (11) | 24 | 26 | 22 | 8 | 8 | 11 |
| (4) Group interests | (15) | 24 | 20 | 26 | 10 | 10 | 11 |
| (5) Specific issues and policies | (29) | 19 | 24 | 18 | 17 | 11 | 11 |
| (6) Ideological content | (22) | 12 | 17 | 22 | 20 | 14 | 15 |

of the population, but still only 33 percent of those scoring high on the PP scale and 40 percent of those given to orthodox activism. So again the evidence points in favor of the conclusion that it is quite possible to be mobilized in a political cause having only a limited ability to respond meaningfully to simple political stimuli like "Labour" or "Conservative," but the potential protester is somewhat more likely than others to have a fairly good grasp of the political geography around him.

## Efficacy

Another nonpartisan influence on political activism that has appeared in previous research is a sense of political efficacy. This is the feeling that one has the capacity to influence government and the democratic process. Essentially it is a feeling that the individual counts and that one personally counts no less than others. Campbell et al. (*The American Voter*) found this measure a strong predictor of political participation; people do not, after all, vote for and seek the attention of politicians and their civil servants out of a sense of complete hopelessness. They may show a sense of scepticism perhaps, but there remains a kernel of positive expectation among citizens who participate in the democratic process that they will have the ear of those in public life. Even if their opinions are not exactly treasured by those in power at least they will keep in touch with public opinion and not just cynically respect their power to vote once every four or five years. Thus the politically efficacious citizen has not given up on the system, participation will bring attention, if not actual reward.

In the light of this knowlege what prediction should we therefore make regarding protest potential? Surely protest is the outcome of the *failure* of orthodox channels of redress? Surely those who feel the democratic system has turned its back upon their cause (or is habitually prone to do so) will more likely be those who turn easily to protest? But we have already established that people prone to engage in orthodox politics (and so feel politically efficacious) are also likely to engage in protest politics. It may therefore be that efficacy is a *general* sense of optimism about the practitioners of politics and their system that facilitates protest as well as voting and canvassing. That anyway is the hypothesis we offer at this stage.

The measure of political efficacy deployed in this study is an Anglicized version of the efficacy scale developed by the Institute of Social Research, at the University of Michigan. Respondents are asked six questions concerning his or her feelings about relationships with the democratic process of government. These are listed in Table 5.4 and the distribution of responses given to each question is included. Note that to each question, a politically efficacious response is a negative answer which prevents the well-known "yes-saying"

Table 5.4: Distribution of Political Efficacy (in percentages)

| | | Agree Strongly | Agree | Disagree | Disagree Strongly | (D.K.) |
|---|---|---|---|---|---|---|
| (1) | People like me have no say in what government does | 14 | 47 | 32 | 2 | (4) |
| (2) | Voting is the only way that people like me can have any say in the way the government runs things | 15 | 59 | 19 | 1 | (5) |
| (3) | Sometimes politics and government seem so complicated that a person like me cannot really understand what is going on | 21 | 53 | 20 | 3 | (3) |
| (4) | I don't think public officials care much about what people like me think | 14 | 51 | 28 | 2 | (6) |
| (5) | Generally speaking, those we elect as MP's to Westminster lose touch with the people pretty quickly | 18 | 49 | 24 | 1 | (7) |
| (6) | Parties are only interested in people's votes, not their opinions | 19 | 48 | 26 | 2 | (7) |

effect from inflating artificially the numbers of those appearing efficacious and ensures that those giving efficacious answers really mean it. It does, however, encourage people who may not be very efficacious in the first place to appear not at all efficacious.

Those who are certain of their ability to influence their government and are confident in the responsiveness of their politicians are not very numerous. Each question attracts a majority view that politics is remote and an unresponsive system run by cynical and aloof politicians. For a country respected for its allegedly high rate of democratic consensus these are not very encouraging results. Efficacy has been declining sharply in the United States (see Miller, A., 1974) and seems likely to have done so here equally precipitously. The political elite are seen to be drifting away from the influence of the mass base of society; they are out of touch and do not care very much that they are.

Likert scaling techniques (see Appendix) were applied to the six efficacy items and, following much informed prevarication concerning the twin elements of the efficacy scale (i.e., efficacy and system responsiveness), a single

scale score of political efficacy was derived having the following regrouped
distribution:

| Efficacy: | Very Low | Low | Moderate | High | Don't Know | |
|---|---|---|---|---|---|---|
| | 18% | 23% | 29% | 16% | 15% | (= 100%) |
| | 21% | 27% | 34% | 18% | (= 100%) | |

Like conceptualization, efficacy is positively linked to education (r=.28), but
again it is by no means the exclusive property of the better-educated young;
levels of efficacy scarcely differ across the three major age groups.

Our initial hypothesis is substantiated by the results, but not very convincingly. Efficacious citizens show only a marginally greater propensity to
protest (r=0.16). The effect is not present among retired people, and generally the impression given is that efficacy discourages *in*action rather than
spurs action. This is a reasonable result related to an equivocal hypothesis.
Though a general sense of efficacy reflects some optimism among protesters,
it must certainly contain also a core feeling of loyalty towards the legitimate
orthodox system, and while protesters may feel efficacious, many more
efficacious people may feel far more attached to the legitimate system and
are wary of protest. This probability is increased by a positive relationship
between efficacy and orthodox behavior (r=.22) though again the stronger
effect is to inhibit uninterest rather than to promote action. Also imbedded
in the concept of personal efficacy is the notion of system responsiveness.
That is to say, some people, protesters included, may downgrade their own
sense of efficacy not because they feel that they *personally* are not able to
make the right approaches to authorities nor even that they do not know how
to get those complaints actually heard, but because they feel that politicians
are not prepared to respond even to the efficacious citizen. For this reason we
turn explicitly to this problem in the next topic.

## Political Trust

One of the more sophisticated bodies of theory in political psychology
centers around the concept of political trust. William Gamson has done much
to formulate this idea. He proposes that trust is the *output* dimension of the
same body of political attitude of which efficacy is the *input* dimension. This
requires a little explanation. Efficacy is described above as essentially the
feeling that "someone up there" can be made to listen if only the citizen
exercises his rights of expression. They, the authorities, do not have to listen
very hard, but efficacy requires the basic self-assurance that the authority

system is democratically responsive to the active demands (i.e., the inputs) of the citizenry. Trust on the other hand comprises the citizens evaluation of the general outputs of the authorities. This is not merely a measure of performance, of "how well the government is doing" but a general measure of confidence in the competence of the authorities to achieve the greatest good for the greatest number and in the authorities' general good intentions in achieving that end. Trust is therefore a "positive set of preferred outcomes."

Venturing beyond Gamson's original formulation we propose that these output stimuli are further divided into two types: intrinsic trust behaviors and pragmatic trust behaviors. Intrinsic trust refers to a notion of honesty: that the authority system is conducted by men of goodwill and high probity, that they should quite literally be unimpeachable. Pragmatic trust outcomes are much more worldly in character; that the authorities are, one way or another, fulfilling their duty and doing things like encouraging industrial output by the fraction promised, restoring collective bargaining or curbing the unions, introducing (or abolishing) comprehensive education and a thousand other functions; in a modern cliché: keeping their promises. The distinction is easily illustrated by the fact that many Americans clearly thought former President Nixon's moral worth to be a shade suspect. The term "Tricky Dick" was often used affectionately within the ranks of the Republican party because he was expected to exercise some of his risqué skills in obtaining their preferred outcomes (honourable withdrawal from Indochina, containment of Communism, continued laissez-faire economic policies etc.) *one way or another*. Only when those skills were found to have been applied to the even more highly valued institutions of the democratic political system of America did the intrinsic dimension of trust start to assume a greater importance than the pragmatic.

So efficacy and trust are two faces of the same coin which has been variously described as "political alienation" (Lane, Schwartz, Finifter, and many others), "diffuse support" (Easton), "allegiance" (Dahl), "output alienation" (Almond and Verba), "political disaffection" (Citrin) or "cynicism" (Miller), depending on whether the presence or absence of trust is referred to and the particular theoretical area to which the concept is applied. Gamson uses the word trust solely to refer to *output* alienation. This is just as well because the reader may have detected already that there is a crucial dilemma in the prediction of protest behavior from trust and efficacy. "Input" trust (efficacy) is positively related to protest activity and will of course be related positively to "output" trust, i.e., people who believe politicians and the political system are fair and responsive and within the citizen's range of influence will also tend to believe that politicians are reasonably honest and well-intended people, who will do the right things. Yet, as Gamson spells out very clearly, the initial level of output trust will determine the choice of political action between what he calls "constraint" (protest), "inducement" (bargaining within the system) and "persuasion" (moving authorities to act by moral or reasoned argument) and therefore it is *low* trust that leads to protest. There is already evidence for this.

Miller found that receding political trust was a live nonpartisan force in American politics and that "cynics of the left *and* right" were retreating from participation in orthodox politics and expressed a wide range of dissatisfaction with the system of government, including a subjective sense of distance from the major parties. Citrin, however, contests that trust is not entirely unalloyed with partisan sentiment and, as we shall see, he is right. Michener and Zeller on the other hand found that inducement and persuasion were more likely to be chosen by high-school students to seek redress from their school authorities even though initial trust may be low because of the high costs incurred by the use of constraints against an authority who possesses usable actions. This of course was in the closed authority system of a school. In the general political arena, authorities have only limited sanctions outside the issue being contested, i.e., to do or fail to do what the protesters demand.

To determine the effect of trust upon protest in Britain, respondents were asked (immediately following the efficacy scale items) four questions which reflected the two elements in output trust. These are listed in Table 5.5

**Table 5.5: The Extent of Political Trust in Britain (in percentages)**

|  | Just About Always | Most of the Time | Only Some of the Time | Almost Never | (D.K.) |
|---|---|---|---|---|---|
| (1) How much do you trust the government in Westminster to do what is right? | 7 | 32 | 47 | 10 | (3) |
| (2) When people in politics speak on television or to the newspapers, or in Parliament, how much in your opinion do they tell the truth? | 3 | 22 | 60 | 10 | (4) |
| (3) How much do you trust a British government of either party to place the needs of this country and the people above the interests of their own political party? | 7 | 28 | 45 | 15 | (5) |
| (4) Generally speaking, would you say that this country is run by a few big interests concerned only for themselves or that it is run for the benefit of all the people? | Few Interests 48 | D.K. 15 | All the People 37 |  |  |

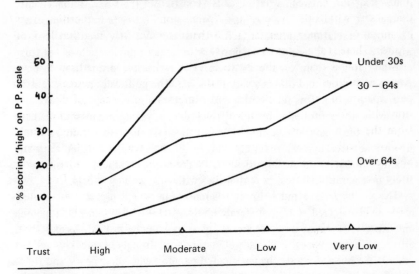

Figure 5.1.

together with the extent of trust feelings associated with each. The results are unequivocal. Political trust in Britain is at a very low ebb. A clear majority of those responding expressed their belief that Britain is governed and administered by self-interest men (of *both* parties) acting on behalf of a "few big interests" and who cannot be relied upon to do the right thing in most circumstances. Furthermore, fully 70 percent of the total sample thought "people in politics" were habitual liars. Thus we find both intrinsic and pragmatic trust are low whereas it might reasonably have been expected that British politicians are held more culpable for poor performance than for deliberate dishonesty.

Gamson uses the analogy of a bank's credit system to describe how the electorate deposits "trust" with a government (evidenced by the well-known "honeymoon effect" that an incoming administration enjoys in the opinion polls). The government is always asked to do more than it can possibly fulfill and so is always technically "insolvent" except that many ameliorative and administrative systems exist to ensure that the government can please at least a fair proportion of the people most of the time and remain politically in business. Now it seems that any party that takes up the mantle of government in Britain picks up at the same time a residue of political debt that considerably inhibits its freedom to trade in the political market. If earlier passages of this thesis did not fully dispose of the notion that the British electorate is composed of people deferent towards political authority, then these expressions of cynical resentment and mistrust ought to end the myth completely.

What effect, then, does this low level of output trust have upon protest potential? Clearly there are too many cynics and too few protesters to expect a one-to-one relationship, but a lack of trust is a modestly good predictor of protest potential. Those of the majority with weak or moderate levels of trust have an average score on the PP score. The cynics are divided, some have quite a high score and others a very low score. The politically trusting mostly have a low score. This relationship like the results of conceptualization and efficacy is not confounded by age differences: the young and middle-aged are equally cynical and the retired only a little less so while within each age group, the very cynical generally have a PP score much higher than the trusting. But it is interesting to see how the *point* at which cynicism takes effect in generating protest potential rises with age (see Figure 5.1).

The young have a much lower tolerance for cynicism and their protest response is triggered at even moderate levels of trust while among older people much higher levels of mistrust are required to generate protest. As expected, efficacy (input trust) and output trust are strongly positively related (r=.40). So we have found the anticipated paradox wherein efficacy and trust, although different aspects of the same feeling of allegiance towards the political system and its practitioners, have *opposite* effects upon protest. Diagrammatically, the problem is expressed in Figure 5.2. Such an arrangement is possible because the sheer amount of variance explained by the zero-order correlation between protest and efficacy and trust is quite small (r=.16 and -.13 respectively). (Again it should be borne in mind that an analysis geared to detect shifts in minority characteristics in skewed distributions does not thrive on product-moment correlation analysis; it takes a fairly massive relationship to produce even a modest correlation.) Thus it seems

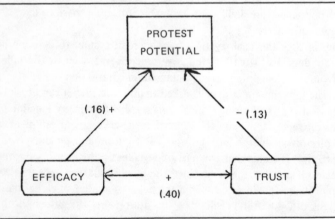

Figure 5.2.

quite likely that some kind of interaction occurs between the two measures of political confidence which provides a dynamic explanation of protest. Paige has demonstrated that *low* trust and *high* efficacy provide a "potent combination" to explain the participation of black citizens of Newark, U.S.A., in the riots of 1967-1968. Among efficacious blacks, the proportion active in riots increases sharply as trust declines, but among those with a low sense of efficacy, participation declines with cynicism. The measure which Paige calls efficacy is based on political information corresponding more closely with our own measure of "level of conceptualization," but his results provide the first clue to understanding the dynamics of protest instead of just describing its corrrelates. What comparable results are available for this study?

Trust and efficacy do have an interactive impact upon protest potential. Among those with high trust, protest potential is low regardless of efficacy. Thus even people who feel well able to influence the course of political events will not turn to protest provided they feel also that their politicians are thoroughly trustworthy and able people. However, among many of this efficacious group, the least feelings of cynicism seem enough to provoke the willingness to engage in protest behavior and it is especially interesting to note that this willingness is associated especially with just low levels of trust rather than with total cynicism. If you believe that politicians are complete rogues, then it is difficult to feel efficacious as well. (This is the problem of the notion of system responsiveness getting entangled with trust as well as efficacy that we mentioned earlier and deal with in the Appendix.) In contrast with the efficacious group, among those who feel much less able to influence events it is only the most cynical that are prepared to protest in greater numbers. This makes sense insofar as feelings of inefficacy can be reinterpreted very specifically as conventional-party-political inefficacy by someone who feels the country is in very untrustworthy hands and thus lead in turn to a willingness to protest. Although the process is not yet clear in this argument, we can say for the moment that protesters will tend to be people who feel that politicians cannot be trusted to get on with their task of government unsupervised by public opinion but believe nonetheless that the same politicians will be likely to make some response (however reluctantly) when opinion makes itself heard—especially if their own voice is raised loud enough.

Conceptualization is only slightly related to efficacy (r=.15) and not at all to trust but has a very similar interactive effect upon protest combined with political trust. Again, high levels of trust inhibit protest regardless of conceptual sophistication; even ideologues who trust the system of government pretty well implicitly have a low protest potential. That Paige was measuring conceptualization rather than efficacy is shown by the lowest conceptualization group ("none" or "intrinsic values") whose PP score actually *declines* among the most cynical in their ranks and this replicates Paige's findings exactly. These people produce a shoulder-shrugging reaction to virtually any political stimulus. They do not trust what goes on "up there" but they "don't know and don't care," and they certainly do not care enough to protest. Nor are they all older people retired from life as well as their jobs. Many of them are working-class teenagers and their low conceptualization and low trust condition explains quite a lot of the residual inaction among the young. Among the remainder of those with low trust, protest potential is associated strongly with higher levels of conceptualization and especially the ideologues among whom anything less than nearly complete trust is associated with high scores on the PP scale.

These results suggest the possibility of a three-way interaction between efficacy, trust and conceptual sophistication. The hypothesis is simply this: Protest potential will be highest when individuals having higher than average ability to conceptualize politics, *and* who feel personally able to voice dissent effectively, feel *also* that politicians are not to be trusted. Yet the arguments supporting the hypothesis are not at all simple. What is being proposed is that an apparently contradictory set of beliefs is coalescing in a curious way to produce a clear behavioral outcome. There is a strong tendency for the trusting to be efficacious or, to state the view of the majority, for a sense of inefficacy to be accompanied by a feeling of cynicism. Yet, as we have seen, it is *efficacious cynics* who are most easily recruited into protest. They are joined in protest by inefficacious extreme cynics. Why should this be so? We must argue, of course, that it is because they share something in common with their efficacious co-sceptics and that the linking characteristic we seek is most likely to be a basic form of political consciousness. They share the same level of cognitive complexity, the same ability to manipulate complex political stimuli in simultaneous configurations. This may sound very clever; a rare political dexterity. But all that this means is that they feel they know "what is going on" and particularly in the case of the inefficacious extreme cynics, they do not like it very much. Such a coalescence of cognitive skill, negative affect, and positive behavioral competence revives, coincidentally, the basic attitude-behavior model (see Allport) of cognition, affect, and behavioral disposition and points toward a very potent source of protest motivation. So what is the evidence?

Figure 5.3 represents in a simplified manner the proportion of respondents scoring high on the PP scale by four levels of trust, high or low efficacy, and four levels of conceptual sophistication. The results are very clear:

(1) *A high level of political trust inhibits protest regardless of efficacy or conceptualization.* If even politically sophisticated and politically self-confident people trust their politicians to get on with the job honestly

and well, they will discard the possibility of protest together along with everyone else who shares their confidence in our elected custodians of parliamentary democracy.

(2) *Lower levels of trust produce high levels of protest potential when conceptualization and efficacy are high.* When reasonably sophisticated and politically self-confident people feel suspicious of politicians, protest behavior becomes an imminent possibility.

(3) *The lowest levels of trust produce high levels of protest potential when conceptualization is high but not necessarily when efficacy is high.* Those convinced that politics is crooked *and* have a sophisticated set of ideas of what politics is about will also be very likely to protest even if they are not very self-confident about whether they will be heeded.

Put another way, we can say that efficacious people who have even a reasonable grasp of the political world are quickly provoked into protest when they become even somewhat cynical of politicians. Among the inefficacious, however, only those who are politically sophisticated *and* highly cynical will be likely to protest.

The simplified diagram in Figure 5.3 shows with impressive clarity the main effects described above of how protest potential maximizes under conditions of low trust, high efficacy, and high conceptualization, and almost disappears when confidence is high. One difficulty that these results now present is that they may appear to contradict our earlier assertion that protest was not the outcome of political alienation. If mistrust among the politically aware is not alienation, what is? The answer, of course, is that many social and psychological conditions have been described as "alienation" and taken together they would make no sense at all. On the one side theorists like Kornhauser speak of alienation in terms of social distance from the mainstream of the normative value system and normative lifestyles; the alienated are the outsiders, *l'étrangérs*. Another body of theory (cf., Finifter) regards political alienation more accurately as a political phenomenon and thinks in terms of withdrawal of system support among politically aggrieved minorities. Neither of these approaches to alienation fit the approach adopted here to the study of protest nor do they fit our data. Protest is more likely to occur when people feel efficacious. Those inclined toward the use of protest in Britain have not given up on the system nor do they feel they have been excluded from it. They are voters, joiners, and do-ers who usually have a clear idea of what the basic features of political change are like, and most of them remain reasonably confident that their role as citizens still counts for something. But in addition they feel that politics is far too important to be left solely to the politicians, most of whom they actually mistrust. If this feeling of positive scepticism is alienation, then alienation may be said to be associated with protest. But the attitude syndrome we describe lacks that essential ingredient of distance from the norm, deviance if you will, that characterizes most satisfactory definitions of alienation and so it would be misleading to use the term here.

This apparent theoretical confusion is more easily resolved if it is accepted that alienation has probably a curvilinear relationship with political activism in general and protest potential in particular. Seeman's model of alienation—a

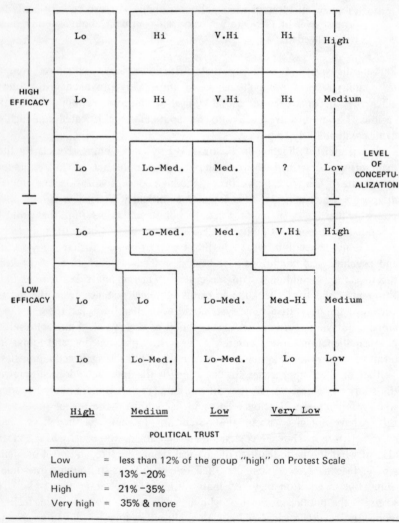

Figure 5.3: PROTEST BY EFFICACY BY TRUST BY LEVEL OF CONCEPT

model having a powerful hold over current conceptualizations of alienation—specifies five basic elements of alienation: estrangement, powerlessness, normlessness, meaninglessness, and social isolation. There is much in this partitioning model that is confusing and almost clumsy. For example, where participation in unorthodox behavior is concerned, the last of these—social isolation—is more likely to be a consequence than a cause of protest. We have demonstrated earlier that the propensity towards unorthodox political behavior is much more a characteristic of socially and politically well-integrated people than of isolates. What is much more likely to be occurring is this: The potential protester in the British political community is a *partial* alienate. He has accomplished the first element of alienation and feels *emotionally estranged* from the orthodox political world *as currently practiced*, i.e., he does not *trust* those elected to govern (nor even those most likely to replace them) and this supplies a strong source of *negative affect*. But he has not accomplished any of the following states of alienation. He does not experience powerlessness. On the contrary, he is quite likely to feel he still counts for something in the political process. Nor does he experience meaninglessness. Again on the contrary, he knows only too well what is going on and where it might all lead and expresses his likes and, more often, his dislikes of the parties in an articulate manner. In a way perhaps he is a *frustrated* alienate. Affectively he feels inclined to withdraw from the party political process but he is bonded by habit, upbringing, and the depth of his own political cognitions to the mainstream of politics. His only possible response is therefore to respond to the need for specific redress or for general reform through whatever means may seem useful. To the political protester, unorthodox political behavior *is* useful and he is motivated thereby to add protest to his range of political resources.

This nonalienation interactive model (cf., Muller) of the nonpartisan influences upon protest may be extended to other measures of political behavior: orthodox and super-orthodox politics. Thus the following hypothetical matrix suggests itself:

|                 | Trust |   | Efficacy |   | Conceptual Sophistication |
| --------------- | ----- | - | -------- | - | ------------------------- |
| Protest =       | low   | + | high     | + | high                      |
| Orthodox participation = | high  | + | high     | + | high                      |
| Repression =    | high  | + | low      | + | low                       |

Paige found that among his efficatious and well-informed black citizens the initial level of trust (qua Gamson) determined the choice of political behavior: High trust led to high conventional activity (i.e., voting, lobbying congressmen etc.) while low trust led to high protest activity (i.e., rioting). We would expect a similar though less spectacular configuration of results from these data. Repression potential, on the other hand, will be associated with the high output trust in the political system but low efficacy. We reason that those high on repression potential are likely to have less concern for individual rights of participation in politics; they feel that government should be left in trust to the authorities, and the authorities should have the freedom to quash interference or threat. The cognitive simplicity implied by such a view of political participation would lead to an expectation of *low* conceptual sophistication among those with high repression potential.

At the aggregate level the hypothetical relationships implied in the above matrix are substantiated though, as we have seen earlier, none of the relationships attain great magnitude. Taken one at a time, these nonpartisan influences are slight but significant; significant, that is, in the wider sense than the statistical. The model shows once more that protest and orthodox participation have similar roots in personal feelings of confidence and understanding but that the choice between, or better perhaps the inclination toward, one or other of the two courses of action is determined by the initial level of trust in the political authorities. This finding is exactly in line with the Paige-Gamson theory. This result maintains that constraint (protest) will be the preferred course of action under low trust and high efficacy conditions while persuasion and inducement (conventional participation) will be the characteristic of high trust and high efficacy conditions. It is interesting also to note that the otherwise weak influence of education upon participation is amplified through the trust, efficacy and conceptualization scales, especially through efficacy. As was found by Almond and Verba, increased exposure to formal education has the effect of raising citizen self-confidence that personal participation is relevant and rewarding.

At the interactive level the relationships implied by our model are sharpened but modified a little. The results for protest potential scores are as already known: At each level of comparison, protest scale mean scores are higher when trust is low and efficacy and conceptualization are high. For the orthodox participation scores, the combined effects of efficacy and conceptualization are clearly the dominant influence upon rates of orthodox participation; though higher trust usually increases participation a little further. In respect of conventional participation, the differences between the low and high conceptualization groups are very considerable. Those who do take an active interest in the workings of conventional politics go into the field with their eyes open. The results for repression potential are more equivocal and indicate that the interaction between trust and conceptualization is the dominant influence. Cynical ideologues are especially unwilling to unleash authority power against protesters or strikers and even trusting ideologues are very hesitant to do so. Clearly, an ideologue in a democratic system is likely to be someone who values civil liberties at least as highly as public order and often more so. It is of course possible to describe an active right-wing ideologue who is eager to use state authority for repressive purposes, but the majority of inactive people (and they *do* tend to be inactive) who support such a view tend not to be ideologues, or the contrary, they tend to be low conceptualizers.

At this point in the analysis it is possible to claim that the first progress has been made towards an *explanation* of protest potential rather than an examination of the correlates of protest. Support for protest behavior and, just as importantly, opposition to repression, arises from a feeling of political self-confidence among people who are at least initiated into the habit of political thought and who commonly try to make sense of political stimuli rather than just ignoring them. Among these people, support for conventional political activities will also be high, but the emphasis of direction in the kinds of action they may favor, to move toward protest or toward continued persistence with the conventional system, will be determined by the extent of the individual's trust in the political authorities. As the sense of cynicism grows in the politically conscious and self-confident individual, so a critical point is reached where direct action will hold more promise of redress than continued persuasion and inducement tactics. This process occurs in each age group and even among the retired to a limited extent. But among the young the critical level is reached at really quite modest levels of cynicism even though the aggregate level of cynicism among the young is no higher than that prevailing among their parents' generation. This three-levered trigger of protest potential is just a lot more sensitive among the young.

To describe this process is more than merely saying that people will try legitimate methods of political action until they are fed up with getting nowhere and turn to protest instead. It is a fundamental shift in political orientation which may well be occurring intergenerationally. The continued growth of political cynicism is coupled with the effects of education which continually raises levels of personal political efficacy and awareness. This intersection of forces can only accelerate the development of much wider parameters of license for protest activity in the political community in the future.

Before this discussion is concluded, it is necessary to explore the extent to which this coalescence of trust, efficacy, and conceptualization is genuinely nonpartisan and free of ideological associations. Even though careful efforts were made to politically neutralize the questions, it would be surprising if it were completely unalloyed with partisanship. Political trust is the most suspect in this regard since it correlates with the left-right scale (r=.28) in a leftward direction, and this occurs most clearly at higher levels of political conceptualization. Therefore, increasing cynicism is quite strongly associated with a left-wing ideological position and with support for the Labour party, which actually commands a majority of support over both the other parties among those who are consistently mistrustful of "the government." This could scarcely be otherwise, particularly at the time of asking.

Yet, the other two factors under consideration are paradoxically related to ideology and partisan choice in the *opposite direction*. Despite the fact that higher efficacy is associated with protest, right-wingers are *more* efficacious than left-wingers (r=.15) and hence Conservative supporters are considerably more efficacious than Labour or Liberal supporters. Sixty-six percent of the Tories score high on the efficacy scale compared with 42 percent of Labour supporters. The relationship between conceptual sophistication and ideology is particularly intricate. Conservatives and right-wingers are disproportionately numerous among those with a high level of conceptualization and among those lower down the scale expressing their views in terms of intrinsic values ("I was brought up a Conservative . . . ."). Labour supporters and left-wingers are quite well represented among ideologues but occupy the mid-level conceptualization point of "group interests" almost as their own ("Labour looks after the poor/workers/unions/etc."), and are also more numerous than Tories among those with the lowest level of conceptualization ("No idea," "Never think about any of them") as also are Liberals and centrists. This complexity notwithstanding, the relationship between partisanship, conceptualization and protest is fairly straightforward. We examined those scoring high on the protest scale separately for left, center, and right self-placement and for Labour, Liberal and Tory supporters across the four main levels of conceptualization. Protest potential rises as a result of higher conceptualization regardless of partisanship but especially for Labour and Liberals (equally so, which is surprising) and left-wingers generally. The result is similar for centrists, Conservatives and right-wingers though these latter are clearly operating, as groups, much lower down the protest scale.

Returning to the efficacy-trust interaction for a moment, we examined the proportion scoring high on the protest scale across the four levels of trust separately for high and low efficacy groups each further divided by left- and right-wing self-placement. For all four groups, protest potential rises as a function of greater cynicism, at greater orders of magnitude on the left than on the right, with the exception of the efficacious but very cynical right-wingers. These are a small group (n=23) of considerably older working-class Tories, who have apparently excluded themselves from the ranks of potential protesters simply on grounds of age. Interestingly too, the separation of left and right is not at all complete, disregarding the exception just mentioned, and some efficacious right-wingers respond to cynicism with increased protest potential *more* strongly than the inefficacious left.

In order to pull together some of those apparently conflicting trends in the data, it is necessary to refer back to the simplified schema presented in Figure 5.3. Here the 24 cells generated by the intersection of four levels of trust, two levels of efficacy, and three levels of conceptualization divided quite fortuitously into three nearly equal eight-cell blocs having relatively high, medium and low protest potential (n=450, 414, and 387 respectively). The mean left-right score was calculated for each bloc and yielded a right-inclined mean score of 6.1 for the low-protest bloc, an exactly neutral score of 5.58 for the medium-protest bloc, and a left-inclined score of 5.27 for the high-protest bloc. These figures, though certainly reflecting the known leftward inclination among potential protesters, should be compared with the range of 4.23, 5.57, and 7.32 scored respectively by the Labour, Liberal and Conservative supporters. Thus the three-way interaction discussed in this chapter occurs across the boundaries of political partisanship. For example, marginally the largest cell in the high protest bloc (moderate trust + high efficacy + high conceptualization) has a mean LR scale score of 6.0, which reflects again the presence of the aggressive young Tories among the ranks of potential protesters. Conversely, the low-protest cell determined by the intersection of moderate trust, low efficacy and medium conceptualization has a mean LR scale score of 5.1, which is well to the left. Also, among the cells in the average or medium protest bloc the range of LR scores is 4.7 to 6.3.

A similar cross-partisan picture emerges for the other measures of political action but overall there are some partisan influences that should not be glossed over. Orthodox political behavior rises as a function of increased trust, efficacy and conceptualization more certainly on the right than on the left. Repression potential on the left is depressed quite readily by a combination of increased personal efficacy and conceptualization (especially the latter) but on the right high levels of repression potential are much more resistant to this influence. At higher levels of conceptualisation, cynical right-wingers do have a lower repression potential than the trusting; they are unwilling to augment the political authority of politicians whom they regard as dishonest incompetents. Yet there is a vast difference between cynical *efficacious* right-wing ideologues and cynical *inefficacious* right-wing ideologues. The former have a very low repression potential and a relatively high protest potential, but the latter have an opposite and deeply repressive configuration. This almost certainly reflects two very different kinds of right-wing ideology. On the one hand among the efficacious ideologues there is an active, participatory concern for political liberties, characteristic of younger Liberals (some of whom placed themselves right of center) and others who do not trust politicians with too much power. On the other hand we have a group of "real" right-wingers who have probably grown tired of the steady socialization of British society under both parties and mistrust pro-

foundly what they probably regard as permissive modern Toryism. Consequently, they feel that the political authority of, the state should be
reestablished by a show of force. During the time of the survey such views
were not uncommonly heard.

Despite a number of discontinuities, two complex and powerful forces
may be seen through these data. These forces are at work shaping changes in
the participation patterns of the British polity. Both forces are pulling
behavior away from the ideal model of parliamentary democracy. By this
ideal model we imply a state in which people listen, discuss freely, vote and
make representations in person or through formal interest groups but do little
also to modify the behavior of the political and civil authorities. That is to
say, there is an ideal model wherein there is always a consensual preference
for inducement or persuasion over constraint. The first force is pulling in the
direction of constraint or protest behavior. It draws its power from increasing
levels of political cynicism and is maintained through residual feelings of
personal political efficacy, coupled with higher levels of political conceptualization. This force is concentrated on the political left but is supported by
some who traditionally identify with the democratic right but who have also
become disillusioned with the conduct of politicians though they still retain a
belief in their own ability to influence political events. Efficacious ideologues
on both left *and* right tend to prefer protest and orthodox participation over
repression. In contrast, efficacious low conceptualizers of both left and right
show the opposite configuration and in this result we see clearly the undertow of the second force which is pulling in the direction of the antidemocratic suppression of attempts by citizens to use constraint upon authorities,
i.e., repression. This second force draws power from a feeling of faith in
political authority, of political trust, that "they" can be trusted to "do what
is right" and rule honestly for the benefit of all above squalid party interests.
It may seem that this is a naive view of politics and, especially when it occurs
on the political left, it arises concurrently with an unsophisticated political
belief system and *tends* to occur, though too irregularly to be of great
significance, along with lower levels of personal efficacy.

The suppression of dissent in the political community offers a cognitively
simple solution to the vexing complexities of modern politics which appeals,
to be candid, to the cognitively simple. It is Cantril's view that it is unlikely
that the Naxi party rose to power in Germany because of an implicitly
antidemocratic culture in that country. The full explanation is very complex,
as Cantril's own work on the subject acknowledges, yet one very simple fact,
carefully researched by Bendix,[2] demonstrates clearly that there occurred no
sudden reversion to type among a naturally authoritarian electorate. The
Nazis' electoral success in 1930 owed much less to a transfer of votes in their
favor from traditional parties than to the Nazis' ability to mobilize new voters

to their cause among recently enfranchised young people, and many others who had failed to vote in 1928. Herbele's research indicates that most prominent among the latter were ill-educated farmers and peasants and old people not formally in the habit of voting. Thus Converse feels safe in concluding, "the mass base of the Nazi movement represented one of the most unrelievedly ill-informed clienteles that a major political party has assembled in a modern state."

It will not be concluded here that the second of the two forces described above is moving the less sophisticated part of the British electorate along a right-wing populist path towards a position imminently receptive to fascism, any more than the first force described is plunging the more involved sectors of the electorate leftward into revolution. As Chapter 4 indicated, the parliamentary model is still the dominant model for political involvement even if the majority do not get involved beyond the ballot box. What is being suggested here is that these nonpartisan forces, unseen and unheard, can count for just as much in the process of political change as the apparently more powerful forces of specific ideologies. The picture that emerges for the British political community is that the freedom to govern in the traditional manner, to capitalize on trust and high consensual participation of a politically self-confident electorate is becoming as clearly constrained as is the freedom of the British economy to expand at will. Freedom to coerce is denied by mistrust and challenged by the protest potential of aware and able young citizens while the freedom to bargain can be constrained just as much by demands for repression. The willingness to listen patiently, to reason and to represent views constitutionally is still present but it is under some pressure.

# NOTES

1. My work on this topic derives directly from my collaboration with Hans-Dieter Klingemann of Zentrum für Unfragen Methoden und Analysen, University of Mannheim, Germany.

2. Some scholars doubt that the Nazis' electoral success after 1928 was quite as straightforward as Bendix describes. For example, Lipset (*Political Man*) says that the initial rise in turnout was shared more or less equally among all parties, and only later did the Nazi party mobilize formerly inactive sections of the population and claim the allegiance of the young.

*Chapter 6*

# DISSATISFACTION AND PROTEST

It is axiomatic in the research literature that protest behavior arises from a subjectively held sense of dissatisfaction. How could it be otherwise? A political protest is, almost by definition, the expression of a grievance and grievances are expressed by aggrieved persons. Thus the current incidence of protest behavior is held inter alia to be a negative indicator of the level of political contentment and even of generalized satisfaction within the polity. The assumption has passed into the culture that outbreaks of political rebellion and revolution occur when generalized and hitherto undirected levels of frustration and human unhappiness within a society reach some critical and insupportable level. The storm signals of impending revolution are recognized in increasingly frequent expressions of frustration and dissatisfaction. These are met by official repression which in turn generates additional frustration until the whole thing boils over into chaos and revolution. In Peter Weis' play, De Sade taunts Marat—the intellectual apologist for the French Revolution—with this simple selfish motivation for popular rebellion:

Their soup's burnt
They shout for better soup
A woman finds her husband too short
She wants a taller one
A man finds his wife too skinny

He wants a plumper one
A man's shoes pinch
but his neighbour's shoes fit comfortably
A poet runs out of poetry
and desperately gropes for new images
For hours the angler casts his line
Why aren't the fish biting
And so they join the revolution.

The echoes of that revolution which disrupted France in May 1968 were similarly interpreted this time both eloquently by intellectual apologists like Aaron: "Protests, renewal of partisan passions, result from a contradiction between aspiration towards the absolute and rejection of the transcendent" and convincingly by participants like Cohn Bendit: "Yes, we are in rebellion. Yes, we are fed up with everything."

Cavanna reminds us that "when a Frenchman—a 'continental'—speaks of revolt, revolution or 'events,' an Englishman translates such words by 'protest and dissatisfaction.' " The question asked in this chapter therefore is to what extent is the propensity to engage in unorthodox political behavior fueled by a sense of dissatisfaction experienced by potential protesters? Such a question has been asked before by empirical political scientists and, for such an apparently simple question, a remarkably tangled and confusing literature has been generated. To help clear the undergrowth, a short account of the theoretical background is required:

The persuasiveness of the *dissatisfaction* ————➤ *protest* model lies in its obvious motivational basis. As Gurr will have us believe, it seems actually to answer the question of "Why men rebel." For the political psychologist, the obvious source model for this paradigm is the work of the Yale school led by Dollard in the 1930s. Their well-known basic postulate is that "aggression always follows frustration." Frustration itself may produce other reactions ranging from self-pity to a psychosomatic rash but aggression of some kind will always be one of the consequences of frustration. Leonard Berkowitz has quantified much of the Yale theory and, finding only a weak direct link between frustration and aggression, has placed more stress upon the role of some "releasing cue" which may elicit overt aggressive behavior from a frustrated person. He demonstrated that experimentally frustrated subjects will exhibit much more aggression in the form of electric shocks to their frustrator if firearms are left around in their sight than if these aggression-associated stimuli are absent. Berkovitz is emphatic that he is observing a process of learned responses and not the provocation of some innate aggressive drive. Thus he has faith that interaction between frustrations and aggressors that produce political aggression, violence, and rioting may also be unlearned especially through the removal of aggression-provoking cues. This is in contrast to the theories of Lorenz and Ardrey who maintain that man possesses some innate aggressive and destructive impulse to defend what is his alone, which, however sophisticated our society becomes, will always burst forth and turn competition into conflict, confrontation into war, and so on.

As it stands, the application of the frustration-aggression model to the study of political aggression has had uneven results and has drawn critical reactions. On a priori grounds Nieburg is scornful of the idea; he says: "The simple frustration-aggression syndrome represents a very primitive state of the psychological art." While he agrees with Hoffer that "leaders cannot conjure a movement out of the void" (cited in Leiden and Schmidt 1968, p. 676) he stresses that "discontent and dissatisfaction exist all the time and only under special conditions does the dissatisfaction-political aggression link become relevant."

Dahl too is suspicious of the equally obvious deprivation————————→ protest model:

> To the dismay and astonishment of activists who struggle to organise a disadvantaged group to oppose its lot, the human psyche does not invariably impel those who are deprived of equality to seek it, or sometimes even to want it (p. 95).

It is certainly the view taken here that the *politicization* of personal frustration and dissatisfaction is a very complex process. As Hobsbawm says:

> Individual rebelliousness is itself a socially neutral phenomenon and consequently mirrors the struggles and divisions within society (p. 13).

Thus we may dismiss the naive idea that human conditions which appear objectively frustrating, miserable and oppressed to the analyst are necessarily experienced as such by the oppressed themselves. Even Dollard concedes that frustration should be experienced as such to produce aggression. Berkovitz from a position of empirical strength points clearly to the role of *relative deprivation* as the key frustrating agent in political aggression:

> Poverty-stricken groups who have never dreamed of having automobiles, washing machines, or new homes are not frustrated because they have been deprived of these things; they are frustrated only after they have begun to hope.

Davies picks up this crucial subjective stage in the realization of deprivation and reminds us that a mature Karl Marx rejected his earlier insistence that deprivation (conceived of by Marx as "immiserization") inevitably leads to political aggression among the oppressed and pointed instead to a *socially* derived sense of deprivation:

> Although the enjoyments of workers have risen, the social satisfaction that they give has fallen in comparison with the state of development of society in general. Our desires and pleasures spring from society. . . . Because they are of a social nature they are of a relative nature (p. 5).

Similarly, Alexis de Tocqueville was puzzled as to why no evidence could be found for an increase in oppression during the period preceding the French Revolution while on the contrary considerable evidence existed for improvements in the common lot through improved distribution of what modern economists now call the gross national product. His answer was clear: that these very improvements, together with some naive attempts by the government to ameliorate the worst excesses of aristocratic exploitation of the peasants, lifted the people's eyes up from the daily business of survival to gaze upon the horizon of the possible; upon the chance of a world actually free of misery and oppression. So theirs was the first revolution of rising expectations.

The confusion we spoke of earlier then, centers around two distinct conceptual and empirical questions:

(a)  What constitutes subjective relative deprivation?
(b)  In what way does this source of frustration lead to political aggression?

Different conceptualisation of relative deprivation produces quite different linkages to political aggression and the impression should not be given that the concept has been considered useful only on the context of political aggression. On the contrary, Hyman, Stouffer, Merton, and others made relative deprivation a key concept of social theory by the 1950s and there is no doubt that the experience of deprivation of some source of expected gratification, be it material goods, status, security, recognition, esteem, or whatever, is indeed frustrating and has all kinds of motivating properties. Necessarily though, we shall concentrate this narrative upon the way in which subjective deprivation becomes translated into political aggression.

Two schools of research have looked at the problem on a systemic level. Ivan and Rosalind Feierabend synthesized the more flexible aspects of the Yale model with techniques for the measurement of *national* relative deprivation from Lipset (1959) and related these cross-nationally using Lerner's (1958) threefold classification of traditional, transitional, and modern societies. They found that transitional societies experience heavy doses of relative deprivation. They conceptualize relative deprivation as "systemic frustration," this being the discrepancy between "social want formation" and "social want satisfaction." Thus systemic frustration is generated in developing nations by the inability of development to keep apace with rising expectations, and this in turn generates much higher levels of political instability and leads to increasingly frequent incidents of public turmoil.

A similar approach more directly addressed to the *relative deprivation*————▸*aggression* linkage is contained in Gurr's prodigious analysis of 114 nations. Gurr spells out the basic postulate of RD theory with admirable clarity:

> Relative deprivation is defined as actors' perceptions of discrepancy between their value expectations (the goods and conditions of the life to which they believe they are justifiably entitled) and their value capabilities (the amounts of those goods and conditions that they think they are able to get and keep). The underlying causal mechanism is derived from psychological theory and evidence to the effect that one innate response to perceived deprivation is discontent or anger, and that anger is a motivating state for which aggression is an inherently satisfying response (Gurr 1971, p. 218).

Yet his operationalization of cross-national comparative measures of RD, like the Feierabends', is strangely indirect, involving eighty-eight measures of economic and social ill-fare (inflation, balance of trade, dependence upon foreign capital, ratios of doctors to patients, hospitals, educational opportunities per capita and so on). These inferred collective states of RD are then compared with indices of political aggression of varying intensity: peaceful protest, turmoil (violent and nonviolent), strife, and rebellion. Gurr is equally clear about his results:

> Levels of peaceful protest are not significantly affected by *any* of the deprivation measures. Total turmoil, violent as well as non-violent, is not associated with economic deprivation but, like total strife, somewhat affected by political and persisting deprivation, r's = .40 and .37, respectively. The strongest causal connections by far are with rebellion. Here both economic and political deprivation are important, correlating .44 and .73 with magnitude of rebellion, respectively, while persisting deprivation correlates .55 (Gurr 1970, p. 134).

So Gurr's work would *not* lead us to form an hypothesis that political aggression in Britain is a direct function of RD since it has been established beyond doubt that the prospects for "rebellion" are as distant as are the circumstances of economic desperation measured by Gurr in some underdeveloped nations.

Another well-known theory of a similar kind locates the key source of frustration in a sudden reversal of the capacity of an economy to satisfy rising expectations. This is Davies' "J-curve" theory:

> Revolutions are most likely to occur when a prolonged period of objective economic and social development is followed by a short period of sharp reversal (Davies 1962, p. 5).

Davies produces some evidence to support his hypothesis and Tanter and Midlarsky demonstrate that Davies' theory may subsequently have held good in the case of Cuba. But Davies goes even further out along the fragile limb of inferring mass-psychological feeling states from historical and aggregate data. No evidence is produced to support the contention that those *engaging* in political aggression or overtly supporting unorthodox activism are *themselves* experiencing subjective RD. It remains a fairly remarkable leap in the dark.

The case of the American black revolt in the 1959-1969 period provided researchers with a better subject of analysis. Pettigrew was quick to point out that what appeared at first glance to be real material gains during the postwar period faded rapidly into psychological losses when compared with the gains accruing to the white population at the same time. It was this acceleration of frustration that brought forth first protest, then rioting. It should be noted at once that here RD is conceived as deprivation *relative to others* which may have different properties to *deprivation relative to some personal standard of expectation.* This idea provided the key interpretation of the blacks' response to discrimination. Thus the Kerner Commission:

> He [the black rioter] feels strongly that he deserves a better job and he is barred from achieving it not because of lack of training, ability, or ambition, but because of discrimination by employers (Kerner, p. 129).

The more Whites pleaded that substantial progress had been made in elevating the blacks, the more angry the blacks became at the slowness of that progress.

Geschwender applied the full range of deprivation theory to the "Negro revolt" as early as 1964. He examined the social and economic conditions of black Americans and argued that an objectively steady improvement in black living standards dismissed both the "vulgar Marxist" (i.e., increasing deprivation) *and* the Davies J-curve hypotheses since no reversal was evident. The data supported instead the "sophisticated Marxist" (relative deprivation), the "rising expectations" hypotheses and the "status inconsistency" theories of Lenski. Geschwender concluded that "relative deprivation is the essence of all three hypotheses that are consistent with the observed data," and that the negro in the United States is handicapped by blockage in the circulation of the elite. He is acquiring the education which is normally the key to occupational mobility and economic gain. He is not experiencing as rapid a rate of occupational mobility and economic gain as he feels entitled to. As a result he is becoming increasingly status inconsistent and sees himself falling further and further behind the White. He feels relatively deprived and justly so. Therefore he revolts in order to correct the situation (p. 256).

What was sorely needed though was some hard empirical evidence to link political aggression in individuals to their own reported sense of relative deprivation. Attempts by psychologists and political scientists to measure the relationship between frustration and political aggression on the *individual* level have been facilitated by the use of "self-anchoring striving scales" developed by Cantril and Free. The respondent is shown an image of a ten-rung ladder and asked to imagine "the best possible life" (or job, income, house, or whatever) for himself which corresponds to the topmost ladder position and "the worst possible" corresponding to the foot of the ladder—what the Chinese poet Tsang K'o-chia once called "the zero degrees of life."[1] The discrepancy between the respondent's self-placement on the scale and the top of the ladder is taken to represent what Feierabend calls the "want-get gap" or subjective relative deprivation.

Cantril discovered that, across fourteen nations, the poor and disadvantaged were by no means unaware of their situation and placed themselves well down the scale. So do American blacks. Relative deprivation arises where one would objectively expect it to. Using this method Free was able to demonstrate that severe and *unchanging* relative deprivation was a possible antecedent of turmoil in the case of Dominica, Nigeria, Cuba, and the American blacks. Campbell and Shuman also found widespread dissatisfaction of the same nature among American blacks.

Bowen et al. obtained similar measures from a mainly black sample of Cleveland, Ohio's poverty area dwellers and uncovered at the same time links with a series of attitudes indicating favorability towards the use of protest methods. They report: "Table 2 indicates . . . there is a statistically significant relation between current relative felt deprivation and positive rank on the protest factor." Unfortunately "Table 2" shows nothing of the kind; the differences they report are minute and insignificant ($\chi^2 = 3.676$ with 2 d.f. $P = .10$), but later they do demonstrate much more convincingly that those blacks who expect a currently deprived situation to continue were much more likely to favor protest than those expecting continued gratification or at least some improvement. Goffman and Muller also demonstrated that shifts in relative gratification over time are more important than static measures. They found from a disproportionately sampled group of black and white citizens of

Waterloo, Iowa, that current RD was a poor predictor of protest potential but, strangely, those expecting improvements in their situation *and* those expecting decreased gratification in the future had a higher protest potential than those expecting no change at all. They explained this "V-curve" phenomenon in terms of differential motivation of the two groups: The decreasing-gratification group are straightforwardly fearful and angry, while the increasing-gratification group have more to lose and are prepared to protect their rising prospects and push for more. The no-change group are resigned to the status quo.

Among the few researchers to find an unambiguous relationship between Cantril-scale deprivation and protest militancy were Crawford and Naditch from a sample of adult male Detroit blacks under the age of forty-five. Those with high discrepancy scores were twice as likely to support protest methods and sympathize with Black Power. Given what it means for a young black man to be relatively deprived within central Detroit any other result would have brought this line of inquiry to a universal halt. Similarly, a study of the highly successful Maryland sit-in movement in the 1965-67 period by Von Eschen et al. found that participants who felt most relatively deprived (on a simple measure of whether they felt their present achievements exceeded, equaled, or fell short of their expectations) were also the most active in the movement even though, objectively, they were less deprived than nonparticipants. This was true for both black and white activists.

One of the most sophisticated applications of this technique was accomplished by Bwy, who combined the Cantril-scale measures with the aggregate-data techniques common to Gurr et al. and produced a complex account of political instability in Latin America. He found that political instability divides empirically into "turmoil" (riots, clashes, strikes, domestic violence) and "internal war" and that

> in provinces where respondents rate themselves *low* on the Self-Anchoring Striving Scale, or when they rate themselves as '*worse off* today than in the past', Demonstrations, Riots, Strikes, and clashes are high (p. 50).

We may conclude from this brief account of major findings that the concept of relative deprivation and the Cantril technique of measuring it have utility for explaining political militance and may do so in Britain. But RD is likely to be a qualitatively different experience in Britain than it is in the slums of Detroit and the shanty-towns of Latin America so we must proceed with extreme caution.

Though he did not use Cantril's methods, much of what we know about the experience and implication of RD in Britain we owe to Runciman's classic survey. He found that the "relative deprivation" generated by the economic inequalities of British society was greatly attenuated by the tendency to judge one's lot within a narrow range of social groups close to one's own. Bricklayers do not spend much time feeling deprived relative to millionaires but watch carefully the rewards gained by plumbers, plasterers, or car workers. The concern for "relativities" among skilled and artisan unions has consistently exemplified Runciman's thesis. Thus those at the top of the manual strata are *least* likely to feel relatively deprived whereas middle-class people are most likely to feel the prosperity of others a grievance since they are thrown much more upon their own resources to maintain their relative prosperity.

The following qualifications and exactitudes seem appropriate for the use of Cantril RD scales in Britain:

(1) Given the high material base of British living standards and the welfare state provisions which ameliorate deprivation in this country, a conceptual and actual distinction should be made between material gratification and an overall sense of life-fulfilment. This latter concept may have more relevance for protest motivation than crude material deprivation, especially for middle-class groups.

(2) Following tradition in the field, measures should be obtained for three points in time: five years ago, now, and five years hence.

(3) A fourth measure should be obtained indicating the level of gratification that the respondent feels *entitled to*. (We agree with Muller that "there is no good reason to believe—much less is it tautologously true—that the top of the self-anchoring scale represents the level of achievement the individual would regard as his just deserts." Indeed, Abrams and Hall have demonstrated that it is true for less than half the population.)

(4) Profiting from Runciman's work, the concept of entitlement should be carefully linked to the respondents own reference group and thus to his personal field of social vision.

(5) Such a generalized and unspecified measure should be taken **before** the respondent has been encouraged to think on politically partisan lines by other questions in the interview.

Thus the respondents were asked for Cantril self-anchoring scale scores first for material satisfaction ("the things you can buy and do; all the things that make up your material standard of living") for the present, five years ago, five years hence and entitlement ("the right level for people like yourself"). These measures were repeated ("leaving aside what we have just discussed") for "satisfaction with your life as a whole." Achievement scores were then subtracted from the entitlement score to produce a subjective relative deprivation index.

Table 6.1: Extent of Relative Deprivation in Britain (in percentages)

| | Respondent has | |
|---|---|---|
| | Material Satisfaction | Overall Satisfaction |
| More than Entitlement | 8 | 8 |
| As much as Entitlement | 29 | 36 |
| 1–2 Points Less | 30 | 32 |
| 3 Points Less | 13 | 10 |
| 4 or More Points Less | 20% (=100%) | 14% (=100%) |
| | W/N = 1,297 | W/N = 1,291 |

The two measures produce similar distributions. A third report complete gratification or even a surfeit. Somewhat over a third of the sample experience a little deprivation, while the remaining third experience a noticeable shortfall of gratification relative to entitlement ranging between three and all ten points on the Cantril scale. The two measures are also quite clearly correlated at $r = .53$ which indicates that the sense of overall satisfaction is still strongly imbued with a materialist interpretation of gratification. That is to say, the extent to which people feel they are enjoying a fulfilled life overall is strongly related to the extent their material gratification approaches the level they feel entitled to. While correlations do not prove causality, the implications of this finding are difficult to avoid. But this is *not* to say that relative gratification is a *direct* function of disposable income—that money brings happiness if you will—in fact material and overall gratification are only weakly linked to income level at $r = .11$ and .06 respectively. In the case of the poor therefore, a process of rationalization akin to that implied by Dahl and described by Runciman is working and many poorly rewarded people feel entitled to only a little more or even no more than what they have. This is also reflected in the class distribution of relative gratification. It is certainly true that people with lower-status occupations experience more deprivation than those in high-status jobs. Only 8 percent of the higher professional and managerial group feel noticeably deprived whereas 25 percent of the remainder of the nonmanual group and 36 percent among manual workers feel they are not receiving their just deserts. Yet on the other hand, fully 34 percent of the unskilled manual workers and their families feel no sense of deprivation at all.

As far as age is concerned the groups *least* likely to feel relatively deprived are the retired and some of the most-deprived are those in their 20s and 30s, especially among working-class people with young families, where rates of material deprivation approach 70 percent with 40 percent feeling severely deprived.

These measures of deprivation are also linked to partisan choice. Conservatives—whose social and economic philosophy has long held it necessary for the good of the country that most people should be content with their lot—are somewhat less prone to feelings of relative deprivation than supporters of other parties.

Generally, the picture given by these single measures is that relative deprivation is more likely to be expressed relative to material concerns and is more likely to be found among younger working-class people. Given this pattern of deprivation experience and weighing carefully the foregoing review of theory and relevant findings, the following hypotheses seem appropriate:

(1) Protest potential will increase as present relative deprivation increases, but not very sharply.

(2) Protest potential will be *high* among those who have experienced *increasing* RD over the past five years.

(3) Protest potential will also be *high* among those who expect *increased* RD in the next five years.

(4) Protest potential will be *very high* among those who have experienced increased RD and expect this to persist in the future or get even worse.

(5) Protest potential will be *highest* among those who have experienced *rising* gratification in the past but expect decreased gratification in the future (i.e., the Davies "rise and fall" model).

(6) Given the presence of unofficial strikes in the protest scale, each of the above relations will be stronger in the case of material relative deprivation than overall deprivation.

With respect to hypothesis (1), people who feel they are receiving their just deserts do have a marginally reduced propensity to engage in unorthodox political behavior while those who feel deprived relative to their entitlement are more likely to protest—though the intensity of deprivation seems to make only a little difference in accelerating the desire to protest. The differences are not large and lend only weak support to the first postulate. But surely it is not reasonable to expect such a relationship to hold great explanatory power for the population as a whole? It is more likely, for example, that the deprived group is made up of old people, placidly resigned to deprivation and young people yet to make their impression on the world and aggressively prepared to resist it. But this is not the case: When the relationship is examined separately for each age group, what little predictive power relative deprivation has for protest potential tends to disappear altogether for people under thirty. Young people in general do not require to feel an abiding sense of dissatisfaction for them also to feel favorably disposed towards protest.

Among the 30-64 age group dissatisfaction remains a modest predictor of greater protest potential but, interestingly, this is much more true for *overall* satisfaction than for material satisfaction scores. So hypothesis (6) receives no support from these static relative deprivation tests. This is particularly surprising since it is among the middle-aged group that the presence of strikes in the protest scale ought to have maximal impact on the styles of protest most commonly engaged in by that age group. Strikes have also obvious material and monetary links whereas sit-ins and blocking traffic are less materially linked and are more likely to be appropriate to younger protesters.

Since the matter is of such obvious theoretical importance (does relative deprivation cause protest or does it not?), the relationship between these two RD scales and the PP scale were explored in great detail throughout the important social and political cleavages in society reflected in the stratification of the sample by age, social class, and political partisanship. Table 6.2 summarizes the results of this analysis for the overall satisfaction measure (the results for material satisfaction are substantially similar but a little less marked).

Table 6.2: The Effect of Deprivation on Protest Potential by Age, Class, and Party (in percentages)

| | Middle-Class | | | | Working-Class | | | |
|---|---|---|---|---|---|---|---|---|
| | Low | Medium | High | (n) | Low | Medium | High | (n) |
| **Over 65** | | | | | | | | |
| *Tory* | | | | | | | | |
| Deprived | 42 | 52 | 6 | (34) | 75 | 20 | 5 | (40) |
| Satisfied | 55 | 40 | 5 | (40) | 68 | 42 | 0 | (43) |
| *Labour* | | | | | | | | |
| Deprived | 42 | 33 | 25 | (9) | 67 | 24 | 11 | (54) |
| Satisfied | 48 | 33 | 19 | (9) | 59 | 27 | 14 | (29) |
| **30–64** | | | | | | | | |
| *Tory* | | | | | | | | |
| Deprived | 40 | 42 | 13 | (78) | 31 | 43 | 26 | (61) |
| Satisfied | 43 | 48 | 10 | (70) | 52 | 39 | 9 | (54) |
| *Labour* | | | | | | | | |
| Deprived | 18 | 26 | 56 | (29) | 43 | 35 | 22 | (165) |
| Satisfied | 27 | 42 | 31 | (20) | 48 | 31 | 21 | (103) |
| **Under 30** | | | | | | | | |
| *Tory* | | | | | | | | |
| Deprived | 28 | 33 | 38 | (30) | 21 | 25 | 54 | (28) |
| Satisfied | 30 | 51 | 19 | (31) | 31 | 62 | 7 | (13) |
| *Labour* | | | | | | | | |
| Deprived | 22 | 17 | 61 | (18) | 26 | 28 | 46 | (61) |
| Satisfied | 17 | 39 | 43 | (7) | 31 | 44 | 25 | (36) |

The impact of relative deprivation upon protest potential is seen in these results to be confined to a few interesting subgroups while among majority groups like middle-aged working-class Labour supporters, no effect is present. Among middle-class supporters of the Labour party—a group noted earlier to have a surprisingly high protest potential—a majority feel deprived even though they are an objectively well-off group. Fifty-six percent of our "deprived" middle-class radicals would consider illegal forms of protest compared with 30 percent of those who feel satisfied.

Deprivation also has an effect upon middle-aged working-class Tories, who have a significantly higher protest potential than those who feel satisfied, a little higher in fact than Labour supporters in the same age and class group. It is also only among the working class that deprivation has an impact on young people. Among manual workers under thirty, relatively deprived Labour supporters have a significantly higher protest potential than their more satisfied peers while the effect of deprivation upon young working-class Tories is quite dramatic: 54 percent of deprived members of this group would consider illegal protest while only 7 percent of those who feel satisfied would do so. Thus the two groups which drew attention in Chapter 4—older middle-class Labour supporters and young working-class Tories—as having much higher levels of militance than would be predicted from traditional theories, now prove to be the two groups most susceptible to the mobilizing effects of relative deprivation. While the small numbers involved leave these findings a little fragile, it is possible to speculate that the feeling of relative deprivation tends to be associated with politically aggressive tendencies only in the absence of more immediate and obvious justifications for militancy. Neither of our politically deviant groups (nor indeed the middle-aged working-class Tories who show similar tendencies) have a basis to support their political aggression in any traditionally "militant" correspondence between class-habit and party-political tradition. Thus the politically aggressive among them will tend to be the kind of people who are unusually sensitive to feelings of personal injustice and deprivation of entitlement.

As a post hoc argument, this class-party noncongruence explanation has a certain appeal but breaks down rather when the Liberal supporters are brought into the argument. They are too few to include in Table 6.2 but if we look merely at the magnitude and direction of the effect of deprivation upon protest using the gamma correlation coefficient, we find the following:

| | Middle-Class | | | Working-Class | | |
|---|---|---|---|---|---|---|
| | 16–30 | 30–64 | 65+ | 16–30 | 30–64 | 65+ |
| Conservatives | +.21 | +.07 | +.23 | +.38 | +.12 | +.23 |
| Labour | +.47 | +.37 | +.12 | +.04 | +.15 | +.24 |
| Liberals | −.46 | +.42 | +.39 | −.33 | +.02 | −.47 |

Few of the relationships are statistically significant from zero but the signs, at the given magnitudes, ought to be reliable and they suggest that, among Liberal supporters and especially the young Liberals there is a distinct tendency toward protest potential being associated with relative *gratification*. This, among other incidental findings we shall refer to in this chapter, foreshadows the argument to follow in Chapter 7.

For the moment, then, the balance of the argument seems to lie with Nieburg and Dahl; the RD————→ protest model applies only under special social or psycho-political conditions.

We turn now to the more complicated argument (hypotheses 3-5) that the experience of relative deprivation is more relevant when considered dynamically. Considerable empirical evidence exists that unrest and dissatisfaction will lead to widespread protest activity when people feel that their present state of grievance will persist in the future or get worse (though of course other evidence exists that under some circumstances, protest will spring from optimism about the future).

Measures of relative optimism were constructed by the linear combination of the Cantril scores given by respondents for each of the three points in time relative to entitlement level. There are, of course, numerous logical possibilities for such a combination, and considerable experimentation was required to achieve the most economical and clearly operationalized measure. The method that proved most effective provided for a seven-fold classification of rising or falling relative gratification over the ten-year time space ranging from the most stressful experience of a rise in gratification to be followed by an expected fall, up to the least stressful experience of the opposite pattern—a reversal of a downward trend. It was found especially useful to score these categories in terms of movement between gross levels of entitlement gratification. For example, a respondent was placed in the "severely falling" category if he reported that previously he had enjoyed at least as much gratification as he felt entitled to, now enjoyed somewhat less (i.e., 1, 2, or 3 points less) and expected that in five years time he would experience even more deprivation than at present.

Very few people feel their rate of relative gratification to be in decline, 25 percent in the case of material gratification, and only 18 percent feel an overall sense of increasing deprivation—whereas 31 percent and 40 percent respectively feel they are and will continue to maintain their present standards, and 44 percent and 43 percent respectively expect continued improvement. For a country held at the time of the survey to be convulsed by confrontation and the urge to challenge for improved living standards in the face of official demands for restraint, these figures might suggest widespread and unexpected complacency.

Whatever might be the wider implications of those expectations, Figure 6.1 shows that, in Britain, the traditional view of the effect of economic and social threat, in the form of increased relative deprivation, upon popular militancy is not merely unfounded, it is strongly reversed. The tiny minority of people actually experiencing their own personal "Davies J-curve" of the sudden reversal of a recent improvement in standards have the *lowest* protest potential. With the single (and only partial) exception of those experiencing a sharp decline in their material standards, higher levels of protest potential are a linear increasing function of *optimism,* both in the material and generalized senses.

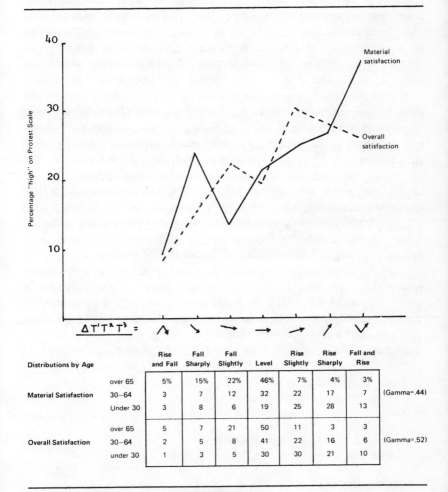

| Distributions by Age | | Rise and Fall | Fall Sharply | Fall Slightly | Level | Rise Slightly | Rise Sharply | Fall and Rise | |
|---|---|---|---|---|---|---|---|---|---|
| | over 65 | 5% | 15% | 22% | 46% | 7% | 4% | 3% | |
| Material Satisfaction | 30–64 | 3 | 7 | 12 | 32 | 22 | 17 | 7 | (Gamma=.44) |
| | Under 30 | 3 | 8 | 6 | 19 | 25 | 28 | 13 | |
| | over 65 | 5 | 7 | 21 | 50 | 11 | 3 | 3 | |
| Overall Satisfaction | 30–64 | 2 | 5 | 8 | 41 | 22 | 16 | 6 | (Gamma=.52) |
| | under 30 | 1 | 3 | 5 | 30 | 30 | 21 | 10 | |

Figure 6.1: PROTEST POTENTIAL BY OPTIMISM

Why should those who feel that their lives are set on an upward trend of increasing relative gratification be so politically aggressive? The image of the protester, surly and aggrieved, pressing his unheard demands for redress upon uncaring authorities is not one easily transformed in the mind by even the strongest empirical data into an image of someone working comfortably towards a rewarding future. Until, that is, these data are controlled for age. Figure 6.1 includes the distributions on the optimism scales separately for the three main age groups. These tables show very clearly that optimism is chiefly a characteristic of young people; the zero-order correlation between age and optimism is +.30. When the question is put separately to these three age groups, the relationship seen overall tends to neutralize. That is to say, pessimistic and optimistic young people differ only a little in militancy, and older pessimists and optimists differ not at all. Does this mean that young people are prone to protest because they are aggressive young optimists? No, we have no way of describing such a relationship even if a causal connection could be proved. But we can say this much: Young people display considerable capacity to use unorthodox political methods notwithstanding their overwhelming conviction that life is getting better. Fully 60 percent of people under thirty were confident that their feelings about life in the future would correspond much more closely with their present entitlement than they did in the past and only 13 percent admitted the possibility of a poorer future, and 26 percent expected their situation to remain unchanged (though most of these young people were *already* satisfied). But this simpler formulation of optimism (disregarding the intervening "present" measure) does show a small but significant relationship with protest. Young people pessimistic about the future compared with the past have a low protest potential while those generally optimistic show a significantly higher level of protest.

For young people, the possibility of happiness must involve optimism; few among them will look back five years and reminisce about "good old days"—for half of them, they are recalling school and it takes more than five years for nostalgia to establish the cliché about the best years of one's life. This mood of active optimism that might well go hand-in-hand with the willingness to engage in protest was captured by the Beatles:

I used to get mad at my school.
The teachers that taught me weren't cool.
You're holding me down, turning me round,
Filling me up with your rules.
But I've got to admit it's getting better,
A little better all the time.

Significantly, the thing that is "getting better" and that is also associated with the optimistic activity of political protest is an overall sense of satisfaction rather than gratification of a purely material kind. Again, the implications of this finding foreshadow the next chapter.

Another question that may usefully be asked of these data is whether there is any interaction between optimism and *present levels* of relative deprivation. To be a dissatisfied optimist may be quite different from being a satisfied optimist or a dissatisfied pessimist. It is also possible to predict that those who feel their circumstances will remain unchanged during this ten-year span will have quite different attitudes to protest if what they expect to experience is continued deprivation than if they expect to preserve a satisfactory life-style. To test this hypothesis we examined the change-over-time data for satisfied and dissatisfied people separately. Protest potential is strongly associated with *dissatisfied optimism*, i.e., people who feel they are currently not receiving their just deserts but expect to remedy this in the future are far more likely to be high on the protest scale than those who are satisfied and expect to remain so. Again the only exception to this trend is the higher protest potential among satisfied people who are fearful of a precipitous decline in their *material* gratification.

But again, the rich theoretical implications of this finding are considerably dimmed by the fact that dissatisfied optimism is very much a characteristic of the young and this supplies the bulk of the significant trend observed for the sample as a whole.

Thus the caution expressed initially has so far proved justified. What British people experience in the form of relative deprivation and the changes they experience or hope for tend to be so dependent upon their position in the life-cycle that its effects upon political aggression are very difficult to discern. What is certain however, is that the bulk of political theory relating to how political instability arises in mass polities, as a function of various kinds of relative deprivation experience, has no simple application for Britain. Yet, to be fair, the fundamental *frustration⎯⎯⎯⎯→aggression* model from which this theory derives has not really been tested by these data. There are few people in the sample who are frustrated in the proper sense of the thwarting of goal-directed activity. Among those who are not receiving their just deserts, two distinct groups are evident: old people who for many other reasons are not interested in political protest and young people who are willing to protest but are also overwhelmingly confident that their aspirations will be met in the foreseeable future. This is not to say that these same young people will not revise upward their estimates of entitlement in the future and so have greater things to aim at, but this still does not amount to frustration in the true psychological sense.

Previous experience with scales of these kinds had indicated that relative deprivation as measured by the striving scale was not widespread in Britain and often as not reflected a personally high standard of gratification rather more than actual deprivation of a commonly accepted standard. A very much more straightforward measure of economic frustration was therefore devised for this survey. Respondents were asked how much extra money they might need "to live without money worries, in health and in comfort." Those who reported some figure more than zero were then asked just how *urgently* they needed the money and also to estimate their chances of getting it within the next two years. People who reported themselves in urgent need of extra income but saw little chance of obtaining it in the foreseeable future are experiencing frustration in the classical sense. They are striving after a salient goal (money) with a sense of urgency and they perceive a blocking of that activity.

Considering the extent to which the question invited flippancy, it is gratifying that most people estimated their cash needs with great deliberation. Exactly one-third of the sample reported that they needed no extra money and that, by implication, they already lived "without money worries, in health and in comfort." A further 17 percent thought a sum less than £10 a week would relieve them of all financial anxiety; 23 percent needed more than £10 but less than £15; while the remaining 25 percent gave estimates that ranged up to £500 per week in one case but were mainly less than £30 per week. Although inflation will have rendered these figures quickly obsolete, even in 1974 they did not give a picture of widespread avarice in the nation. In face, the overall mean estimate of the increment that would spell freedom from *all* financial anxiety was about £ 11 or about 25 percent of the average family income. The average income shortfall by income level indicates that, apart from the highest income groups (who tend to ask for a great deal or none at all) the cash need remains at a similar proportion to cash received up to the middle-income groups and declines thereafter.

A straightforward relative deprivation hypothesis would suggest that the greater the perceived cash need, the greater will be the individual's protest potential. We find qualified support for this hypothesis. Among those who needed extra money at all, the greater the figure named the more likely it is that they score high on the protest scale, but those who denied any financial need do not fit this linear trend and show instead a level of protest potential in line with the overall average. The same data for each of the three major age-groups shows that those demanding higher levels of extra cash are disproportionately young to an extent sufficient to neutralize the effects observed in the sample as a whole.

The questions concerning the urgency of need and the chances of obtaining extra cash were put to the 67 percent of the sample who needed some extra income and, surprisingly perhaps, proved to be unrelated.

Only 10 percent of those reporting some cash need (6% of the total sample) report feeling exceptional stress in that they need the extra money "very urgently" and see no chance of getting it. A further 18 percent (11% of the total sample) feel they will be denied extra money they feel they need "fairly urgently" while another 19 percent (12% overall) need cash at least "fairly urgently" but see only a slight chance of getting it. This still leaves 71 percent of the total sample reporting very little monetary stress in their lives, of whom 51 percent need no extra cash, 21 percent need cash and will get it, and 22 percent view their poor financial prospects with calm complacency. Thus the distribution of monetary frustration looks like this:

| Severe Frustration | Moderate Frustration | Slight Frustration | No Frustration |
|---|---|---|---|
| 6% | 23% | 38% | 33% |

Considering the full range of frustrative nonreward conditions, the following hypotheses are appropriate:

(1) Highest levels of protest potential will be associated with the "very urgent need—no chance" condition.
(2) Moderately high levels of protest potential will be associated with the "very or fairly urgent need—slight or no chance" condition.
(3) Lowest levels of protest potential will be associated with the "not very urgent—fair chance" condition.

Each of the above hypotheses is quite false. What nonsignificant trends do exist in the data actually point in the opposite direction. Respondents in the economically frustrated condition are *least* likely to protest. The reason for this is quite obvious: as would be expected from the considerable optimism shown by the young in contrast to the equally striking pessimism of old people, those in the frustrative nonreward conditions are disproportionately old (30% of those over 30 compared with 19% of those under 30) and therefore record lower levels of protest potential. But since the generality of young people are optimistic of exercising their own power to increase their income (as opposed to the old who have usually to await the pleasure of the chancellor of the exchequer) surely those young people who are still frustrated may be expected to show unusually high levels of protest potential? This expectation too is dismissed by the facts.

The trend for those under thirty is in the direction favorable to the basic hypothesis but by no means statistically significant. What is more interesting is that the most frustrated groups of young people share a higher protest potential with their *least* economically frustrated peers. This again foreshadows the next chapter.

One remaining possibility for frustration to show the predicted direct impact upon political aggression lies in the interaction between categories of frustration and the level of frustration reflected in the *amount* of money being denied. The hypotheses follow therefore that

(1) Protest potential will maximize under frustrative nonreward conditions when significant sums are needed but not when small sums of money are denied.

(2) Protest potential will minimize under nonfrustrative conditions irrespective of sums mentioned.

Again there exists only the most qualified support for the first hypothesis. Those in the frustrative nonreward category ("urgent need—no chance") do show higher levels of protest potential to be associated with increased levels of demand (needs more than £10 per week). Yet, those in the high demand condition overall show no significant increase in protest potential between frustrative and nonfrustrative conditions. Support for the second hypothesis is a little less equivocal in that people whose modest and nonurgent needs are likely to be met show a distinctly diminished protest potential compared with most other groups. Yet, these effects too are considerably dependent upon the fact that among those who need the extra cash, young people tend to ask for larger sums regardless of their prospects of getting them, while older people make much more modest demands.

## The Politicization of Dissatisfaction

The failure of "relative deprivation" and "frustrative nonreward" to provide more than a highly qualified explanation of protest potential is not too surprising. The consequences of deprivation in Britain may well be ameliorated both subjectively by individual rationalization and objectively by the high base-line of material security provided by the welfare state. Even those in Britain who feel severely relatively deprived may certainly be denied what may reasonably be considered to be their just deserts but rarely do they face starvation, the deprivation of basic needs like shelter or even of "basic" luxuries like more than one pair of shoes, private accommodation, or even television. Taken at face value, this is not the stuff of which revolutions are made, nor even a respectably aggressive demonstration. In an industrially developed country which has a mature participatory political system, what counts surely is who is getting the *blame* for any deprivation that is felt. A number of scholars have argued that only when "deprivation-induced frustration is accompanied by attribution of responsibility for the condition to socio-political structural arrangements will men become sufficiently motivated to protest" (Muller 1969). Thus subjectively felt dissatisfaction must become politicized before protest behavior is a *relevant* possible antecedent of frustration. The individual must somehow feel he is not personally to blame for his failure but "the system" (or whatever) is operating in a manner unfavorable to him. Again, unfortunately for formal theory building, the "socio-political structural arrangement" in Britain that is most likely to receive blame for deprivation is Her Majesty's Government, and the act of protest which is the most obviously relevant antecedent is provided at least every four or five years: an unfavorable vote in a general election. "The system" is not a word often heard in popular vocabulary in Britain and experience has shown that it is extremely difficult to ask questions about the "political system" and especially about the quality of its performance and ability to meet individual material demands without thoroughly implicating the government of the day and thereby arousing all the partisanship associated with such a judgement.[2] The best strategy therefore is to implicate the party in power anyway and try to determine to what extent dissatisfaction with government performance has an effect upon protest potential independent of basic partisan preference and then attempt to establish linkages between subjectively felt dissatisfaction and objectively expressed dissatisfaction with the government at the individual level.

Respondents were asked to consider ten specific areas of domestic government activity: health, education, care of the elderly, the provision of full employment, good housing, and protection from crime, pollution control, and movement toward equality in rights for colored immigrants, women, and in the distribution of wealth. (The technique used owes much to Milbrath's formulation.) With the partial exception of these last three items, the overwhelming majority of people reported that each issue was "important" or "very important" to them (usually the latter) and was either an "important" or "essential" government responsibility.

There is widespread agreement that the provision of health and education facilities are good, and that at least a reasonably good job was being done to control crime. Care of the old and the security of full employment are two areas riven by partisan sentiment in that few Tories believed their government was doing a bad job but a majority of Labour and Liberals thought so. A similar though weaker trend is observable for "equal rights for women," and here also the Labour and Liberal supporters were more likely than Tories to believe the government had a responsibility in the matter. This was also true of judgements about the government's treatment of the rights of colored immigrants, but only the young middle-class Labour supporters contained a majority who thought the government's performance on the immigrants' behalf was poor.

The most obviously nonpartisan issue is pollution control and this tended to draw unfavorable comment from young people of all persuasions and especially from Liberals. Labour and Liberal supporters of all ages reserved special condemnation for the government's record of "providing adequate housing" and "trying to even out differences in wealth between people." Yet, surprisingly, these items also drew unfavorable ratings from supporters of the Conservative party. A majority of young middle-class Tories thought the government's housing record was bad and a majority of working-class Tories of all ages thought that equality of wealth should be greater. Now to these respondents an increase of material equality may represent no more than an increase in their own standard of living that they feel they deserve. Yet, Rokeach has demonstrated that the word "equality" is a negative stimulus object for supporters of the moderate right and the policy pronouncements of the Conservative party would certainly indicate that material equality was a low priority for them. While Tories did express more satisfaction with equality of wealth than did supporters of other parties, the evident levels of dissatisfaction among especially their younger supporters points again to an ideological rift between party and followers of a kind that is supposed to be more characteristic of the Labour party. At least we may assert that dissatisfaction with a Conservative government performance is by no means a sentiment exclusive to Labour and Liberal supporters. But what effect does it have upon political action?

No one area of government responsibility has an outstanding impact upon protest potential. Rather, several areas have attracted the kinds of dissatisfaction that are associated with protest. These are: education ($r = 0.24$), care of the elderly ($r = 0.27$), pollution control ($r = 0.22$), housing ($r = 0.24$), and economic equality ($r = 0.21$). These topics have nothing special in common that suggests an issue-oriented protest syndrome. Indeed, two issues that are popularly associated with protest, equal rights for women and for colored immigrants, show rather less tendency to link dissatisfaction with protest ($r=0.09$) than the basic issues like housing. This echoes the findings of Chapter 4 that protest is not exclusively the property of the politically exotic.

To pursue this analysis more economically, a single index of dissatisfaction with government performance was constructed (see Appendix) by adding the four-point "very good-good-bad-very bad" item scores and dividing the distribution obtained nearer to the average inter-item satisfaction proportion (63%) and dividing satisfied and dissatisfied groups to form a single four-point scale. When this new overall satisfaction-with-government index is divided by age, class, and party, we see that whereas older Conservatives accumulate significantly lower dissatisfaction scores, younger Conservatives—especially those of the working class—show quite high levels of overall dissatisfaction

**Table 6.3: Protest Potential by Overall Dissatisfaction with Government Performance (in percentages)**

|  | (n) | No Pro-test | Peti-tions Only | Lawful Demon-strations | Boy-cotts | Rent Strikes/ Strikes | Occupations Blockades |
|---|---|---|---|---|---|---|---|
| Satisfied | (500) | 27 | 25 | 21 | 15 | 7 | 5 |
| Partly Satisfied | (397) | 17 | 19 | 24 | 20 | 10 | 10 |
| Dissatisfied | (324) | 16 | 20 | 19 | 13 | 13 | 19 |
| Very Dissatisfied | (245) | 17 | 19 | 17 | 15 | 12 | 21 |

which, (though a little lower) do not differ statistically significantly from the dissatisfaction expressed by young Labour and Liberal supporters.

Table 6.3 reports that the dissatisfaction with government performance index (DGP index) is a moderately good predictor of protest potential; only 12 percent of those generally satisfied with government performance have a high protest potential compared with 33 percent of those scoring higher on the DGP index. This relationship is consistently true of each major age-group (even for the retired group) and more than 50 percent of young people high on the DGP would consider illegal forms of protest. As we have found earlier, quite wide differences in the tendency to move toward the higher levels of the activity scales are reflected in only modest product-moment correlations but as a useful test of independence, Table 6.4 reports the correlations between all three behavior scales and the DGP index, controlled for left-right self-placement and age, separately and simultaneously.

We find that the relationship between DGP index and protest is significantly independent of age and ideological disposition and it is even a slightly better predictor of repression potential—i.e., those who are satisfied with the government, young or old, left or right, tend to feel that the government should have more power to deal with dissent. Thus the DGP index seems to

**Table 6.4: Dissatisfaction with Government Performance and Participation**

|  | Protest Potential | Repression Potential | Orthodox Participation |
|---|---|---|---|
| Zero order correlation with DGP index | .22 | −.27 | .10 (n = 1,589) |
| Partialled on age | .18 | −.25 | .08 (n = 1,530) |
| Partialled on L-R placement | .20 | −.23 | .08 (n = 1,325) |
| Partialled on age and L-R placement | .16 | −.21 | .08 (n = 1,325) |

NOTE: All correlations significant beyond 1% level.

be behaving in a similar fashion to the political trust/cynicism index employed in Chapter 5. Indeed, the two measures are quite closely correlated at r=+.43 although DGP is not nearly so closely related (r=+.14) to personal inefficacy as is cynicism and (unlike cynicism) is linked more to personal dissatisfaction (r = .22).

Table 6.5 examines the effect of dissatisfaction with government performance upon protest potential controling for age, class, and left-right self-placement. High DGP scores have no effect upon the low protest potential of "right-wingers" over the age of thirty. Among older "left-wingers" the impact of dissatisfaction is greater among middle-class leftists than upon the scores of working-class leftists. Among younger respondents (under 30s) a quite striking picture emerges. Among younger leftists, dissatisfaction is clearly a key accelerating factor in the high protest potential associated with this group. Among younger people who place themselves on the right, dissatisfaction has no effect upon the moderately low protest potential shown by middle-class rightists but has a dramatic effect upon young working-class rightists. Among this group (who are mostly young working-class Tories) of those who are dissatisfied with the government, only 9 percent would *not* consider protest while 60 percent would consider illegal forms.

Thus we may conclude that among groups of people who have some will to use protest methods, the potential for action is greatly accelerated by a

**Table 6.5: Effect of Dissatisfaction with Government Performance upon Protest Potential Controlling for Age, Class, and Left-Right Self-Placement (in percentages)**

| | LEFT | | | | | RIGHT | | | | |
|---|---|---|---|---|---|---|---|---|---|---|
| | Low | Med | High | (n) | γ | Low | Med | High | (n) | γ |
| **Over 30s** | | | | | | | | | | |
| *Middle-class* | | | | | | | | | | |
| Satisfied | 38 | 41 | 21 | (61) | .47 | 39 | 51 | 10 | (222) | -.17 |
| Dissatisfied | 15 | 42 | 43 | (53) | | 54 | 32 | 15 | (53) | |
| *Working-class* | | | | | | | | | | |
| Satisfied | 53 | 30 | 17 | (171) | .26 | 51 | 39 | 10 | (207) | |
| Dissatisfied | 40 | 30 | 30 | (128) | | 54 | 30 | 16 | (89) | |
| **Under 30s** | | | | | | | | | | |
| *Middle-class* | | | | | | | | | | |
| Satisfied | 13 | 59 | 27 | (24) | .66 | 34 | 49 | 17 | (51) | .20 |
| Dissatisfied | 8 | 17 | 75 | (25) | | 31 | 37 | 33 | (34) | |
| *Working-class* | | | | | | | | | | |
| Satisfied | 29 | 46 | 24 | (51) | .38 | 40 | 41 | 20 | (47) | .68 |
| Dissatisfied | 25 | 18 | 57 | (41) | | 8 | 33 | 60 | (32) | |

sense of dissatisfaction with the government's provision of improvement in key sectors of its domestic responsibilities. Overtly political kinds of dissatisfaction have, therefore, a more significant impact upon protest potential than do subjective and personal feelings of deprivation and frustration. We are now in a position to look for linkages between the two kinds of frustration which have an interactive effect upon protest.

To return to our earlier theoretical discussion of the nature of the *dissatisfaction* ⎯⎯⎯⎯▸ *protest* relationship, we can now say with more certainty that some process of politicization intervenes between the subjective experience of motivating forms of dissatisfaction or frustration and the acquisition of the disposition to protest. To make further progress we turn again for the help of Dahl, who attempts to map out the general nature of these linkages. Given that some objective inequality exists (which of course from a psychological point of view is not actually necessary), he suggests that affirmative answers must be given to each of five sequential questions before even the likelihood of protest may be present (Figure 6.5).

The operationalization of the deprivation variable (material and overall RD) met conditions A-C in that people judged their perceived deprivation condition relevant to "people like themselves" against a personal standard of legitimacy (entitlement). Anger is a difficult emotion to capture with a questionnaire but the carefully constructed implied-frustration variable

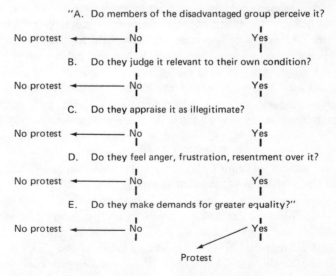

SOURCE: R. A. Dahl, **Polyarchy: Participation and Opposition.** 1973, p. 95.

Figure 6.5.

seemed to meet condition D. What about condition E—the extent that demands are made for redress? We did not ask people to state their own history of demand-making and would have obtained rather thin data if we had, but we did ask their opinion upon movements toward material equality and the condemnation of the government's record in this field, especially if linkages A to D are complete in respect of this demand, may be said to form a demand. Also, it is difficult to disentangle the making of a demand with the intention to protest that we wish to predict. There is something tautologous about that.

Our task is to try to determine the extent to which these linkages are traceable in latent form in the general population. Furthermore, a second type of behavior-emergent condition is missing from Dahl's formulation that is crucial to the case of a mature democracy such as Britain, wherein individuals have a measure of personal responsibility for their own lives and destiny while the power of the authorities *to endow or to deprive* is somewhat limited. This is: To what extent are the authorities held responsible for ameliorating the condition of felt deprivation?

We may combine this condition with a demand condition to provide a sequence of conditional linkages for material deprivation using a series of responses in the questionnaire having to do with the basic issue of economic equality. This issue ("trying to even out differences in wealth between people") drew the most controversial response from the sample—in that 64 percent thought the government was failing in this area (even 41% of older middle-class Tories thought so) while at the same time leaving the sample evenly divided as to the extent of the government's responsibilities in the area and even of the degree of importance the issue held for the respondent. In Dahl's opinion, also, economic equality is the key demand relative to protest. Figure 6.6 maps out our adaption of Dahl's formulation of conditional linkages between dissatisfaction and political action stage by stage alongside the appropriate question answered by our respondents. Note particularly that it is not at all necessary that objective deprivation should exist; only that it should be felt to exist by the respondent. The experience of nonlegitimate deprivation is expressed in the feeling that the respondent is not getting what people like himself feel entitled to in the area of material satisfaction and is coded in this analysis as (1) as much and more than entitlement; (2) one to three points less than entitlement; and (3) more than three points less than entitlement. The remaining linkages are complete for deprived respondents who feel personally involved in inequity (the issue is important to them personally) and that the government has failed in its responsibilities to redress the balance of wealth generally and, in particular, in their direction. Note also that it is not theoretically necessary for each linkage to be independent of each other linkage (though of course complete interdependence would render

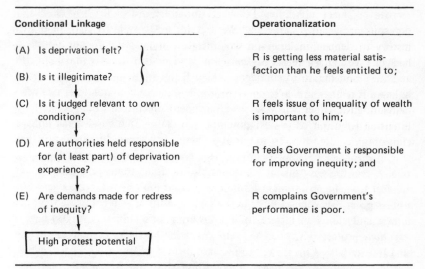

| Conditional Linkage | Operationalization |
| --- | --- |
| (A) Is deprivation felt? | R is getting less material satis- |
| (B) Is it illegitimate? | faction than he feels entitled to; |
| (C) Is it judged relevant to own condition? | R feels issue of inequality of wealth is important to him; |
| (D) Are authorities held responsible for (at least part) of deprivation experience? | R feels Government is responsible for improving inequity; and |
| (E) Are demands made for redress of inequity? | R complains Government's performance is poor. |

High protest potential

**Figure 6.6: CONCEPTUALIZATION AND OPERATIONALIZATION OF CONDITIONAL LINKAGES BETWEEN DEPRIVATION AND PROTEST**

the step by step formulation redundant and substitute instead a multiple-bloc "either-or"-condition). Nor in this case is it empirically true. The extent to which the government is held responsible for solving inequity and the feeling that the issue is personally important *are* closely correlated and so will be analyzed in bloc form. On the other hand, the experience that the respondent is not receiving the amount of material satisfaction to which he is entitled does not predict very strongly the extent of "personal importance" and "government responsibility" nor do these latter predict in turn the extent to which the government will be harshly judged, beyond a rather modest negative correlation of .26. But it is interesting to note that these interrelationships occur independently of ideological left-right self-placement. It is not only the left who feel economic equity is important *and* hold the government responsible for doing something about it *and* tend to be critical of failure.

The general hypotheses attached to the conditional linkage model are these:

(1) Protest potential will maximize when all linkages are complete.
(2) Protest potential will be accelerated as a linear function of the amount of deprivation (moderate or severe) that is felt and when all linkages are complete and not when they are incomplete.

Table 6.6 provides information relevant to these hypotheses. The marginal distributions of this table provide valuable background information. Those who feel that inequity effects them personally and feel the government is responsible for doing something about it are not very much more likely to experience relative material deprivation than those who do not complete linkages C and D. There is a tendency for deprived respondents who complete linkages C and D also to complete linkage E and see the government's record as one of failure and a strongly reversed tendency for nondeprived, non-completing respondents to view the government's record favorably.

The distribution of protest potential scores for each conditional linkage lends only qualified support to our hypotheses. It is especially interesting that people who feel severely deprived, feel equity is important to them personally, feel the government is responsible for doing something about it, yet still feel that the government have done a good job (n = 43) have a very *low* protest potential whereas those in the same condition who complete the final linkage and complain bitterly of the government's failure (n = 103) have a *very high* protest potential. Yet, elsewhere in the table, completion of the final linkage shows the power to increase protest potential even when earlier linkages remain in the negative condition, but our hypothesis may rest acceptance on the fact that only in the two linkage-complete conditions does the effect upon protest potential attain statistically significant levels, especially so where the level of initial deprivation is very high. So, while it is possible to conclude that personal material deprivation and critical lack of support for authority performance do interact positively to accelerate the willingness to use protest methods, the exclusivity implied in our hypotheses is not upheld, and these results do not amount to a very convincing demonstration that even politicized *material* deprivation is a central factor underlying the parameters of protest in British politics.

Earlier we found that where subjective relative deprivation had an effect upon protest, *overall* deprivation tended to be marginally more important than material deprivation. Is it possible that the effect we are seeking is more general in character and that on an overall sense of dissatisfaction is more likely to coincide with a generally jaundiced view of the government's performance? We examined the relationship between dissatisfaction with government performance and protest potential separately for three levels of overall satisfaction and found that dissatisfaction with government is a more powerful influence than overall dissatisfaction. That is to say, personally satisfied people who are very dissatisfied with the government have a higher protest potential than dissatisfied people who are satisfied with the government. But a particularly fascinating aspect of this result is that it shows that it is *moderate* levels of overall dissatisfaction that have the optimal impact upon protest (unlike material dissatisfaction which is a linear function) and does so independently of dissatisfaction with the government (DGP index). Those who are really depressed with their lives are no more moved toward protest

**Table 6.6: Conditional Linkages Between Subjective Material Relative Deprivation and Assessment of Government Performance in "Trying to even out differences in wealth between people"**

| | | GROUP A | | | | | GROUP B | | | | |
| | | *Respondents who feel Government has an "essential" or "important" responsibility for equality of wealth and feel the issue is "important" or "very important" to them personally (n = 676)* | | | | | *Respondents who do not feel as Group A (n = 694)* | | | | |
| Subjective R.D. | Protest Potential → Government Performance is | (%) | Low (39%) | Med 37% | High 24% | Gamma | (%) | Low (44%) | Med 34% | High 20% | Gamma |
|---|---|---|---|---|---|---|---|---|---|---|---|
| **No deprivation** | good or very good | (35%) | 50 | 38 | 12 | | (56%) | 51 | 38 | 11 | |
| (n = 253) | bad | (37%) | 37 | 46 | 18 | .20 | (31%) | 47 | 37 | 14 | .03 |
| | very bad | (28%) | 37 | 38 | 25 | | (13%) | 52 | 25 | 23 | |
| | | | | | | (n = 217) | | | | | |
| **Some deprivation** | good or very good | (29%) | 38 | 35 | 28 | | (41%) | 38 | 45 | 17 | |
| (n = 208) | bad | (40%) | 48 | 34 | 18 | .19 | (47%) | 40 | 28 | 32 | .08 |
| | very bad | (32%) | 27 | 38 | 35 | | (13%) | 40 | 33 | 28 | |
| | | | | | | (n = 209) | | | | | |
| **Considerable deprivation** | good or very good | (17%) | 52 | 34 | 14 | | (36%) | 40 | 40 | 21 | |
| (n = 215) | bad | (40%) | 35 | 39 | 27 | .30 | (44%) | 33 | 39 | 27 | .07 |
| | very bad | (43%) | 31 | 31 | 38 | | (20%) | 42 | 26 | 32 | |
| | | | | | | (n = 268) | | | | | |

than those who are satisfied. This makes good psychological sense. It has been established in learning theory, for example, that drive states (especially anxiety in humans) have their optimal motivating impact upon behavior at moderate levels. All this also conforms to mild commonsense expectations but adds little of real weight in favor of the general theory that protest arises from the growth of generalized dissatisfaction among the polity.

## Summary and Conclusions

This chapter extrapolated conventional theory regarding the nature of the linkage between dissatisfaction and protest into a formulation appropriate to British political culture and compared some basic measures of individual dissatisfaction with the protest potential scale scores. The evidence considered raised more questions than it answered. Although a slight general tendancy was confirmed for dissatisfied people to show more political aggression than satisfied people, why do so many people who feel they are getting their just deserts still score very high on the protest potential scale? Why should great optimism *and* political aggression go hand-in-hand with youth? Although a plausible linkage between the experience of material deprivation and protest potential could be traced through overt political dissatisfaction, the motivational and attitudinal structure of these linkages were by no means self-evident. And having stated these questions with deliberate naivety, the basic inadequacy of conventional theory becomes evident when applied to British politics. At the outset, caution was expressed that the exotic social and political circumstances whence the *deprivation*————▸*protest* model is derived have scant resemblance to the stable and supportive socio-economic system that is serviced by British politics. Unlike those who question the inhabitants of riot-prone North American cities, or revolution-prone Latin American societies, we found that the sense of relative deprivation was not widespread in Britain. Concentrations of deprivation tended to be expressed mostly in material terms among working-class people who had not yet reached retirement age. This is a wide-based group with no obvious monopoly on protest behavior.

The important point is that the real extent of deprivation in Britain and the conditions of life that perceived 'deprivation' actually implied do not amount to the same kind of social-psychological motivation that a black protester or a Latin American activist may experience. The British potential protester who also reports that he is getting much less than he feels entitled to is far more likely to be stating a general demand than reporting objectively miserable conditions of life. It is symptomatic of a refusal to accept an ordinary scale of reward and it reflects a certain truculence with life that goes naturally with the fact—and the optimism—of youth. We can state with confidence, then, that the psychological motivations of protest potential in Britain do not derive in simple and direct fashion from the relative deprivation of material well-being, nor in a political community as complex as Britain should they be expected to.

# NOTES

1. Quoted by Chomsky in *Problems of Freedom and Knowledge,* p. 64.

2. It is much easier in Germany of course where the word "Der Stat" refers to much more than the partisan incumbents of government and also in America where "Washington" represents a network of authorities which may be shared between the two main partisan groups.

*Chapter 7*

## A SILENT REVOLUTION?

Despite the equivocal results of the preceding analysis of the relationship between relative deprivation and political action, it is still difficult to dismiss the expectation that potential protesters should feel a sense of dissatisfaction about something. We do not mean that they must necessarily be the kind of people who will produce a well-practiced list of political grievances to the most casual enquiry but simply that a theory of political action must surely be incomplete without a universalistic motivational base. Relative deprivation provided us with some specialized and particular insights into the protest motivation of some sectors of the political community but little more than that. The weight of traditional theory combined with the thrust of contemporary research on the revolt of the deprived (especially North American blacks) compelled us to pose the question, but far too many objective indicators point in the opposite direction to lead to a realistic expectation that deprivation causes protest in Britain. Whereas the American black fits the classic definition of a member of an oppressed community and the conditions of relative deprivation in which he lives seem designed almost as a field experiment for the social sciences to test the traditional theories of discontent and revolution outlined in the previous chapter, few people in Britain do so and many of those who do (old people, for example) are among the least likely to protest. Indeed, the strangest irony of the European protest movements of the 1960s was the recurring fact that the group universally most likely to resort to unorthodox political methods, including every conceivable form of illegality and even violence, were middle-class undergraduates who are often among the most advantaged members of the community.

At the macropolitical level it is easy and attractive to entwine the student revolts at Berkeley, the Sorbonne, Berlin, and even Tokyo with the black revolt and the struggles of the low-paid in a single movement whose levels of active indignation were constantly recharged by painful outrage over the prosecution of the war in Indochina. Certainly students in Europe and America demonstrated their indignation, sympathy, and their identity with these struggles. White students were present at some of the earliest boycott movements in the deep South and the French and German students were desperately anxious to carry young workers with them, and in May 1968 it looked for a while as though the French students had succeeded. Yet, while it may appear from many points of view that all the protest movements of the 1960s hoisted the same essentially anticapitalist, antiimperialist, antiauthoritarian banner, there are some important discontinuities in the motivation of the young middle-class elements.

The most important of these discontinuities is the value that is placed upon the consumer society. One of the more orderly bodies of thought that guided the movement was the New Left. This movement started in the 1950s in England and was developed eagerly by a number of American activists who desired to embrace an egalitarian creed without appearing to accept totalitarian forms of government. Its principal achievement was to add considerably to the range of targets appropriate to left-wing activism. While the New Left acknowledged that the control of the means of production and capital formation still held the key to political power, they stressed that if socialism was to be about freedom, then something had to be done about the authoritarian use of passive media systems, the deadening hand of alienative bureaucracy, the miserable trap of life on an automated assembly-line, and all the other aspects of modern industrial consumer society that crushed the will of people to question authority and to participate, even a little, in the shaping of their own lives. As such, these forces in any industrial society are ideologically neutral and it is no coincidence that the embryonic student movements in Eastern Europe found it possible to lay very similar objections against the Stalinist organization of their equally materialistically motivated society.

But the strongly antimaterialist content of rhetoric of the middle-class youth movement contrasted strangely with the cheerfully materialistic ambitions of those disadvantaged groups on whose behalf they sometimes demonstrated. Certainly blacks, for example, demanded political as well as material advancement. But Daniel Cohn-Bendit's strictures upon the evils of material consumption would have drawn a wry response from a black rioter busily "liberating" several weeks' groceries from a Jewish-owned ghetto store. Many contemporary commentators saw the whole protest movement of the 1960s as a strange alliance between people who had not enough money and others who had too much. For the British case, we have examined the first hypothesis in the previous chapter, the second will be the subject of this chapter: to what extent is protest potential in Britain associated with a shift in basic value orientations away from the traditional materialism of the industrial consumer society towards the "postmaterial" values of a "postindustrial" society?

One of the very few empirical researchers to attempt a comprehensive study of the effects of value change upon political behavior is Ronald Inglehart. Inglehart (1971) presents a persuasive thesis to describe "a transformation" in political value priorities occurring in Western Europe. He argues that in Europe since 1945 young people have increasingly been freed of the urgency of material acquisition by sharply rising industrial affluence. Consequently these younger Europeans are held to be far more sensitive than their elders to the "higher-order" needs predicted by Maslow's theory of the need hierarchy of human motivation. They have been freed to demote safety and material needs among their personal priorities and concentrate instead upon fulfilling their "belongingness" needs and intellectual and aesthetic drives.

According to Inglehart, among the political outcomes of this shift in value priorities has been the desertion of their traditional class loyalties by the young middle classes and especially those who have had higher education, causing them instead to embrace the ideology and goals of what may in some places be loosely called "the left" and in others more precisely "the New Left." They will tend also to support student radicalism and supranationalism and generally hold to an articulated set of "postbourgeois" values. Correspondingly, a process that Lenin described as "embourgeoisification" has increasingly led the older skilled workers into an unaccustomed alignment with parties of the right, who appeal more strongly to their "lower-order" needs. Their value priorities remain dominated by the need to protect and augment their material and physical security whose enjoyment is still a welcome novelty for those who lived through the Depression years and the Second World War. Theirs is an "acquisitive" view of life.

Inglehart sought out and identified his two "pure value types" by asking respondents in the five major (preenlargement) EEC countries plus Britain to choose two out of four statements representing alternative national goals. Those choosing "maintaining order in the nation" and "fighting rising prices" were assigned to the "acquisitive" position, and those choosing instead "protecting freedom of speech" and "giving people more say in important political decisions" to the "postbourgeois" position.

Inglehart does not appear to take the position that there is anything *intrinsically* "postbourgeois" about free speech and political participation.

These notions have been worn smooth by generations of "liberal" and not-so-liberal politicians, and few indeed would regard them as absolutely unimportant. It is the choice itself that is postbourgeois: the assignment of greater *relative* importance to freedom and participation over basic material and civil security. Expressed in political terms, such a choice represents an initial step towards Maslovian self-actualization.

The proportion of "pure" acquisitive choices compared to postbourgeois choices occurring within each age cohort from country to country across Europe gave strong support to Inglehart's hypothesis that the rise of post-bourgeois values is linked fundamentally to the prevailing economic conditions experienced by the members of each national age cohort during their childhood and adolescence. Britain experienced a steady erosion of her prewar economic supremacy in Europe and, consequently, has atypically *fewer* postbourgeois types among her young age cohorts whilst retaining an unusually *high* proportion among her older cohorts. Elsewhere in Europe industrial advance has apparently wrought a real transformation, creating profound intergenerational differences in value priorities; for example, among the under-25s in mainland Europe, postbourgeois types actually outnumber the otherwise dominant "acquisitive" group, and do so most noticeably in countries where economic advance has been most dramatic—especially in Germany. Hence the evident signs of intergenerational stress, hence the European student revolution, hence the growth of the young middle-class New Left, and so on. For example, Inglehart found that postbourgeois were four times more likely to be favourable toward the students' use of demonstrations than were the acquisitives.

There is little doubt that Inglehart regards the postbourgeois phenomenon as a seminal force in modern radical politics and the postbourgeois (as we may refer to them individually) themselves as the parvenus of political change in postindustrial society. His view seems credible. Indeed, it is attractive to press the Maslovian underpinnings of the silent revolution thesis further than Inglehart does himself and. point out that the industrial and commercial processes that are taking society toward a postindustrial situation and are facilitating the growth of postacquisitive values are at the same time unavoidably imposing a set of societal conditions least likely to satisfy the equalitarian, humanitarian, and naturalistic relations implied in Maslow's high-order needs. These inhibitors include the nuclear family as the principal consumer unit, the growth of an alienative bureaucracy, passive media systems, standardized and automated production, and so on—all recognizably the bêtes-noirs of the New Left. The more efficient becomes industrial production, therefore, the more postbourgeois types will appear *and* the more things they will find offensive in society. Opening up this paradox introduces a sense of crisis—a dynamic singularly appropriate to the theory's theme of intergenerational stress.

Perhaps unfortunately for our purposes, Inglehart's theory casts Britain in an atavistic role. The impression is created that the choice of postbourgeois values in Britain is an eccentric response in the face of economic stagnation, the highest inflation rate in Europe, five years of continuous violence in Northern Ireland, and a stubborn tradition of class-based but moderate politics. Indeed, at the time of writing (Summer 1975) to describe British politics as other than predominantly materialist would be to risk derision. So the small group of young Britons who place these problems of material and civil security aside and accord instead a higher priority to freedom and participation must surely have their reasons. Inglehart's data, resting rather starkly upon value-choices, provided few insights into those reasons but since we know also that postbourgeois priorities are associated with high social and economic status, the question then arises: Does the postbourgeois phenomenon really "tap a relatively well integrated and *deep-rooted* aspect of the respondent's political orientations" and is it "*integrated* into the individual's attitudinal structure—a fact which suggests attitudinal stability"[1] or is it merely a fashionable and perhaps slightly cynical pose adopted by those who, actually or potentially, can afford to be less concerned with their personal material security?

The results of our second pilot study (Marsh 1975) indicated in favor of the second conclusion. The British postbourgeois, compared with acquisitives, revealed no sense of material repletion, on the contrary, they tended to make fairly strident material demands and valued the material aspects of their lives as highly as did the acquisitives. Whatever priority they really do give to "postindustrial" political values, they have developed the ability to maintain these feelings coexistent with the continued defense of their privileged economic position. Therefore we suggested that they may be rather more interested in power than in postindustrial enlightenment. Maslow was always rather imprecise about the real nature of "self-actualisation" and it is perfectly possible that to young, protest-prone, middle-class radicals the ability to take decisions on behalf of the community is as much self-actualisation as they desire.

Inglehart (1975) has argued in reply that it is incorrect to assume that postmaterialists (as he now prefers to describe the postbourgeois) will show a sense of material satisfaction. He writes:

> The [Maslow's] need hierarchy model states that those who have obtained *objective* satisfaction of a given set of needs will, after a time, shift their priorities, giving greater attention to the pursuit of other needs . . . not that they would necessarily manifest relatively greater *subjective* satisfaction concerning the "lower-order" domains

but he acknowledges that

the emergence of a large Postmaterialist minority among the younger age cohorts does not reflect the appearance of an essentially nobler, more altruistic generation.[2]

Therefore, although our pilot study called into question the *fundamental* characteristics attributed to a shift from materialist to postmaterialist value choices, Inglehart has regained his position by claiming that whether the postmaterialist phenomenon is just radical chic, or whether it is a fundamentally new psychopolitical orientation, or even a confused mixture of both, the phenomenon itself is still important because young people *are* concerned to maximize goals other than continued economic growth and this development, however superficially, still "fits" the Maslovian need hierarchy model. While this represents to some extent a shift away from a theoretically well-modeled position towards a more empirically dependent position, it does keep the silent revolution theory afloat.

Support for the value-shift theory of political radicalism has come in from other quarters. Knutson operationalized the Maslovian hierarchy and compared people who had achieved a high level of "self-actualization" (i.e., people able to maximize higher-order goals in leisure pursuits, self-expression, mutual affection, and so on) with those who did not ("low self-actualizers") and those who were so bound up with basic security needs as to be "physically deprived." Knutson takes a position akin to Lane that political participation is a positive function of ego strength and, indeed, one finds that her self-actualizers have significantly higher rates of political participation than the other two groups. The direction of this heightened political consciousness was, very generally speaking, leftward and included a tendency to score significantly lower than average on Rokeach's dogmatism scale and on various versions of authoritarianism scales. In American terms, self-actualizers tend to be liberals and are usually well-educated and young.[3]

Rokeach too has completed impressive work relating basic value choices to political dispositions. He produces a two-value theory of the left-right, radical-conservative dimension which may be summarized diagramatically (Figure 7.1).

| | Extreme Left | Moderate Left | Center | Moderate Right | Extreme Right |
|---|---|---|---|---|---|
| Value maximized: | EQUALITY | EQUALITY AND FREEDOM | UNCERTAIN MIXED VALUES | FREEDOM | |
| Value minimized: | FREEDOM | | | EQUALITY | FREEDOM AND EQUALITY |

Figure 7.1.

Freedom and equality feature in his sixteen-item terminal values battery which is largely concerned with personal values like love, happiness, salvation, self-respect, friendship, accomplishment, security (personal and national), recognition, and so on. . . . He finds strong support for the two-value model. Those on the left do maximize both of the "higher-order" terminal values, those on the right maximize freedom at the expense of equality. Also, content analysis of Lenin and Hitler's work indicated that the former maximized equality at the expense of freedom and the latter minimized both equality and freedom in favor of the aims of the Nazi party. Also those who tend to maximize *either* of these "higher-order" political goals tend towards a higher-than-average level of political activism of some kind. This confirms Knutson's findings.

Both Knutson and Rokeach quote Inglehart approvingly. Rokeach in particular notes that his equality/freedom model aligns very well with Inglehart's four-item battery, which maximizes freedom and participation as higher-order values compared with material and civil security which maximizes lower-order values. But it is Knutson who most sharply points out the relevance of this line of enquiry: young middle-class people in a materialist society whose basic value inheritance was constructed in the nineteenth-century world of the unquestioned preeminence of material progress have developed higher-order needs of which they are constantly *deprived, relative to their expectations.* They expect to find their institutions of higher education havens of total freedom of expression and untrameled liberalism and are disappointed when careerism and materialism impinge upon their lives. Put as simply as possible, it is proposed that, whereas relative material deprivation may to a certain extent explain working-class protest, relative psychic deprivation of higher-order needs may explain middle-class protest. We know already that the middle-class radical in Britain is not immune from feelings of material deprivation, but is he, and not the working-class protester, also sensitive to psychic deprivation of higher-order needs?

Inglehart's results are of course in the same direction as predicted by both Knutson and Rockeach's results, but Inglehart's four-item battery does seem to exclude consideration of the difference between the center ("middle American" in Rokeach) and the moderate right because no combination of Inglehart's goals maximizes freedom while minimizing equality. The next stage in this field of enquiry was clearly to be concerned with instrument development.

## Measuring Values

The reader should consider carefully the conceptual diagram Figure 7.2. The essential features of the Maslovian need hierarchy are illustrated, ranging from the "lower-order" sustenance and security needs, through the post-

materialist or self-actualizing threshold to "belongingness" needs (for affection and friendship), "esteem" (the feeling of respect received from others)
and to the most obviously higher-order needs, which require the satisfaction
of the intellect and aesthetic sensibilities. Alongside these are aligned first the
original Inglehart battery, each item occupying its obvious position, then a
development into a single battery of two further four-item choice questions
used by Inglehart in his 1973 survey (see Inglehart 1975). Then, on the far
right of the diagram are aligned ten value objects of a much more clearly
defined *personal* nature. This battery was developed by the writer especially
for this survey and is based upon the following hypotheses:

(1) Those concerned exclusively with lower-order sustenance and security
    needs will maximize their health, the quality of their housing and
    their material standard of living. "Job" too is likely to feature highly
    in these needs though, as Inglehart has insisted, many aspects of
    employment values like fulfilment and contributing to the community
    are more appropriate to higher-order needs.

(2) "Esteem" and "belongingness" needs will be reflected by the items:
    "the respect other people have for you" and "family and social life."

(3) The unequivocally "higher-order" needs of intellectualism and aes-
    thetic drives will be reflected in the items: "your education," "the
    level of freedom and democracy in this country," "your hobbies and
    leisure activities" and "the arts."

The four-item battery was administered verbally. The eight- and ten-item
batteries were administered with the help of cards. Each value stimulus was
described briefly upon a two-inch square card and, for each battery separately, the respondent was asked to select the three items he felt were *most*
important to him and then rank these most, second most, and third most
important and then to select from the remaining cards the three *least* important
items and then rank them least, second least, and third least important. Un-
ranked items thereby obtained a neutral score: neither important nor unimportant. It should be noted that the importance/unimportance scores thereby
generated are scores of *relative* importance, not absolute importance; therefore items ranked *relatively* unimportant by a respondent may nonetheless be
held by him to be very important in a wider context. When basic values are
concerned a certain amount of "armtwisting" is needed to pin down a
respondent's final value preferences among an array of highly salient stimulus
objects. Even then, about one-fifth of respondents failed to complete the
"least important" rankings for the public-values battery protesting that such
important matters could not attract any kind of *unimportant* judgment. It
should also be borne in mind that the private-values battery was explicitly

| Maslovian Hierarchy | Q.9: Four-item Battery | Q.10: Public Values | Q.2: Private Values |
|---|---|---|---|
| Social and Self-Actualization Needs ["Postmaterialist"] | | | |
| AESTHETIC INTELLECTUAL | "Protect free speech" | D. Beautiful cities<br>H. Ideas > money | J. the Arts<br>C. Hobbies and leisure |
| ESTEEM | "Give people more say in Government" | G. Less impersonal society | G. Freedom and democracy<br>H. Education |
| BELONGING | | C. More say in work and community | D. The respect of others<br>I. Family and social life |
| | "POSTMATERIALIST THRESHOLD" | | |
| Physiological ["Materialist"] | | | |
| SAFETY AND SECURITY | "Maintain order" | B. Strong defenses<br>F. Fight crime | B. Job<br>A. Housing |
| SUSTENANCE NEEDS | "Fight rising prices" | A. Economic growth<br>E. Stable economy | F. Material standard of living<br>E. Health |

Figure 7.2: CONGRUENCE BETWEEN MASLOVIAN THEORY AND VALUE-PRIORITY CHOICES

linked to the life-satisfaction measures and was administered immediately following the life-satisfaction questions with the introductory phrase:

> Here is a list of things people have said are important in determining how satisfied or dissatisfied they are with their lives.

Thus, each item is being judged *as a relatively important source of life satisfaction.*

The need to deploy a "private" values battery alongside the public (i.e., explicitly political) value items derived from the apparent paradox brought to light by the pilot study in that the postmaterialists seemed to be demanding "freedom and participation for the nation and cash and security for themselves." In this study we are now in a good position to draw a distinction between the public and personal value domains and to test whether the allegedly fundamental nature of the values-choice typology extends into the personal domain and to test also whether the behavioral outcomes imputed to postmaterialist tendencies (now measured in greater detail) apply in singular fashion in both domains.

## The Nature of Value Priorities in Britain

The explicit relationship between value priorities and political behavior has not been previously investigated in Britain. The word "values" as an explicit concept is absent from the major textbooks on British politics. This is all the more surprising since value priorities are implicit in many of the most commonplace measures of political sentiment used in British survey research. For example, the Gallup Poll's monthly inquiry: "What are the most important problems facing the country today?" have always shown "inflation," "employment," or some other implicitly "material or security" value priority to be the greatest source of concern to the public. Political decisions are supposed to be made on the basis of some long-term goal orientation: the Labour party is supposed to move towards goals that maximize social and economic equality and the Conservative party is supposed to maximize efficiency through free economic competition and to defend traditional values of loyalty toward legitimate authority. Ideologues of both parties are heard to complain when long-term value priorities are sacrificed to short-term expediencies. When Harold Wilson justified cuts in public expenditure in July 1966 in terms of short-term economic emergency, he lamented that the Labour government had thereby been "blown off course"—off its "crusading" course toward social equality outlined in the party's policy documents. Similarly, Edward Heath disillusioned the ideologues of his own party when the expansionist laissez-faire strategy embodied in the Selsdon policy of 1970 was abandoned within two years in favor of interventionist economic policies to stave off worsening terms of trade and growing inflation. But the fact remains that politics is *supposed* to be about basic choices between different ways of organizing society and it is quite amazing that political scientists have not seriously addressed themselves to the task of measuring these basic value priorities before. Whatever may be the final verdict (here and elsewhere) upon Inglehart's silent revolution thesis, he has undoubtedly advanced political science a long way by bringing basic values into the science of mass politics survey research.

As a guiding hypothesis, based on earlier experience, we would expect materialist and security considerations to dominate the configuration of value priorities in Britain.

By the time of the survey (1973-74) retail price inflation was already a serious problem, yet the expected dominance of the "Fight rising prices" item among the original Inglehart four-item battery is not overwhelming: 36 percent of the sample regard it as relatively unimportant. "Giving people more say in important decisions of the Government" was (narrowly) the second choice, followed by "Maintaining order" and lastly: "Protect freedom of speech".

Outstandingly, among the eight-item battery, the need for a stable economy (61% "important") and efforts to suppress criminality (56%) were accorded the greatest priority and these must certainly reflect a need for basic "lower order" Maslovian satisfaction. Yet, the item accorded third priority (46% "important") was "Giving people more say in decisions at their work and in the community," which seems to confirm the configuration of the four-item choice pattern where the need for *participation* was surprisingly strong. Among the remaining items, the Maslovian hierarchical order is preserved in aggregate terms in that economic growth and strong defenses are preferred over environmental improvement (this despite the apparent dissatisfaction seen in Chapter 6 with the government's performance in fighting pollution) and movement toward a friendlier and nonmaterialist society.

The choice pattern among the ten-item personal value battery also contains non-Maslovian anomalies. Overwhelmingly, people recognized the need for good health: 82 percent of the sample place this item among the three most important choices and 55 percent placed it first. Yet clearly the second most important item is "Family and social life," which seems to provide a link between "security and belongingness" that folds the hierarchy somewhat. Critics of Maslow have long pointed out that the nomothetic distance between the need to seek shelter and food and the "higher-order" goal-seeking which maximizes belongingness is probably very small indeed. Even when actually starving, people have been observed to seek the affection and support of their friends and family.

Otherwise, the choice pattern in aggregate terms again confirms that British people are more concerned with their jobs, housing and money and less concerned about democracy, the esteem of others, hobbies, education, and the arts, in that order. In this list, democracy (considered, it should be remembered, in the light of its possible contribution to personal happiness) receives quite an unexpectedly high rating, only 25 percent rank it relatively unimportant, while education, whose power to increase earning power (if nothing else) is fairly obvious, receives a very low rating.

Aggregate rankings, therefore, imply that the British population cleave to a fairly low level of Maslovian development. Yet, intruding into their concern to maximize material and security needs is a concern for participation in the decision-making processes of the community that supersedes their concern for personal and national aggrandizement (i.e., fast growth and strong defenses). The British want to be secure, certainly, but they want to be

**Table 7.1: Estimated Structure of Value Priorities (Unrotated, principal axis analysis)**

|  | Factor I | Factor II | Factor III | Communalities |
|---|---|---|---|---|
| *(A) Personal Values* | | | | |
| Percentage of total variance | 16% | 14% | 12% | |
| The Arts | .472 | −.454 | − | .529 |
| Education | .460 | .389 | + | .467 |
| Family | .351 | + | −.520 | .719 |
| Democracy | .340 | − | .500 | .574 |
| Job | + | .591 | + | .901 |
| Hobbies | + | −.550 | −.460 | .691 |
| Health | − | −.400 | .570 | .545 |
| Respect | −.453 | − | − | .789 |
| Wealth | −.532 | + | + | .535 |
| House | −.600 | + | − | .552 |
|  | Materialist/ Postmaterialist | Achievement/ Leisure | | |
| *(B) Political Values* | | | | |
| Percentage of total variance | 22% | 18% | 15% | |
| More friendly society | .608 | + | + | .662 |
| Ideas > cash | .569 | −.318 | + | .935 |
| More say in decisions | .314 | −.317 | −.739 | .949 |
| Beauty | + | .490 | .408 | .964 |
| Fight crime | − | .719 | + | .670 |
| Stable economy | −.398 | −.457 | .444 | .754 |
| Strong defense | −.577 | .316 | −.464 | .773 |
| Economic growth | −.598 | −.381 | + | .590 |
|  | Materialist/ Postmaterialist | Traditional/ Modern | | |

*consulted* even more than they want to be rich or powerful. This finding seems to accord well with the general theme of this study: that deference is no longer a force in British political culture but has given way to a concern for influence in the decisions of the political community.

But aggregate levels reveal only half of what we need to know. How do these choices *cluster*? Is there any distinguishable tendency for those who include nonmaterialist items among their value priorities to choose others; or do most people opt for a *basic* set of materialist choices and then include (perhaps for the sake of appearances) one or other of the higher-order concerns? Does the idea of a materialist/postmaterialist axis of value priorities which was imputed to the four-item choice patterns by Inglehart find any support in this much more finely attuned set of items? Table 7.1 shows that the idea finds strong support.

A principal axis analysis of the relative importance scores of each value battery shows that for *both* the personal and public value domains, a first axis emerges that clearly reflects a materialistic-vs.-postmaterialist choice pattern. Among the personal values, concern for the arts, education, family and social life, and democracy is clearly juxtaposed to concern for wealth and housing and, surprisingly, "respect." The a priori labeling of this item as corresponding to what Maslow characterized as the highest order for "esteem" was incorrect. The word "respect" clearly reflects economic standing. We would argue that, in a predominantly materialist society, the acquisition of wealth itself bestows the esteem that a materialist set of value priorities has determined as the reward for success. If we had characterized esteem in terms of recognition by others of one's intrinsic moral worth, or perhaps as the love and friendship of others, the result may well have been different. Yet, there is no doubt that the influence of the dominant form of societal organization of a material-dependent society feeds back into the normative value system to cause anomalies in the progressive-hierarchy model to an extent that makes Maslow's "linear" conceptualization very difficult to handle. The problem is simply that a highly developed materialist society finds ways for people to achieve self-actualization in material terms. Pride in achievement is necessarily bound up with material reward. Yet, on the other hand, we see that "job," whose equivocal character as a materialist or a postmaterialist stimulus object was argued about earlier, receives a neutral loading[4] on this first factor as does health (which is everyone's concern) and hobbies (which is no-one's— one way or the other).

Among the political value choices, the pattern is quite unequivocal: the first factor (accounting for 22% of the total variance) juxtaposes participation and movement toward a friendlier and nonmaterialist society on the one side against economic stability and growth and strong defenses on the other. Beauty and the fight against crime are the most ideologically neutral stimuli in the list and so receive low loadings on this factor, beauty is weighted in the direction of postmaterialism, crime in the direction of materialism.

From these choice patterns, four value-type indices were constructed:

(A) The original Inglehart four-item battery which trichotomizes the six possible combinations of four choices into "acquisitives" (order and prices), "postbourgeois" (Freedom and participation) and "intermediates" (mixed choices).

(B) A factor-score distribution for the eight-item battery was derived from the loadings on the first principal axis and divided into five equal-appearing intervals to form a materialist postmaterialist score.

(C) A combined index was constructed by adding two components:
   (1) the number of materialist items mentioned first or second in the four-item battery, or mentioned first, second or third most important in the eight-item battery, and
   (2) the number of postmaterialist items mentioned third or fourth in the four-item battery or mentioned as least, next-to-least, or third-least important in the eight-item battery. The most neutral item—"beauty"—was excluded from this index.[5]

(D) A factor-score distribution for the ten-item personal values battery similar to B was obtained from the loadings upon the first principal axis and divided into four equal-appearing intervals to form a "basic material security and order"-vs.-"higher order" score.

The frequency distributions obtained for these four measures are presented in Table 7.2. The marginal stability of the four item-index is evident in that 10 percent of the sample emerge in the postbourgeois position compared with 7 percent in 1970 and 8 percent in 1971 so, as Inglehart would predict, a slow drift toward postmaterialism is evident. Also the acquisitive group has shrunk significantly from 36/35 percent to 24 percent, apparently as a function of the increased priority accorded to participation and this has occurred despite the possible influence of rising inflation. We attach great importance to this result. Here are data that suggest that the need for political participation beyond voting once every few years is growing rapidly and this militates strongly against the supposedly "deferential" habit of extending freedom of decision to authorities.

The eight-item index indicates a preponderance of materialist concerns with 30 percent having an almost wholly materialist outlook and only 12 percent occupying the postmaterialist pole. The combined index indicates approximately 14 percent in the postmaterialist position but only 18 percent in the highly materialist group. The personal values index, however, indicates a more solid clustering of postmaterialists (whom for the sake of clarity and distinction we have labelled "higher-order" group) of about 20 percent. Not too much should be read into these latter distributions, however, because the

**Table 7.2: Distribution of Value Types**

(A) *Original Inglehart Four-Item Battery*

| Acquisitives | Intermediates | Postacquisitives |
|---|---|---|
| 24% | 66% | 10% (n = 1,726) |

(B) *Adapted Inglehard Eight-Item Battery*
(Equal-internal factor scores)

| Materialist | | Postmaterialist | | | |
|---|---|---|---|---|---|
| 1 | 2 | 3 | 4 | 5 | |
| 30% | 19% | 28% | 11% | 12% | (n = 1,404) |

(C) *Combined Four-Item and Eight-Item Battery*
(Additive measure)

| Highly Materialist | Materialist | Intermediate | Postmaterialist |
|---|---|---|---|
| 18% | 35% | 33% | 14% (n = 1,353) |

(D) *Personal Values Battery*
(Equal-interval factor scores)

| Basic Security and Order | Intermediate I | Intermediate II | Higher Order |
|---|---|---|---|
| 25% | 28% | 27% | 20% (n = 1,674) |

establishment and labeling of the categories rely upon somewhat arbitrary criteria and may not be strictly comparable.

Despite the apparent similarity of distribution, the scales may not be tapping the same aspects of postmaterialist feeling. Table 7.3 describes the intercorrelations between the scales and indicates a surprisingly *low* positive relationship between personal and political postmaterialism. This is forgiveably so in the case of the four-item index which has 66 percent of the sample scoring neutrally, but is very surprising in the case of the elaborated batteries which, after all, appear a priori to be reflecting very similar polarities. Clearly they are not very similar and allow for interesting possibilities for different relationships with the behavioral variables. But before we proceed that far, it is right that we should refer again to our pilot study which asserted that "some hard questions must be asked before Inglehart's theory may be elaborated to accommodate (these) findings" and do so.

The value types generated by the two main value-type indices were analysed for differences according to age, sex, class, income, education, and partisan preference. Some fairly remarkable differences emerge for both scales but they are not the *same* differences. Characteristics that distinguish

Table 7.3: Intercorrelations Between Value-Type Indices

|  |  | 1<br>(4-item) | 2<br>(8-item) | 3<br>(12-item) |
|---|---|---|---|---|
| (1) | 4-item "acquisitive vs. postbourgeois" index | * |  |  |
| (2) | 8-item "materialist vs. postmaterialist" index | .25 | * |  |
| (3) | Combined 12-item index | NA | NA | * |
| (4) | Personal values index | .22 | .14 | .21 |

public postmaterialists from private materialists are not, one for one, the same characteristics that distinguish personal postmaterialists from personal materialists. Age effects are much the same: Postmaterialists are a lot younger than materialists on both scales. Also postmaterialists tend to be richer, better educated, and have a higher social status than materialists on both scales but this is much more the case in the personal value domain than in the public domain. The extent to which working-class people maximize basic material and security goals in their personal value domain contrasts very strongly with middle-class people, who are actually in a majority among personal post-materialists. Among public postmaterialists, however, working-class people still form the majority. This difference in class composition between the two postmaterialist groups is reflected in their partisan loyalty. Public postmateri-alists have a very strong tendency to vote Labour (50%) or Liberal (23%) compared with only 29 percent and 12 percent respectively among public materialists, 58 percent of whom vote Tory, which implies an impressive clustering of working-class Tories in this group. However, the four value types defined by the personal-value battery do not differ at all in their tendency to vote Conservative or Labour. Indeed, those of the postmaterialist group who do not favor the Conservatives show a distinct prejudice *against* the Labour Party and in favour of the *Liberals*. With their class composition, though, one would predict even fewer Labour voters than those present.

The salient characteristics of age, class, and political party were examined simultaneously for each value type on both scales. In the personal value domain, there is an impressive clustering of materialist values among older working-class people of all political persuasions; members of this group are united in their emphasis upon the material needs of life and divided merely on which political party is most likely to meet them. In sharp contrast, young middle-class people all share a strong emphasis upon higher-order values and presumably differ only on the party most likely to meet their needs—if any at all. Between these two extreme orientations, the broad value priorities of young workers and older middle-class people look superficially similar: An uneven balance is struck between materialism and postmaterialism with the great majority having mixed values. In the public value domain, the concentration of postmaterialist priorities is much more clearly associated with middle-class leftism, especially among younger middle-class respondents. True, young workers show a greater tendency *towards* postmaterialism than their elders but, except for the small group of Liberals among them, few break through into an unequivocal postmaterialist position.

A political basis for explaining the discontinuity between the socio-political patterning of public and personal value priorities may lie in the economic input of public policies upon the private purse. Put bluntly, working-class people may embrace equalitarian political values because the most tangible outcome of equalitarian policies may be the material enrichment of the working-class, whose material value priorities *and* material dissatisfaction are self-evident. That, after all, is what the Labour party itself is supposed to be for. For a working-class Labour supporter who is perhaps a little more politically aware than average, the goal, "Moving toward a society where ideas are more important than money," may well imply for him a society where he has personally been enriched and can begin to afford to share Postmaterialist concerns for the higher things of life. He probably would not put it that way but he is likely to covet such a condition for its own sake. The goal: "A high rate of economic growth" does not necessarily guarantee *him* a share in increased national wealth.

Among the middle-class generally and the young in particular, there is a closer correspondence between priorities in the two value domains ($r = .27$) and among young Labour and Liberal supporters it attains the level that an optimistic researcher might predict for the sample as a whole ($r = .45$ and $r = .32$). The three attitude elements of this analysis: political party identity, public values and personal values, are congruent in the case of middle-class radicals. The higher-order priorities of their private domain are actually served by the congruence between postmaterialism and what are for them altruistic Labour sympathies. Older middle-class Tories however are noncongruent in the opposite direction: they tend toward postmaterialistic personal values combined with and perhaps even reinforced by materialist public values. These are doubtless concentrated *upon* the ideas concerning public order that our measure of materialism contains.

To summarize the argument so far: the data support Inglehart's theory to the extent that postmaterialism is associated with middle-class radicalism and this is especially true among the younger groups. Younger working-class people also strain toward a Postmaterialist position but fall well short of their better placed peers in both the public and personal value domains. Materialism on the other hand is clearly associated with older people and particularly those having working-class status. All this is predicted by Inglehart's theory in that those who have enjoyed the most advantaged upbringing in the modern world tend to be those with the highest levels of postmaterialism among whom the postmaterialist phenomenon also tends to be a more coherent reality. Also, there tends to be a sizeable residue of postmaterialist sentiment among the older age cohorts, a legacy of the days when Britain enjoyed a very high relative economic position. We can now ask again: To what extent do postmaterialists manifest their Maslovian development in terms of conscious material life satisfaction?

Unlike our pilot survey, we do not have very elaborate measures of relative gratification with which to probe the feelings of relative deprivation or gratification experienced by each value type. But those we have are deployed in Table 7.4 for both public and personal value domains. Our guiding hypothesis in this analysis is that in both domains, but especially in the personal domain, Postmaterialists will register higher levels of material gratification and lower demand levels for cash, especially in terms of their urgency of need, but will not manifest higher levels of overall life satisfaction because the overall measure of satisfaction must imply the additional inclusion of unmet higher-order needs. Materialists on the other hand should manifest their dissatisfaction in the relative deprivation of material goods, "the things you can buy and do."

**Table 7.4: Relative Gratification among Value Types (in percentages)**

| | Personal Values | | | | Public Values | | | |
|---|---|---|---|---|---|---|---|---|
| | Basic Security | Inter. I | Inter. II | Higher Order | Highly Mat. | Mat. | Inter. | Post-Mat. |
| *Material Gratification* | | | | | | | | |
| Satisfied | 37 | 31 | 37 | 44 | 41 | 37 | 34 | 33 |
| Dissatisfied | 32 | 30 | 29 | 31 | 34 | 28 | 29 | 33 |
| Very dissatisfied | 31 | 39 | 34 | 25 | 25 | 35 | 37 | 34 |
| *Overall Gratification* | | | | | | | | |
| Satisfied | 44 | 43 | 45 | 49 | 50 | 46 | 41 | 43 |
| Dissatisfied | 32 | 33 | 32 | 34 | 32 | 31 | 34 | 34 |
| Very dissatisfied | 24 | 23 | 23 | 17 | 18 | 23 | 25 | 23 |
| *Extra Money Needed* | | | | | | | | |
| None | 28 | 26 | 37 | 45 | 39 | 33 | 30 | 30 |
| Up to £15 p.w. | 53 | 48 | 36 | 25 | 43 | 43 | 40 | 36 |
| More than £15 p.w. | 19 | 28 | 27 | 30 | 18 | 24 | 30 | 34 |
| (a) Urgent, may get | 39 | 33 | 33 | 31 | 31 | 32 | 36 | 34 |
| (b) Urgent, not get | 31 | 31 | 25 | 23 | 21 | 29 | 30 | 21 |
| (c) Not urgent, may get | 17 | 21 | 25 | 28 | 26 | 23 | 19 | 31 |
| (d) Not urgent, not get | 13 | 14 | 17 | 18 | 21 | 16 | 14 | 14 |

Table 7.4 indicates that our hypothesis is broadly true for the private value domain but not for the public value domain. Our predominantly well-off, young, middle-class *personal* postmaterialists (or "higher-order" group) manifest a higher level of material satisfaction and show a much greater tendency not to ask for more money than do the personal-level materialists. At the same time, their material satisfaction is not manifested in significantly higher levels of overall satisfaction. The public domain postmaterialists, however, show a *lower* level of material gratification and have a *higher* propensity to demand extra cash (as they did in our pilot survey), as well as showing a slightly lower level of overall gratification. So again it appears that our new personal values battery is tapping the "postmaterialist phenomenon" rather more successfully (in Maslovian terms anyway) than the batteries developed by Inglehart for the public value domain.

Whereas fairly obvious predictions are possible in the area of personal gratification, satisfaction with government performance is more difficult to estimate. Dissatisfaction with the traditional areas of government responsibility like housing, employment, health, and so on is not necessarily dependent upon personal experience. A postmaterialist is just as likely to criticize the government's housing record even if he is personally well-housed. But we would expect postmaterialists to display a greater sensitivity about "radical" issues like sexual and racial equality, education, and pollution control while materialists might show more concern about crime control, employment, health, and housing.

These expectations are only partly justified. In the personal values domain, the postmaterialists show only marginally greater concern over pollution and education and no more concern about sexual and racial equality. In the traditional areas of government responsibility, however, the materialists—as we suspected—show no greater concern but interestingly they are more critical of the government's record in controling crime. In the public value domain, the postmaterialists are very critical of *every* aspect of government performance. Given their political composition this is straightforwardly a partisan reaction, almost a response set, but there is no tendency for them, compared to the materialists, to concentrate their attack in the radical sector of issue concerns, except perhaps their concern for colored immigrants. On the other hand, the public materialists are surprisingly critical of pollution control efforts. There is a brief and obvious conclusion to be drawn from these data: Public-domain postmaterialism in Britain is as much associated with the Old Left as the New Left; personal postmaterialism on the other hand comes close to being issue-free and ideologically nonspecific.

The extent to which the last conclusion may be true may be judged from Table 7.5, which provides a psycho-political profile of value types in both the

Table 7.5: Psycho-Political Profile of Value-Types

|  | Personal Values | | | | Public Values | | | |
|---|---|---|---|---|---|---|---|---|
|  | Basic Security | Inter. I | Inter. II | Higher Order | Highly Mat. | Mat. | Inter. | Post-Mat. |
| (a) Average left-right self-placement score (L=1, R=10) | 5.63 | 5.84 | 5.73 | 5.76 | 6.33 | 5.80 | 5.50 | 5.09 |
| (b) % cynical about politicians | 50 | 53 | 43 | 37 | 45 | 48 | 54 | 65 |
| (c) % politically efficacious | 44 | 44 | 57 | 71 | 58 | 52 | 47 | 58 |
| (d) % of ideologues and near-ideologues | 16 | 17 | 27 | 36 | 26 | 23 | 22 | 32 |
| (e) % of good or sophisticated con-ceptualization of L-R dimension | 20 | 20 | 27 | 50 | 35 | 26 | 26 | 40 |

| Correlation coefficients | Personal Values | Public Values |
|---|---|---|
| Left-right scale | .00 | .20 |
| Cynicism | −.10 | .20 |
| Efficacy | .21 | .06 |
| Level of conceptualization | .17 | .01 |
| Conceptualization of L-R | .21 | .04 |

personal and public domains and reveals some fascinating differences in the two measures. Essentially, postmaterialists in the public value domain are politically cynical, moderately efficacious, moderately aware, leftists whereas postmaterialists in the personal value domain tend to be moderately *trusting*, highly efficacious, politically sophisticated, and are normally distributed along the left-right continuum, clustering a fraction left-of-center. Politically and personally, then, the majority of postmaterialists in the two value domains are not merely not the same people, they are quite dissimilar people too.

## Values and Political Action

We have arrived at two subtly different measures of the postmaterialist phenomenon. The first, the personal values domain, successfully determines all the social and psychological characteristics of postmaterialism that are predicted by Inglehart's theory (i.e., they are middle-class, well-educated, materially undemanding, self-actualizing young sophisticates) but none of the political characteristics. The second measure, the public political domain, successfully determines the *political* characteristics of postmaterialism (leftism, mistrust of conventional politicians, bitter criticism of the Government, etc.) but reflects the social and psychological characteristics only very imperfectly, except in the case of *age*. Therefore, to predict from these findings the likely relationship between postmaterialism in Britain and political action, especially protest potential, involves an interesting dilemma. Inglehart's theory implies that the closer one penetrates to measuring the *fundamental underlying* nature of postmaterialism (i.e., a profound shift in value priorities away from the dominant values of the consumer society toward higher-order concerns), the more obvious becomes the discrepancy between the postmaterialist values held and the materialist society in which postmaterialists live and, hence, the greater the likelihood they will form unorthodox political tendencies. Therefore it follows that the eight-item public-value battery will be a better predictor of protest potential than will the original four-item scale because it is more finely attuned to the underlying dimension. The twelve-item combined scale may be a better predictor than either alone, but the personal-value battery should be a much better predictor of protest potential than either of the public-value measures because it is even more closely aligned with the core concept of nonmaterial value preferences.

An obvious difficulty with such a prediction is that it contradicts the evidence so far presented in this chapter. The postmaterialists in the *public* value domain are displaying all the combined characteristics we have earlier established as good predictors of protest potential; they are young, cynical, leftists. The postmaterialists in the personal value domain have only their youth and their cognitive sophistication to recommend them as potential protesters while they lack the cynicism and the partisan preferences of protesters, save for their residual sympathy for the Liberal party. Thus the only sensible empirically based prediction is that the public-value scale will predict protest potential far better than the personal value scale whereas theory suggests the opposite. Such a dilemma will not be resolved by further conjecture so we must turn hopefully to the data for an empirical solution.

The relationship between postmaterialism and protest potential is analysed in Table 7.6, and no simple answer to the above question emerges. The most parsimonious predictor of protest potential is, after all, the original four-item Inglehart value scale. Exactly in line with his 1970 findings, the postbourgeoise group are almost four times more likely than the acquisitives to favor nonlegal forms of protest. This finding is also independent of the powerful age effect in that postbourgeois over thirty years of age are almost twice as likely to favor protest than acquisitives *under* thirty. Combined with age, the effect is very impressive: Only 15 percent of young postbourgeoise would go no further than petition signing and more than half would engage in illegal forms of protest.

Table 7.6: Protest Potential by Postmaterialism Scales (in percentages)

| | (n) | No Pro-test | Peti-tions Only | Demon-strations | Boy-cotts | Strikes/Rent Strikes | Occupations Blockades |
|---|---|---|---|---|---|---|---|
| *Original Inglehart Four-Item Scale* | | | | | | | |
| Acquisitive | (387) | 27 | 23 | 24 | 14 | 8 | 4 |
| Intermediates | (1,078) | 22 | 23 | 19 | 15 | 10 | 12 |
| Postbourgeois | (164) | 9 | 10 | 21 | 17 | 17 | 27 |
| *Eight-Item Political Value Scale* | | | | | | | |
| Materialist (1) | (30) | 22 | 21 | 25 | 14 | 11 | 7 |
| (2) | (19) | 18 | 18 | 23 | 16 | 14 | 12 |
| Intermediate (3) | (28) | 21 | 19 | 17 | 16 | 11 | 16 |
| (4) | (11) | 19 | 24 | 20 | 15 | 8 | 14 |
| Postmaterialist (5) | (12) | 10 | 10 | 29 | 13 | 17 | 20 |
| *Twelve-Item Combined Value Scale* | | | | | | | |
| Highly materialist | (18) | 27 | 19 | 26 | 13 | 10 | 5 |
| Materialist | (35) | 20 | 23 | 20 | 17 | 10 | 10 |
| Intermediate | (33) | 21 | 20 | 20 | 15 | 11 | 14 |
| Postmaterialist | (14) | 14 | 13 | 16 | 16 | 13 | 29 |
| *Ten-Item Personal Value Scale* | | | | | | | |
| Basic material security and order | (25) | 35 | 22 | 18 | 13 | 6 | 7 |
| Intermediate I | (28) | 23 | 22 | 23 | 13 | 10 | 9 |
| Intermediate II | (27) | 20 | 25 | 19 | 13 | 12 | 11 |
| Higher-Order | (20) | 8 | 13 | 21 | 22 | 12 | 23 |

It would be surprising if this were not so. The scale determines postbourgeoise choices as a preference for freedom and participation in politics as opposed to the acquisitive's preference for public order and material security. But does this really imply anything fundamental about values and protest? That the former preference should be associated with the tendency to engage in unorthodox political behavior has a face validity that does not require an hierarchical theory of Maslovian development to explain it. Protesters are simply more likely to place a higher value on freedom and participation than upon public order and material security. No more need really be said. That is why the second-order value batteries were developed.

The prediction that the eight-item postmaterialism scale should prove an even better predictor of protest potential is unfounded. Those scoring highest on the scale do have a significantly higher protest potential than those scoring on the materialist side, but the trend in the remainder of the distribution is discontinuous and nonlinear—especially among the young. Since the weighting determined by the factor analysis of the individual scale items emphasized a distinction between (a) materialist priority for economic stability and growth with national security and (b) postmaterialist priority for community and work participation together with movement towards a friendlier society where ideas are more important than cash, there can be no denying that the scale has very strong face validity. If postmaterialism has anything to do with movement away from unrelieved concern with material security toward a more warmly human and concerned society, then this scale measures it and does so more keenly than the four-item scale. So this finding suggests that the underlying dimension of postmaterialism has fewer implications for political change than the overlying concern for freedom-vs.-order.

The combined twelve-item scale, however, does provide a clearly linear positive relationship with protest potential that is at least partially independent of age and which isolates the potential of young postmaterialists with even more clarity (59% of postmaterialists under 30 score high on the protest scale), but it would be difficult to determine whether the overlying or underlying dimension was the greatest influence; the only evidence we have so far holds the "order-vs.-freedom" element to be the greater influence.

We know the personal value scale evidently cuts even closer toward the underlying dimension of postmaterialism than the developed public-value measure and does so in a highly individual context, i.e., the extent to which the individual's overall life satisfaction is derived from his house, his money, or his material standing versus his education, friendships, his love of the arts and the value he places upon democracy. Neither is it related to partisanship or cynicism. Thus, given the evidence that the nearer the public battery approaches the underlying value dimension, the poorer its predictive qualities for protest potential, we would now expect quite unequivocally that the personal-values scale will not predict protest potential. But it does. The group who place higher-order concerns before material security are three times more likely to engage in nonlegal forms of protest than are those who cleave to basic material concerns (36% vs. 12%). Since the personal values scale defines a much larger group (20% of the total sample) in the "higher-order" (postmaterialist) condition, than does the public value scale (14%) this is a very impressive relationship to find between so abstract a psychological concept and so behaviorally specific a measure as protest potential. Moreover, the relationship is wholly independent of political ideology. The personal value scale correlates positively with protest potential at +.30, which is modified merely to +.29 when the effects of left-right self-placement are partialed out. In contrast, the public-value scale correlates with protest at only +.22, and this reduces sharply to +.13 when the effects of the L-R scale are partialled out.

We examined more closely the relationship between values and all three political action scales (protest, repression, and orthodox participation). On each postmaterialism scale, protest potential rises smoothly as a function of increasing postmaterialism and so does orthodox political participation. This lends support to Knutson's finding that the tendency toward self-actualization increases all forms of political participation. But the most interesting feature of this analysis is that repression potential is more strongly associated with materialism in the public values domain ($r = -.28$) than in the private domain ($r = -.20$). The element of "pro-public order" in the public-values battery may well be responsible for this and reemphasizes that the order-vs.-freedom political value dimension is strongest in the public domain while sheer personal efficacy and perhaps self-actualization is the strongest influence in the personal value domain.

What if those feelings should coincide? We noted earlier that there is only a modest correlation between respondents' positions in the two value domains of +.21. It is possible, however, that this low correlation is just an artifact of the skewed distributions of the two scales (especially at the postmaterialist end of the public value scale) combined with the strong tendency for intermediate, or neutral scores to accumulate ("neither important nor unimportant"), which contribute nothing to the linear association properties that are measured by the correlation coefficient. This would conceal the much closer relationship among extreme scorers who may coincide on both scales.

This must be a doubtful proposition because we know already that postmaterialists in the personal value domain do not share very similar social and ideological characteristics with postmaterialists in the public, political domain. This doubt is confirmed by analysis since we find that only 25 percent of postmaterialists on either scale are postmaterialists on both. These people will be referred to below as "integrated postmaterialists," and their scarcity may be due to a factor which drew speculation earlier. There is possibly quite a high proportion of public-domain postmaterialists who take up this position at least partly because they have unsatisfied personal *materialist* goals which they believe may be gratified by a movement towards a more equalitarian, less profit-motivated society. Materialism, on the other hand, is generally a less complicated outlook than postmaterialism and so we should expect a far greater proportion of materialists to take up a consistent position on both scales. But this is not so: "Integrated materialists" constitute only 16 percent of all materialists. Therefore the conclusion remains intact that the two value domains, contrary to Inglehart's thesis, are discontinuous. Yet, the curiosity we have expressed in the political behavior of those who take an integrated, consistent position in both value domains merits some persistence. It is possible that those in whom reside a complete set of postmaterialist choices may well possess special characteristics that exemplify, in a small group, the general trends that this chapter has explored so far.

A single, seven-point categorical variable was constructed thus:

|     |                              | %  |
| --- | ---------------------------- | -- |
| (1) | Integrated materialists      | 5  |
| (2) | Personal materialists        | 16 |
| (3) | Public materialists          | 9  |
| (4) | Intermediates                | 46 |
| (5) | Public postmaterialists      | 6  |
| (6) | Personal postmaterialists    | 14 |
| (7) | Integrated postmaterialists  | 5  |

Table 7.7 shows these combined value groups distributed by protest potential. Among the seven value groups, the integrated materialists are the least likely to protest but are only marginally less likely to do so than those who are materialists on only one scale—especially the personal values scale. Those having no strong preferences on either value scale (by far the largest group, of course) have an exactly average protest potential. But the situation at the other end of the scale, among the postmaterialists, is startlingly clear. Those showing postmaterialist preferences on one or the other scale show, as expected, a high protest potential but neither scale has a much greater impact upon protest than the other. Among our small group of integrated post-materialists, however, the commitment to protest behavior of some kind is almost total. Only 10 percent of the integrated postmaterialists would go no further than signing a petition compared with fully 60 percent (three times greater than average) who would consider illegal forms of protest and 46 percent (four and a half times greater than average) who would engage in every item in the scale.

Even more remarkable are the integrated postmaterialists' attitudes towards the repression potential scale items. Whereas less than 5 percent of all the materialists would deny the authorities' right to move in some way against noncompliant protesters and still only about 12 percent of the intermediates and (surprisingly) of the nonintegrated materialists would with-hold their consent for authority action, fully 49 percent of the integrated postmaterialists would do so. This finding may indicate that, unlike the generality of protesters that have been described so far, the commitment to protest of the integrated postmaterialists has a distinctly anarchic quality. Is this group the true representative of the popular idea of the protester as one who has departed entirely from the orthodox pathways of political redress? Not at all; even they have a higher-than-average conventional political participation score: 55 percent of them score high on the scale compared with 31 percent overall.

One obvious explanation of this finding would be that we have managed to isolate a small group of very young people. There are in fact 86 people in the group which weights down to 55 when the oversampling of the middle-class areas is taken into consideration. But this is not so. Certainly, only 7 percent of them are over the age of 64 compared with 65 percent of the integrated materialists and 23 percent overall, but only 17 percent of the integrated postmaterialists are under 21, and only a further 25 percent are under 30. Thus a narrow majority of this protest-prone group are actually middle-aged. Nor are they a group of extreme leftists. While it is true that only 20 percent of the integrated postmaterialists say they feel closest to the Conservative party, still less than a majority (37%) prefer Labour and a very large minority (30%) support the *Liberal party*. A majority of them are, of course, middle-class, and fully 42 percent enjoy full "professional and managerial" status, mostly in their own right or at least come from households who do.

Through an almost unreasonable persistence, then, we have isolated what may be described as quintessentially postmaterialist protest potential. But, in so doing, we have not explained protest; only a small minority of potential protesters fall into this rather specialized category: About 13 percent of all those who will consider illegal forms of protest are integrated postmaterialists. But to have isolated this group of young, middle-class, highly efficacious,

Table 7.7: Combined Value-Scale by Protest Potential (in percentages)

| Combination of Personal and Public Value Scales | (%) | No Pro-test | Peti-tions Only | Demon-strations | Boy-cotts | Strikes/ Rent Strikes | Occupations Blockades |
|---|---|---|---|---|---|---|---|
| (1) Materialist on both scales | (5) | 34 | 19 | 20 | 15 | 8 | 5 |
| (2) Materialist on private values | (16) | 36 | 21 | 18 | 12 | 7 | 7 |
| (3) Materialist on public values | (9) | 25 | 20 | 26 | 13 | 10 | 6 |
| (4) Neither materialist nor postmaterialist on either | (46) | 19 | 23 | 22 | 14 | 11 | 11 |
| (5) Postmaterialist on public values | (6) | 21 | 17 | 15 | 18 | 11 | 19 |
| (6) Postmaterialist on private values | (14) | 11 | 17 | 22 | 21 | 11 | 17 |
| (7) Postmaterialist on both scales | (5) | 3 | 7 | 17 | 13 | 15 | 46 |
|  | (100%) | | | | | | |

nondoctrinaire, integrated postmaterialist protesters has served a number of causes. It retrieves the essence of Inglehart's thesis insofar as demonstrating that when postmaterialism does thoroughly seize the minds of men (and they are mostly men, 69% in fact), it has remarkable properties to impart to their political motivation. If this value orientation should become more widespread, so also will protest potential. But the present scarcity of the phenomenon, occurring as it does among evidence of more widespread postmaterialist attitudes of a less well-integrated nature, casts more permanent doubt upon Inglehart's key theme that a new configuration of value preferences has lodged itself widely in the minds of the young *in a "stable and well-integrated" form.*

This finding also retrieves the reputation of survey research for penetration into specialized and subtle intersections of multitrait attitudes. Yet it would be difficult to press this line of inquiry very much further since it would necessarily drift into overspecialization and away from the macropsychological processes that are the central themes of this study. Instead, we shall try to advance our understanding of the relationship between political values and political behavior by returning to the parallel analysis of the two value scales. This return is made, however, in the surer knowledge that there lies at the intersection of the two scales a vastly accelerated, nonlinear function which has the power to impel the postmaterialist trend toward protest into an impressive commitment.

The differing nature of the influence of the two value scales suggests that the two different elements of postmaterialism that lie outside their crucial intersection will influence protest potential quite independently. Regression analysis determined that the multiple correlation between personal values, public values, and protest is greater than each zero-order relationship at +.34. The possibility still remains that this combined power to predict protest potential in a nonspecific, diffuse manner is still heavily dependent upon the other combined effects of age and social class. When the two demographic variables are added to the equation, the result in Table 7.8 is obtained.

While age remains the dominant influence on protest potential, the value scales each retain their power to predict protest independently of social class; the four variables together explaining 16 percent of the total variance. This

**Table 7.8: Stepwise Multiple Regression on Protest Potential**

| P-P score | Age | + | Personal Values | + | Public Values | + | Social Class | + | Constant Term |
|---|---|---|---|---|---|---|---|---|---|
| b (coefficients) | (.34) | + | (.18) | + | (.09) | + | (.09) | + | (3.17) |
| Standardized betas | (.33) | + | .21 | + | .11 | + | .07 | | |

Multiple correlation - .40; variance explained = 16%

may not sound a great deal, especially to a reader not familiar with the very high amount of random error variance present in general population survey data. But the equation does imply strong support for our original proposition that postmaterialist values are a powerful force in the growth of unorthodox political behavior. It follows then that strong support exists for Inglehart's basic thesis. Political change in Western Europe, characterised especially by the growth of new nonclass issues concerning participation, liberation, anti-industrialism, and the growth of unorthodox political behavior has been fueled by the growth of new value orientations.

One especially interesting implication of these data is that they reflect a continuity in British political culture rather than a new departure. On the Continent, especially in Germany, Inglehart's data describe a rupture in the political value system. Postmaterialist values appear suddenly among the youngest age cohort and materialism is the value of the old. Britain on the other hand has plenty of older postmaterialists *who also favor political radicalism*. The growth of postmaterialist protest among the young has not created a new constituency of age-based politics but has expanded upon an established constituency of middle-class radicalism. There is little conclusive proof we can offer for this suggestion, but it is appealing to think that the smooth continuity of change attributed to conventional British political life should also apply to British political aggression.

## Values, Dissatisfaction, and Protest

We began this chapter seeking an alternative conceptualization of relative deprivation that would carry more relevant political implications and which may predict protest potential better than does the straightforward deprivation of material and social advancement. The idea was simply that those whose political and personal needs included more than daily striving for material reward would find little opportunity to express their "higher-order" needs in the class-based and economically obsessed party politics of Britain. Being more aware and interested people generally, self-actualizers in Maslow's terminology, they would prove to be the people most likely to favor unorthodox experiments in political behavior. With many subtle and interesting qualifications, this seems broadly to be true. The most salient qualification is that postmaterialism is a stronger reflection of middle-class radicalism than of protest potential among working-class people.

These general conclusions raise one more important question and one which is difficult to conceptualize clearly. The problem concerns the linkage between subjective dissatisfaction and value priorities. We should expect the small number of protesters among the materialists to be especially sensitive to material deprivation in their lives. That is to say, materialists who feel they are receiving less than their proper entitlement of material rewards are obviously under pressure to protest and especially to strike. Not all of them will of course, but more of them should favor protest than materialists who feel relatively gratified. This is fairly straightforward. The position of the postmaterialists is more problematic.

We should expect that the postmaterialists who favor protest will be far more sensitive to *overall* relative deprivation. That is to say, the extra sources of life satisfaction that postmaterialists, or anyone else for that matter, will bring into focus when asked to judge his life as a whole will tend to resemble those things Maslow has characterized as higher-order concerns. Deprivation of overall life satisfaction will imply deprivation of higher-order needs. Those who say that they derive their life happiness more from the gratification of higher-order needs than from the gratification of material things, i.e., those who are postmaterialists on the personal-values scale, and who report overall relative deprivation, ought to be experiencing exactly the kind of motivation that spurs political aggression and protest.

Respondents were divided into three material satisfaction groups: "satisfied" (as much or more than entitlement), "dissatisfied" (one to three points less than entitlement) and "very dissatisfied" (more than three points less), and further divides each material satisfaction group into each value-type separately for each of the public and personal value scales and illustrates those high, medium and low on the protest scale for each group. This analysis was repeated for *overall* satisfaction groups.

From our analysis we are able to illustrate the effect of material dissatisfaction. The prediction is that dissatisfied materialists will show much higher levels of protest than satisfied materialists. This is so, but the effect is not great and is surprisingly more likely to occur in the *public* value domain than in the personal value domain. Because the personal value domain was consciously attuned to the life satisfaction measures themselves, it is logical to expect personal values to modify the behavioral outcomes of dissatisfaction far more effectively than public values but in the case of the materialists this is not so.

The complementary prediction is that postmaterialists will be unmoved by material satisfaction and those who feel they have achieved their *material* entitlement will be just as likely to protest as will those who feel materially deprived. This prediction is not supported by the data. Material satisfaction has a distinct dampening effect upon protest potential among postmaterialists in both value domains. This would be less surprising in the public domain than in the private-domain because public postmaterialists indicate they are *less* materially gratified and more materially demanding than the private-domain materialists. But material gratification also has the same dampening effect upon protest potential in the important personal sphere where postmaterialists indicated greater material gratification and are less demanding, as befits the advanced Maslovian development imputed to them. Postmaterialists ought not to be "bought off" in this way, even if gratified Postmaterialists do still have a higher protest score than the (extremely low) score of gratified materialists.

Certainly, the postmaterialist effect is far more powerful than the effect of material satisfaction to the extent that *materially satisfied postmaterialists* have a marginally higher protest potential than *materially very dissatisfied materialists*, in both domains. Perhaps also it is rather pious to expect postmaterialists to appear in a saintly light, pushing aside their chances of material gratification to grapple personally with the social and political problems of the day. Yet there is no doubt that this kind of result casts new doubts upon the real nature *underlying* motivational properties of postmaterialist value priorities. We turn now to the results of the overall satisfaction measure.

If the results of the second analysis with the overall dissatisfaction measure had been presented alone, the doubts discussed above would not arise. Postmaterialists who are dissatisfied with their lives *overall* are very much more likely to protest, by a factor of two, than are postmaterialists who feel they are achieving full satisfaction in their lives whereas materialists are relatively unmoved in the direction of protest by overall dissatisfaction. But the patterning of the results is similar to that obtained for material satisfaction which suggests strongly a theoretically inconvenient conclusion that material satisfaction is as great a component of overall satisfaction for postmaterialists as it is for materialists. This can be easily tested.

The squared correlation coefficient estimates the amount of variance in overall satisfaction that is explained by material satisfaction. For the sample as a whole, this estimate is 28 percent but we should predict that this figure will be much lower among postmaterialists than among materialists and that this will be especially true for postmaterialists in the personal value domain. The material-overall satisfaction statistic for each value type was correlated for the sample as a whole and for each of four social groups: young and old, middle-class and working-class. Put in plain terms, our hypothesis is that among materialists there will be few people who are happy but poor or who are rich but unhappy. Among postmaterialists such conditions, and especially the latter, will be far more common, thus lowering the value of our measure of association.

The results lend only meagre support to our hypothesis. The two measures of satisfaction are a little less closely aligned among personal postmaterialists than among materialists but not much difference is observable between postmaterialists and materialists in the public domain. An apparent absence of association for young middle-class postmaterialists is due in fact to the correlation coefficient vanishing due in turn to a small drift of people away from the satisfied/satisfied condition on both scales toward, ironically, a condition implying satisfaction with life *overall* but dissatisfaction with *material reward*. Exactly the same thing happens among young working-class materialists, which is a more suitable result in their case.

The actual magnitude of the relationship between the two satisfaction scales gives us some interesting insights into the problem. Overall, about 48 percent of the sample feel they are getting less than their just deserts on both scales. About 18 percent feel happy but poor, 24 percent feel content on both scales, while only 10 percent feel rich but unhappy. This last figure is no larger among postmaterialists than among materialists, it is precisely 10 percent for each value group, and there is a slight tendency for postmaterialists to be less satisfied on both scales than are the materialists. Our pilot survey concluded:

> Postbourgeois are distinguished from acquisitives by their relative youth, wealth and education, *and by their concern for ideology.* The content of this ideology is likely to be biased toward a liberal and humanitarian disposition. But it seems that the British postbourgeois embraces a mode of ideological thought that is appropriate to his chronological age in *addition to*, not at the *expense of*, the materialism approximate to his times and to his social class.[6]

The results of this far more exhaustive investigation indicate that in the public value domain at least, this conclusion is vindicated. On the other hand, postmaterialists isolated in the personal value domain do seem to have more consistency and slightly less overtly materialistic views, but not very much.

As we said at the outset, Inglehart's developed view that postmaterialists merely set themselves higher standards of subjective satisfaction than materialists is not very helpful to his theory. It simply creates the image of a young, rich, postmaterialist demonstrating for social justice while privately yearning for a second new car and a larger color television. And this image is intended to be only partly flippant; perhaps it captures something of what is occurring. The postmaterialist phenomenon in Britain has caught a generation of young middle-class people desperately trying to maximize both higher-order *and* materialist needs. In a way, the British economy has let them down. If Britain's industrial output, starting from a relatively high base, had expanded and the economy become enriched over the past few years at the same rate as Germany, France, or Italy, it would be a massively rich country. The postmaterialists, whose attitudes were forming when Britain was still a relatively rich and certainly a very secure country, could now relax and get on with maximizing their higher-order concerns without any real personal economic worries. As it is, many of them find themselves with mortgages they cannot afford and a taste for a liberal-bourgeois lifestyle now beyond the pocket of all but the more successful left-wing Hampstead lawyer or publisher. This conclusion is not intended to expose hypocrisy but to explain a puzzling phenomenon. We should not always expect people to have a logically consistent set of views. It is quite possible to demand freedom and participation for the nation and cash and security for oneself and to use aggressive and unorthodox political action to do so, even if one is objectively already better off than one's fellows, and remain perfectly sincere. It just makes one's motivation very difficult to detect unambiguously through the use of survey data.

Nor should these equivocal attempts to probe for a motivational base for postmaterialist protest be allowed to mask the basic and important conclusion of this chapter. The growth of protest potential among the young, while often concerned with demands for better material conditions, is strongly influenced by the need to maximize other goals which include the creation of a more humane, sensitive, and concerned community. This conclusion does not spring from rhetoric, it rests on empirical observation.

But postindustrial politics may have a darker side. Samuel P. Huntington, prompted perhaps by his unsympathetic reception by demonstrators at several universities, speculates that postmaterial politics may not be at all benign. He notes as we do (Marsh 1975) that postindustrial values are both a product of *and* a reaction against postindustrial society. After all, postindustrial society is called such only because greater and more powerful industrial complexes have become more productive to allow the migration of a majority of the workforce into the service sector and other more or less nonproductive areas. Yet, it remains nonetheless a highly materialist and industrial economy and postindustrial values disapprove of crass industrialism; hence the environmental movement. Thus there will develop a conflict between postmaterialist ideology and the institutions that are still required to keep the machines turning. New political tensions will be generated and improved education will further fuel a clamor of articulate demands beyond the capacity of government to satisfy them. The increased redundancy of the economic class-based parties will open up new opportunities for ad hoc leaders to conjure new social movements. Lacking a base in class conflict, these new movements will lack also a coherent and mature body of ideological tradition and will tend easily to take on an idiosyncratic and even neurotic character. An understanding of this thesis would certainly lead one to expect a correspondence between postmaterialist values and protest potential. That it should emerge in a democratic and stable but not especially overadvanced country like Britain is considerable evidence in favor of the thesis that this relationship is part of a serious change in political alignments and political participation.

But it is probably Alain Touraine who provides the most insightful suggestion about the direction in which postmaterialist protest is headed. He characterizes the postindustrial world as a programmed society ruled by technocrats. These will be the new guardians of knowledge, and it is access to the control of the flow of information that will be the key to power in the postindustrial system. Certainly they will try to maximize a much wider range of goals than those, depending upon which traditional orientation they spring from, of profit or surplus value (and it does not really matter which), but their rule, ironically, may be just as authoritarian as the captains of industry and the bourgeois politicians they have supplanted. Huntingdon also agrees that a postindustrial government will need to have access to more obviously authoritarian forms of power if it is to control or even respond effectively to the demands thrown up by an increasingly idiosyncratic polity that becomes less and less amenable to control through institutionalization and incorporation.

We stated earlier that we felt that postmaterialists were interested in power. With their social and educational background it could scarcely be otherwise. It is from the ranks of today's young middle-class postmaterialists that Touraine's technocrats will be recruited. They may not change their views as they approach power. There is good evidence that value orientations are enduring (see Rokeach). Nor may they abandon their present belief in protest methods and may even seek out ways to improve informal channels of communication between the masses and the elite. But the most obvious conclusion about their protest motivation is still uppermost. It has less to do with altruism and much more to do with their urge to hasten the day when the existing elites have been ousted by themselves.

# NOTES

1. Inglehart (1971) pp. 997 and 1001 (my emphasis).

2. Inglehart, R., *The Silent Revolution*. Chicago, forthcoming.

3. It should be noted though, that Knutson's empirical evidence is based upon a self-completion questionnaire survey of timber factory workers, which achieved a response-rate of only 13% (see Knutson, 1972, pp. 178), and so may be open to charges of bias.

4. This is partly due to the retired members of the sample ignoring "job" in their rankings.

5. I am grateful for the help of Russell Dalton in constructing this index.

6. Marsh 1975, p. 28.

*Chapter 8*

# A STUDENT REVOLUTION?

The prospect of yet another discussion of student protest might justifiably provoke a bored sigh from any reader well-acquainted with current political science. Even an adequate review of the literature would double the length of this volume. Equally, no study seriously addressed to the psychology of political protest can ignore the phenomenon. What is required, therefore, is that any fresh contribution should have something genuinely new to offer. So what follows is a systematic comparison between the political attitudes and actions of British students and those of the general population we have examined thus far. Such a comparison is obviously important: Are student activists the self-indulgent outliers of the political community they are often painted as, or are they really an integrated part of a single political process? It is extraordinary, therefore, that such a study has never been attempted before. Accordingly, our general population questionnaire was administered, in the same form, to a sample of 289 university and polytechnic students throughout Great Britain (see Appendix for details).

We have now reached, in this volume, a fairly mature point in our understanding of the factors that contribute to protest potential in the wider political community. We may take the outline of this understanding as the basis for a comparative framework among the student sample, and we shall be guided by a generalized null hypothesis that among students the antecedents of protest will be similar to those found among the national sample, only more so.

First, are students more protest-prone than other people? Yes, of course they are. More than half the student sample claim to have participated in a lawful demonstration of some kind and only 6 percent say they would never do so. This contrasts with only 6 percent among the general population who have participated and 43 percent say they would never do so. Twenty-one percent of students also claim to have participated in some kind of nonlegal demonstration (occupations, etc.) and voice high levels of support for rent strikes (53% approve) and even unofficial strikes (36%). Interestingly though, their views on political violence are far more closely aligned with those of the wider community. Only 2 percent approve of violence and 86 percent say they would never contemplate its use.

As in our pilot study, the same unidimensional structure of attitude toward protest emerges among students as among others ($\theta$ Rep= .97) and this provides an early confirmation of our null-hypothesis: structurally students' attitudes resemble the commonly held pattern. When the protest potential scale is constructed in exactly the same way as described in Chapter 2, the aggregate difference in student attitudes becomes apparent. More than half the students endorse every point on the scale. Students are, of course, much younger than the population average and we know that younger people generally have a much higher protest potential. The following table compares the student sample with members of the national sample of the same age.

| | No Protest | Petitions Only | Lawful Demon-strations | Boycotts | Rent Strikes/ Strikes | Occupations/ Blockades |
|---|---|---|---|---|---|---|
| | % | % | % | % | % | % |
| National sample (18-22) | 9 | 17 | 20 | 17 | 13 | 24 |
| Student sample | 1 | 4 | 11 | 12 | 19 | 53 |

Holding age constant, therefore, we find that students are more than twice as likely to protest than are their peers in the general population. Predictably, then, when we asked students the follow-up question, "Are there ever times when it is justified to break the law to protest?" 86 percent agreed there were. They went on to elaborate many political scenarios they felt might override their duty to the law, concentrating mainly upon situations involving threats to civil rights and political freedom. Thirty percent also thought violence might be justified, much for the same reasons.

This very high protest potential among students was matched by a correspondingly low repression potential (r = -0.41). Whereas only 12 percent of the national sample would withhold all forms of constraint upon protesters (i.e., the use of courts, police, government bans, or troops) 58 percent of students would deny their use, and 92 percent would sanction no action beyond the use of courts or police.

Students are also widely convinced of the effectiveness of protest and their effectiveness-scores predict their protest potential with the same accuracy as was found in the national sample (r = 0.50). Given such enthusiasm for protest and such wholesale rejection of official constraint, one may feel entitled to predict that here we may also locate a rupture between orthodox and unorthodox forms of political action. Yet one would also be wrong. Among students there is a much *stronger* positive relationship (r = 0.41) between the protest scale and the conventional participation scale. This impressive and perhaps unexpected versatility of political action is accompanied by higher levels of conventional party activity among students than are present in the national sample, particularly so, compared with others of their own age.

At this point we may retain our null-hypothesis: Structurally, students share the same *kinds* of attitudes towards political action and differ only in aggregate levels. Before we may proceed further and examine the correlates and causes of this large aggregate difference, a small technical problem must be resolved. So great is the aggregate difference that students' scores on the nationally based protest potential scale are severely skewed toward the upper end of its range. What must be done is to construct an additive scale combining the approval and behavioral intention scores for each scale item using the full four-point item scores. For use in tables, the range of the resultant score from 16 (i.e., a minimum score of one for "disapprove strongly" and "would never do" for each protest item) through 64 (a maximum score of four for each) will be divided into equal thirds. The reader will have to remember that, in comparative terms between the students and the national sample, "low" means at least "medium"; "medium" means at least "high"; and "high" means, well, "student protest."

A seminal finding in the study of the student protest movement in the United States showed that students from wealthier middle-class homes were more prone to protest than were those from less advantaged backgrounds. This sparked off much of the "post-industrial" speculation discussed in the previous chapter. In Britain, though, this is simply not the case. Students from working-class homes are actually a little more likely to protest than others. This too, incidentally, is the case among European students. Comparing German and American students, Klaus Allerbeck has written: "The affluence-radicalism correlation in the U.S. is no causal relation but a by-product of the relations of political ideology and social stratification which are not the same in the U.S. and in Germany." In Britain, the radical traditions of the working class (if such they are) are carried aloft no more vehemently than by those young people it exports into the middle class by way of higher education (cf., Abrams' work on British middle-class socialists).

We noted earlier that while men tend generally to have a higher protest potential than women, this difference is less pronounced among younger respondents. Among the students, this difference actually vanishes; women students are equally as politically aggressive as men students and, compared to women (even young women) in the general population, that is very aggressive indeed.

Another finding common in previous work showed that students reading arts subjects (i.e., the liberal humanities and most social sciences) were much more protest-prone than their colleagues reading material science. This fact has been held to be evidence that, in *choosing* to read arts subjects, these students are reflecting the underlying liberal sensitivity that also makes them easy to mobilize in political protest movements on arrival at college. No-one, however, has really been able to show conclusively whether arts students arrive in this state of radical readiness or whether it arises soon after as a product of their experiences which include of course their teaching.

This survey replicates the traditional finding that arts students are generally more protest-prone than the scientists. The timing of this survey also gives some leverage upon the second problem. Students were interviewed during the first few weeks of the academic year. Table 8.1 compares arts and science students separately for first, second and third years of study. We find, surprisingly, that these students have arrived at university with a uniformly high protest potential undifferentiated by their chosen field of learning. By the second year (assuming, if we may, cross-sectional data to have a measure of longitudinal validity), the arts students have increased their protest potential considerably, but the scientists have not. Among the third-years, arts students have become even more committed to protest, but still the scientists have not responded beyond their initial levels—high though these might be in general terms. One is reminded of a delightful cartoon in *Punch*

**Table 8.1: Protest Potential Among Students by Field and Year of Study (in percentages)**

|  |  | Protest Potential | | |
|---|---|---|---|---|
|  |  | Low | Medium | High |
| First Year | Arts | 33 | 42 | 25 |
|  | Science | 38 | 39 | 23 |
| Second Year | Arts | 37 | 22 | 41 |
|  | Science | 45 | 30 | 25 |
| Third Year | Arts | 26 | 43 | 46 |
|  | Science | 46 | 32 | 22 |

magazine showing two science students, test tubes in hand, gazing wistfully through their laboratory window at a political demonstration in the quadrangle below. "It's alright for these social scientists," one complains, "It's a sort of practical for them."

## The Students and the Left

Students do not shun party political activity, far from it, but what is the ideological direction of their involvement in conventional politics? A common view holds that what real party support comes from students usually benefits parties of the left. Like other conventional wisdoms examined above, this view is mistaken. Twenty-seven percent of students support the Conservatives, an extraordinarily high 31 percent favour the Liberal party, and only 21 percent declare for Labour. The survey was conducted during a brief but strong rise in Liberal fortunes nationally, but to find them the largest single party among students was very surprising. Labour supporters are augmented on the left by 4 percent giving allegiance to the Communist party and 3 percent to other parties of the Socialist left, and by 9 percent who remain politically unattached but not uncommitted. Nearly all the latter placed themselves on the left side of the left-right continuum, as did many Liberals (unlike Liberal supporters nationally) giving an overall impression of a left-leaning body of students. The Labour party, however, is by no means the principal beneficiary of this tendency.

Are these leftist tendencies also associated with very high levels of protest potential? We find, of course, that they are. Only 10 percent of Conservative students score in the "ultra-high" category though many retain a level of protest potential that might alarm the Conservative Central Office, and which has in the past spawned Tory "ginger-groups" like the Bow group. Among the large left-central bloc of Liberals this figure rises to 26 percent, just below the population mean for students. As soon as the left is encountered, however, the "ultra-high" category inflates to 50 percent among Labour students and to more than 60 percent among the Socialist and unattached left. Not one of the non-Communist Socialist left has anything like a low protest potential, even in student terms. Unsurprisingly, therefore, the left-right self-placement scale correlates with protest potential at $r = 0.59$. This is precisely the kind of relationship we looked for in the national sample and failed to find because of unexpectedly high levels of protest potential among young rightists. Student rightists also have their own measure of protest potential, but they are scarcely in the same league as the student protesters of the left. This factor will have to be taken constantly into account as the comparative analysis unfolds.

This very strong association between student protest and leftism may hint to some of revolution. Have we encountered among the student sample a large cadre of the revolutionary left? It seems unlikely. Almost none favor the use of violence against person or property. It is true that 30 percent were not prepared to rule out the possibility altogether, but then 15 percent of the general population also held that view. If we take a generously wide view of revolution and include the British Communist party alongside the International Socialists, the International Marxist Group and others of the openly revolutionary Left, they still muster less than 9 percent of the student body even as sympathizers. A sizeable enough minority, to be sure, but by no means large enough to support the idea that dedicated revolutionary sentiment lies behind the bulk of student protest potential.

Another clue to the ideological quality of student leftism lies in the definitions given of the left and right following their self-placement on the continuum scale. Unlike the general population, students were very articulate, but it was very noticeable that very few students (9%) of the right or the left, specifically mentioned the Labour party as representing the left. Most went further to describe the left as some kind of *non revolutionary* socialist position (55%) coupled often with some elaborated notion of movement toward increased social and economic equity (23%). The key to understanding student leftism probably lies in their attitude towards the Labour party. Table 8.2 compares the sympathy-scores (zero through 100) given by students for all the political groupings with those described in Chapter 4 for the national sample. Comparatively and actually, the Labour party is not well regarded by students. It features well down in the list together with the

Table 8.2: Comparison of Sympathy Scores among Students and
National Sample

| Students | 0-100 Score | National Sample | 0-100 Score |
|---|---|---|---|
| Colored immigrants | 65 | Police | 80 |
| Police | 63 | Small businessmen | 70 |
| Liberal party | 57 | Clergy | 61 |
| Small businessmen | 56 | Civil servants | 56 |
| Student protesters | 55 | Liberal party | 52 |
| Women's liberation | 50 | Labour party | 49 |
| Trade unions | 49 | Trade unions | 49 |
| Civil servants | 48 | Conservative party | 47 |
| Clergy | 47 | Colored immigrants | 46 |
| Labour party | 43 | Company directors | 41 |
| Conservative party | 38 | Women's liberation | 35 |
| Revolutionary groups | 37 | Student protesters | 25 |
| Company directors | 33 | Revolutionary groups | 16 |

Conservative party and company directors. The *least* favored groups, though, are still revolutionary groups even though they are better regarded than they are among the national sample. Less-than-revolutionary-left groups are much more highly rated (e.g., Women's Liberation, student protesters). Blacks receive almost universal sympathy from students, far more than from the general population, but then so do the Liberal party, small businessmen, and most of all the *police*. Even many extreme leftists were prepared to indicate a better than neutral feeling toward the police. This finding must surely draw some of the sting from the image of student protesters as embryonic revolutionaries however left they say they are.

Such an ambivalent picture is typical of a polarized community. When the factor analysis conducted in Chapter 4 is replicated for students including all the sympathy-scores, the L-R scale, and the three behavior scales, the confusion lessens considerably. Table 8.3 shows clearly that, unlike the national sample, student attitudes polarize along a dominant "radical protest" dimension which accounts for 36 percent of the total variance. Loading heavily on this factor are all three behavior scales (with repression potential loading negatively of course along with the Conservative party and "rightism"), the trade unions, students, revolutionaries, Women's Liberation, and the blacks;

**Table 8.3: Factor Analysis\* of Behavior Scales, Sympathy Scores, and Left-Right Scale**

|  | Factor I | Factor II | Factor III | Communalities |
|---|---|---|---|---|
| Protest potential | .71 | −.42 |  | .68 |
| Repression potential | −.40 |  |  | .24 |
| Conventional participation | .43 |  |  | .20 |
| Liberal party |  | .50 |  | .28 |
| Small businessmen |  | .67 |  | .50 |
| Women's liberation | .68 |  |  | .47 |
| Revolutionary groups | .84 |  |  | .74 |
| Labour party |  |  | .60 | .54 |
| Colored immigrants | .57 |  |  | .38 |
| Conservative party | −.53 | .57 |  | .62 |
| Student protesters | .61 |  |  | .38 |
| Civil servants |  | .57 |  | .37 |
| Police |  | .69 |  | .60 |
| Company directors |  | .68 |  | .64 |
| Clergy |  | .50 |  | .26 |
| Trade unions | .70 |  |  | .57 |
| "Right-ism" | −.67 |  |  | .64 |
| Percentage of total variance | 36% | 15% | 6% |  |
| Percentage of common variance | 69% | 24% | 7% |  |

\*Principal axis solution rotated to varimax criteria.

but *not* the Labour party. The second, less important factor reflects the same pro- and antiestablishment factor found in the national sample. This factor attracts high loadings from the Tories (again), the Liberals, small business-men, civil servants, the police, company directors, and the clergy. Again, unlike the national sample, protest potential loads (negatively) on this factor too. Thus protest is a pervasive action concept that features in every dimen-sion of student political thought, except one: We still have not encountered the Labour party, which emerges finally as a single-item third factor all on its own. The Labour party is almost an entirely neutral element among students, it simply will not fit into the major polarities of their political attitudes. There is actually a zero correlation between sympathy for Labour and for the Tories. So, whereas many people in the wider community mutter about the two major parties being as bad as each other, students have actually inter-nalized this sentiment. Like the snapping of a lynchpin in a highly stressed mechanical structure, this studied indifference towards the one major cleav-age in the conventional political system in Britain causes the structure of student ideology to fly into a new pro-and-anti radicalism configuration.

Despite all this, it is still difficult to believe in student protest as a wellspring of socialist revolution. For student leftists, though, there are more alternatives to the Labour party than revolution. What we have found is probably well summarized by the current title of the coalition of Left groups that holds the majority on the executive of the National Union of Students. They call themselves "The Broad Left." Some are "revolutionaries" most certainly, but they are never the dominant influence.

## The Sources of Student Activism and Ideology

### AGGRESSIVE COMPETENCE

If higher education is any preparation for citizenship, it must be supposed that students will have high levels of political competence and that protest potential will be linked to this competence. Their high participation rates would anyway imply this. To take the simplest measure: 67 percent profess more than a passing interest in politics compared with 46 percent among the national sample, and the extent of this interest correlates positively with protest potential ($r=0.42$), and even more so with conventional participation ($r=0.68$) by accounting for the nonprotest political activities of the Tory students.

Students' answers to the two Almond and Verba questions concerning possible actions to oppose new laws that are felt to be unjust brought forth a wide array of efficacious plans. Only 12 percent said they would remain inactive while up to 80 percent would use formal channels of redress (M.P.s, councillors, parties, officials, etc.). Twenty percent would organize petitions, 14 percent would use the news media, 19 percent would create informal action groups, and 12 percent would specifically *organize* marches or other forms of demonstration. This graphically illustrates the versatile duality of student political activity, even on the left. They are not all out of touch with the "system"–whatever they may feel about it.

We have already described the elaborate cognitive skills shown by students in defining left and right. Similarly high levels of political conceptualization are reflected in their likes and dislikes of the two major parties. Sixty-three percent of all students used at least one ideological concept to describe their views and usually more. The use of ideological concepts outnumbered other usages by five to one. It may be concluded fairly, then, that students are vastly more politically sophisticate–in cognitive terms at least–than are the general population and so they ought to be. However, when we turn to the more inferential and affective scale measure of political efficacy used in Chapter 5, the comparison becomes far more problematic.

In their excellent study of British undergraduates in five universities, Citrin and Elkins discuss a fascinating problem. Many politically knowledgeable people–like students–tend to make a distinction between two kinds of political efficacy. They may believe they have high *personal* efficacy, i.e., they are the kind of people with the personal acumen and ability to influence politics. Equally, they may believe also that the political *system* is massively *unresponsive* even to the entreaties of personally efficacious people like themselves. Traces of this problem were found in the general population and are discussed in the Appendix dealing with scale construction. Now among the student sample the problem becomes acute. Students are personally efficacious. They are much less likely than others to agree that they "have no say," that "voting is the only way to influence things," and that "politics is too complicated to understand," but they are much *more* likely to agree that "officials don't care," that "MPs lose touch" and that "parties are only interested in votes not opinions." The cause of this sudden divorce between the two halves of the ISR efficacy scale, between personal efficacy and system responsiveness is *cynicism*. Students are, if it is possible, even more cynical about politics than are the general population. When the political trust scale is constructed in exactly the same manner as previously, the comparison is as follows:

| Political Trust (in percentages) | High | Medium | Low | Very Low |
|---|---|---|---|---|
| National sample | 24 | 32 | 28 | 16 |
| Students | 17 | 31 | 25 | 28 |

Cynicism expressed on the three "system responsiveness" items correlates with that expressed in the trust scale very closely (r=0.62) and each of these expressions of cynicism correlates with the left-right scale at r=0.40 and 0.56 respectively. It follows then that each predicts protest potential comprehensively (r=0.45 and 0.50 respectively). Student protesters are not merely leftists, they are articulate cynical leftists.

Personal efficacy is not directly related to protest potential because it is also common among Conservative students. The interesting question is whether personal efficacy combines interactively with cynicism and high levels of conceptualization to accelerate protest potential into ultra-high levels. Here we may test the general theory of aggressive political competence derived in Chapter 5 from the general population. In this way, the polarized student sample may be used as a crucible to test a general theory. The results are entirely positive. Where high efficacy, high conceptualization, and political cynicism are all present, there too will be found an almost undiluted concentration of the highest levels of student protest. Where only two elements are present, and especially where cynicism is absent, protest potential subsides to more modest levels. Where trust is high and efficacy absent, we find a small haven for inactive apolitical students. The only exception to the pattern is the *same* exception found in the general sample: Highly cynical students with high conceptualization but *low* efficacy still have a very high protest potential. Their cynicism is so complete that they seem to be standing with fists clenched in a state of inefficacious yet politically aggressive rage. Mercifully perhaps, there are only about a dozen of them in the sample.

It would be difficult with such small numbers to try and disentangle this three-way interaction from the pervasive influence of leftism. Yet it may be fairly concluded that the presence among students of this interaction, this three-levered trigger of protest, provides a strong theoretical continuity of the underlying causes of protest potential. The theory works even in the heated atmosphere of the student political community and so predicts with almost clinical accuracy their much higher aggregate levels of protest action.

## POLITICIZED DISSATISFACTION

Citrin and Elkins concluded that "although we surveyed students from many different backgrounds during the peak of recent student radicalism in Britain, very few of their responses could be construed as general denunciations of their country or its government." On the other hand, Citrin and Elkins survey took place in 1968 during a period of Labour government. While we know that the class of 1974 has no great love of Labour, those in this sample were watching a Tory government move into the last fatal moves of a confrontation with a core element of the Labour movement. Therefore the leftist cynicism of student protesters ought to be a strong agent in linking protest action to dissatisfaction with specific areas of government failure.

Overall (cf., Citrin and Elkins) students appear not much more critical of government performance than are the general population. Only in the areas of racial equality, housing, and economic equality is the proportion of students saying the government is doing a bad job significantly greater than it is among the national sample. But these marginal differences conceal much wider partisan differences among students than among the blander and less polarized attitudes of the general population. Tory students were generous in their praise of Edward Heath's government; left students were derisive. Thus each area of dissatisfaction correlates highly with protest potential in a range of $r=0.33$ (caring for the elderly) through $r=0.49$ (economic equality) except for pollution control ($r=0.01$) and crime control ($r=0.19$). These last two items also drew criticism from conservative students. The overall dissatisfaction-with-government index correlates very strongly with protest potential ($r=0.54$) and, of course, also with cynicism ($r=0.61$), system unresponsiveness ($r=0.48$) and leftism ($r=0.57$). What is being uncovered then is a syndrome of aggressive cynical leftism among students that is well polarized in an anti-government direction.

## POSTMATERIALISM

The previous chapter was written with due regard for the student protest movement. Without the fact of the 1968 movement and its aftermath, Inglehart's postmaterialism thesis would have little relevance. Even among the general population we found that the theory had considerable utility in explaining protest potential among those people for whom the idea of postmaterialism was itself relevant, i.e., among the young middle classes. It follows, therefore, that the student sample ought to manifest high levels of postmaterialist value choices. Indeed they do: On the original four-item "order and prices—vs.—freedom and participation" index, those choosing the pure post-acquisitve position are more than three times more numerous than among the national sample (33%) and only 8 percent compared with 24 percent chose the materialist pole. So too with the more elaborated choices: In the political value domain 48 percent of students placed "moving toward a society where ideas are more important than money" among their three most important choices compared with only 19 percent of the national sample. Students accorded similarly higher priorities to movement toward a more friendly society and increased participation while they almost all poured derision on the need for strong defense forces (52% thought it *least* important). They were also far more ready to look askance at the importance of economic growth. Again unlike the national sample they were relatively neutral about the need to fight crime. On the other hand, the pattern of the students' choices revealed among the personal value items, more closely resemble those of the general population. They too placed greatest value upon their health and their family and social life. They assigned much less value to their housing, but this merely reflects their transient status. Other differences are reflected in fairly subtle shifts of emphasis away from the value of personal respect, job, and material standard of living towards higher priorities for freedom and democracy, leisure interests, education, and the arts. All this is predictable enough yet also gratifying from an empirical point of view and from Inglehart's too. The student community is indeed the fountainhead of postmaterialist sentiment and had it not been found to be so, the previous chapter would have taken on a strange aspect. A crucial theoretical question now arises: Is the postmaterialist persuasion also connected to aggressive political action among the student community as were the trends that were found in the national sample or is it after all merely a mood or an affectation common to many students and which has few political connotations?

The evidence favors the first conclusion to an almost spectacular extent. Taking first the four-item scale, we find that among the materialists only 10% exhibit ultra-high levels of protest potential; among the intermediate or mixed-values group this figure is an averagely high 23 percent; among the postacquisitives it leaps to 57 percent ($r=0.40$). Figure 8.1 plots the proportion scoring high on the trichonised protest scale for increasing levels of postmaterialism in both value domains determined by the elaborated batteries. In the political ($r=0.53$) and the personal value domains ($r=.24$) protest potential rises dramatically as postmaterialism increases but the political value scale obviously has the greatest effect on the greatest *number*. Thus the overlying political dimension of postmaterialism seems more important among students. We find too, that the political P-M scale is quite strongly connected to leftism ($r=.30$) and to system unresponsiveness ($r=0.48$) while the personal scale is not ($r=0.14$ and $0.09$ respectively). The two scales are more strongly interrelated than in the national sample ($r=0.30$) but not as closely as one might expect or as the Maslovian aspects of Inglehart's theory would predict. Again the two value domains seem to exercise fairly independent influences upon political action. It is a very powerful influence and fully vindicates Inglehart's original thesis that value change was a seminal force in the radical youth and student movement in Europe in the late 1960s.

Because it is *political* postmaterialism that has emerged uppermost in the student sample, it is impossible to resist the temptation to cast another glance toward the paradox that has haunted the role of the postmaterialism concept right from the pilot project. Are these student postmaterialists—the parvenus of protest—really so materially replete that their motivation to protest is expressed in leftist and equalitarian sentiments solely out of altruistic concern

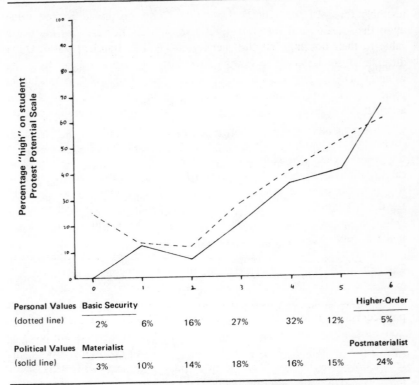

Figure 8.1: PROTEST POTENTIAL BY POSTMATERIALISM/STUDENTS

for those less well placed than themselves? It hardly seems likely and nor is it so. Students are *less* materially satisfied than the general population, scoring a mean of 6.1 on the Cantril scale compared with 6.7. Most students, probably rightly, expect this situation to improve within five years (7.5) but regard this as no less than their due—they presently feel entitled to even more (8.0). This material dissatisfaction is actually *positively* correlated—just—with post-materialism (r=0.10). As evidenced by continual agitation over student grants and rents for campus accommodation, material dissatisfaction is also strongly and directly linked to protest potential (r=0.35). So even among these parvenus of the postindustrial estate, Maslovian development is still contaminated with material self-interest in a distinctly nonlinear progression toward enlightenment. Again we do not wish to claim to have exposed hypocrisy but merely to have described an interesting and complex duality of thought and conflicting motivation of a kind that is perfectly human but quite ruinous to the elegant theories of political psychologists.

## First Steps toward an Integrated Theory of Protest Potential

Comparing this sample of students with the general population, one can see what Converse means by "levels of constraint" in political belief systems. Among the wider community, the search for linkages between personal feelings and circumstances and political action was complex and the answers subtle, even indistinct. Among the students the main effects just leap up off the computer output: an integrated syndrome of aggressive left-wing post-materialist ideological dissatisfaction is clearly responsible for the ultra-high levels of student protest. A basis willingness to protest is certainly present in new undergraduates and is no doubt partly associated with an imitative acceptance of the role of a student as they believe it to be. As soon as they enter student life, many students become socialized into this pervasive syndrome of protest politics. This seems especially true for students whose chosen field of learning involves the study of society. This is not to say that students who adopt this integrated political stance do so because they are looking for something to occupy their spare time and are easily influenced. Many of them choose to enter radical politics for rational and sound reasons. Why does anyone enter politics? Unless they are the complete Machiavellian and (initially anyway) few are, they act because they are *moved* by something: an idea, an issue, a cause, or whatever excites or outrages them. Many student radicals will go on to full political careers, others to professional careers linked closely to the political process. They cannot all be irrationally seduced by a simple leftist creed. The influence of leftism is indeed strong, but is it entirely pervasive? What is now required is some means of assessing the relative independence of the various elements of student protest that have been examined above. Do they function at all independently or is it all down to leftism?

As a first step in considering this question, all the main predictor variables considered above were included in a factor analysis together with one additional variable: dissatisfaction with education. Using the Cantril self-anchoring scale once more, students had indicated how satisfied or dissatisfied they were with their education. The majority indicated some degree of satisfaction but feelings of dissatisfaction were quite closely linked with protest potential ($r=0.37$).

A principal axis solution was obtained and rotated to varimax criteria. Three factors emerged. Protest potential, the DGP index, leftism, cynicism, and system unresponsiveness all loaded on *both* the first two factors. The first factor was dominant, accounting for 30 percent of the total variance and 74 percent of the common variance, and also included both the postmaterialism domains thus indicating a dominant "postmaterialist-leftism" factor linked to protest potential. On the second factor accounting for only 12 percent of the total variance, the core variables were joined by material dissatisfaction and dissatisfaction with education indicating a "dissatisfaction-protest" axis. The third factor (10% of the total variance) was made up of cynicism and system unresponsiveness leading yet again together with personal efficacy indicating that their rather subtle interactive relationship occurs outside the mainstream of leftist politics. Yet, this is clearly an artificial result. There are so many cross-factor loadings, the orthogonality of the factors is a fiction. Excluding the interactive effects of personal efficacy, what is clearly suggested is that a single linear model is the most appropriate explanatory strategy.

The analysis then proceeded by way of stepwise multiple regression techniques to identify those variables having the greatest predictive power toward protest potential accompanied by the least interdependence between them. The technique is deployed more extensively in the following Chapter and is explained there in more detail. Briefly what happens is that the technique selects the best predictor and, controlling for that highest correlation, searches for the variable with the highest partial correlation with protest potential. Then, controlling for these two simultaneously, it looks for the next highest partial and so on. After considerable experimentation it was found that six variables formed the most parsimonious linear model of protest potential and these are set forth in the following equation:

| Protest Potential = | Leftism | + Dissatisfaction with Government | + Political Postmaterialism | + Personal Postmaterialism | + System Unresponsiveness | + Material Dissatisfaction |
|---|---|---|---|---|---|---|
| Beta weights | .30 | + .09* | + .12 | + .11* | + .13 | + .12 |

Multiple correlation $\overline{R} = 0.70$, variance explained = 49%

$* \ p < .05 > .01$, otherwise $P < .01$.

Within this equation, cynicism may be substituted for system unresponsiveness and dissatisfaction with education for material dissatisfaction and a similar result obtained. It appears that basic leftism is not quite as pervasive as it first appears. It combines with personal and political dissatisfaction and with personal and political postmaterialism in an almost symmetrical way to provide a very conclusive explanation of the political psychology of student protest. Linear equations such as these rarely approach explaining 50 percent

PROTEST AND POLITICAL CONSCIOUSNESS

of the variance of the dependent variable in survey data without the use of rather obvious structural variables like age and sex—and often not even then.

We could not expect such an efficient performance of this analysis among the general population. In the first place the unifying syndrome of leftist ideology as a determinant of protest is absent in the general population and in a far more heterogeneous and less polarized sample the levels of constraint are bound to be much lower. Yet, the continuities of attitude structure and function between students and the national sample are more impressive than the differences. They so seem part of a similar political process. So we may now advance from the crucible test provided by the student sample and attempt a similar integration of the elements of political action in the wider political community.

*Chapter 9*

# TOWARDS AN INTEGRATED MODEL OF
# THE SOCIAL PSYCHOLOGY OF POLITICAL PROTEST

Up to this point, the analysis has proceeded through a series of 'micro-theories' of political activism. In this way the influences upon protest potential contributed by respondents' social characteristics; by conventional party loyalty and ideology; by the intersection of political efficacy, level of conceptualization and mistrust; by special forms of relative deprivation; and by the phenomenon of postmaterialism; have each been explored in great detail and assessed. What follows now is an attempt to build upon this finely grained analytical base an integrated theoretical model that will place the results of this survey into the mainstream of current political theory in this field. There will be no grand theory of protest, of course. Instead, the appropriate strategy is to build through an empirical integration of the data using higher-order statistical techniques until either the data are exhausted or the capacity of present survey technology is exceeded and then to permit reasonable conjecture to carry one a little further to a point when the need for new data to answer the new questions raised exceeds the need for further speculation.

The first stage of an integrative strategy is to determine the extent to which the elements contributing to the proposed theoretical model are independent of each other. There is only limited value in integrating variables that are substantially dependent upon one another since they may even be measuring the "same thing." For these purposes the linear additive model is useful even though it will fail to account for interaction effects between variables. Such interaction effects are already known to have an important role in this study and so the use of linear additive techniques will require a brief suspension of disbelief.

Variations of the linear additive model rely upon a simultaneous partitioning of the variance of the dependent variable by any number of predictor, or independent variables. The popular term "independent" can be misleading because one problem with this kind of analysis is that the reliance upon correlational techniques is vulnerable to the effects of multicollinearity or intercorrelations between the independent variables. This effect will be examined closely in the following analysis.

The most common form of linear additive techniques, multiple regression analysis, was adopted for this study and each of the main predictor variables upon protest potential were included in a stepwise multiple regression analysis. Four demographic variables were included: age, sex, education and trade union membership, together with 10 variables that were earlier found to have the most significant influence upon protest ("significant" in he wider sense than the statistical). These are:

(1)   The effectiveness of protest
(2)   The effectiveness of repression
(3)   Personal values
(4)   Political values
(5)   Satisfaction with Government
(6)   Level of political conceptualisation
(7)   Personal efficacy
(8)   Left-right self placement
(9)   Overall dissatisfaction
(10)  Political trust

This initial inclusion list was, of course, subject to considerable experimental variation.

Stepwise multiple regression analysis is a technique that selects the best predictor of protest potential (i.e., the variable having the highest zero-order correlation coefficient with the protest potential scale) and then, controlling for the best predictor variable, selects the next best predictor, i.e., the variable having the highest *partial* correlation with the protest scale and adds this to the equation. Then, controlling simultaneously for these two, the variable with the next highest partial correlation is selected, and so on. The addition of each variable to the equation will increase the multiple correlation coefficient between these variables and the dependent variable and, hence, will add independently to the proportion of variance of the predicted variable that is explained by the whole equation. The magnitude of this additional explained variance is a measure (a) of the predictor variable's original zero-order correlation with the dependent variable and more importantly, (b) a measure of the extent to which the variance explained by this squared zero-order correlation coefficient is *independent* of the preceding variables entered into the equation. It follows, therefore, that a variable that is substantially correlated with variables already entered into the equation will add little to the total explained variance even though its own zero-order correlation with the dependent variable may be quite large. The general form of the equation is expressed in this way:

$$y = c + bx_1 + bx_2 + bx_3 \ldots + bx_n + e$$

Dependent variable = constant + predictor + unexplained
term      variables      variance

The magnitude of the b-coefficient is an estimate of the linear increase in the dependent or predicted variable that may be expected from an increase in each unit of the independent or predictor variable. If the straight line described by these coefficients is constrained to pass through the point of origin of the y and x axis, then the constant term is zero and the new coefficients are thus standardized and are known as beta-coefficients and express the linear increase to be expected in the dependent variable in standardized units. It is this measure that is usually reported in multiple regression analysis.

Table 9.1 reports the results of the "general" equation and indicates that nine variables: youth, sex, union membership, belief in the effectiveness of protest and the ineffectiveness of repression, personal postmaterialist values, dissatisfaction with government performance, high political conceptualization and high efficacy all contribute significant additions to the explanation of protest potential. Variables that fail to add further to the explained variance are education, overall dissatisfaction, cynicism, the left-right dimension, and political values, all having been preempted by their intercorrelations with included variables, especially leftism and the two effectiveness scores.

The influence of the effectiveness scores is pervasive. "Effectiveness of protest" alone explains 27 percent of the total variance of protest potential and boosts the total amount of variance explained by the whole equation to 36 percent. Even so, most of the other elements in this simple additive model still retain power to add to the explained variance despite substantial intercorrelations with effectiveness scores and despite also the additional inclusion of the powerful predictors of age, sex, and trade union membership. This suggests that a social psychological explanation of protest for the general population remains an independently viable proposition.

Table 9.1: General Regression Equation Predicting on Protest Potential

| | Effectiveness of Protest | + | Age | + | Effectiveness of Repression | + | Personal Values | + | Satisfaction with Government | + | Sex | + | Level of Concept | + | Trade Union Member | + | Personal Efficacy |
|---|---|---|---|---|---|---|---|---|---|---|---|---|---|---|---|---|
| Protest Score | .37 | | .15 | | -.08 | | .12 | | -.10 | | .08 | | .09 | | .06* | | .06* |

Multiple correlation = .60   Variance explained = 36%

Standardized Betas = *p < .05 > .01, otherwise p < .01

Variables excluded by the analysis are:

(1) Political values
(2) Left-right self-placement
(3) Overall dissatisfaction
(4) Education
(5) Cynicism

Table 9.2: Nondemographic Predictors of Protest Potential

| | Effectiveness of Protest | + | Personal Values | + | Satisfaction with Government | + | Effectiveness of Repression | + | Level of Concept | + | Personal Efficacy | + | Left-Right |
|---|---|---|---|---|---|---|---|---|---|---|---|---|---|
| Protest Score | .40 | | .15 | | -.10 | | -.11 | | .08 | | .07* | | .05* |

Multiple correlation = .57   Variance explained = 33%

Standardized Betas = *p < .05 > .01, otherwise p < .01

Variables excluded:

(1) Political values
(2) Dissatisfaction
(3) Cynicism

Table 9.3: Nondemographic Predictors of Protest Potential, Excluding Effectiveness Scores

| | Personal Values | + | Satisfaction with Government | + | Level of Concept | + | Left-Right | + | Personal Efficacy | + | Political Values | + | Cynicism | + | Dissatisfaction |
|---|---|---|---|---|---|---|---|---|---|---|---|---|---|---|---|
| Protest Score | .22 | | -.13 | | .13 | | .10 | | .12 | | .09 | | .05* | | .04* |

Multiple correlation = .42,   Variance explained = 18%   Standardized Betas = *p < .05 > .01, otherwise p < .01

When the demographic (or classification) variables are removed from the equation, the total of variance explained still remains high at 33 percent (Table 9.2) while the four demographic variables analyzed alone contribute an independent explanation of only 14 percent. This indicates that, among the measures deployed in this study at least, psychological explanations of unorthodox political actions are, even in simple linear-additive form, a superior prediction of protest than social or structural explanations. Moreover, even when the pervasive and direct influences upon protest supplied by the subjective belief in its effectiveness coupled with the ineffectiveness of repression are also removed from the equation (Table 9.3), the remaining variables of the model together explain 18 percent of the variance. For a set of highly specialized social psychological variables deployed in a general population survey, this is a very high figure. Moreover, when the generalized influence of the effectiveness scores is removed, all the other variables enter the equation and add significantly to the total of explained variance. This too is encouraging and the performance of the social psychological elements of the model is even more creditable when it is remembered that their zero-order correlations with protest potential are anyway rather unimpressive. In fact, the total variance explicable by the variables in the equation in Table 9.3 would be only 25% if each variable proved to be completely independent (i.e. to have a correlation coefficient of zero) of each other variable in the equation, i.e. other than the predicted variable.

It is interesting to speculate whether the emphasis of certain elements in the model would vary significantly according to different groups of people in the population. We repeated the stepwise multiple regression analysis in Table 9.3 (i.e., the main social psychological elements of the model less the influence of the effectiveness scores which appear as a constant) for each of six social groups, dividing the sample by age and social class. It is of course difficult and often actually misleading to read much substantive meaning into an analysis of this kind and the early inclusion of one variable at the expense of others often depends on rather insignificant chance variations in the partial correlations. But the basic message seems reliable. Among young middle-class people, the influence of leftist political sympathies is the most important direct influence upon protest potential. This influence is expressed in two independent ways: left self-placement on the left-right scale (indicating the young middle-class Labour supporters) and the additional influence of post-materialist political values (possibly indicating the additional influences of young middle-class Liberals).

Among the numerically much larger working-class groups (who tend to have many nonprotesting leftists) the *un*importance of partisanship and ideology in predicting protest potential is underlined once more. Instead, a combination of dissatisfaction with the government's performance and with basic aggressive self-competence is the obvious pathway to protest for them but which is accelerated somewhat by the addition of personal postmaterialism. Though not generally a working-class attitude, where it does occur among working-class youth, postmaterialism retains an independent power to influence political aggression.

There is a number of reasons to expect that men and women may differ in the emphasis they place upon aspects of the model and may take differing pathways toward protest. For example, the growth of the Women's Liberation movement is surely not unrelated to the development of postmaterialist values. Women are anyway known to have a lower degree of involvement in active politics and are generally less "politically conscious" (see especially Di Palma 1970, Table 7.1, p. 134). Therefore it is predictable that high levels of conceptualization and postmaterialism *when they occur among women* will have a more powerful impact upon protest potential, independently of other factors, than among men, and that leftism will have less impact. These expectations are only partly justified and differences, though in the predicted direction, are not significant. The more valid conclusion is that attitudes towards protest have a very similar structure among both men and women despite differing aggregate levels.

Beyond the known class differences, the elements of the model are fairly *consistent* within the general population so we may be entitled to conclude that the model "works" to the extent that it does not only provide an understanding of the motivation of the minority of the population who use protest methods frequently (i.e., those normally thought of as deviants) but will explain also the much more generalized tendency of the readiness to use unorthodox political behavior present in the community and even the *negative* motivation (if such a term may be allowed) of those who will not protest. This is not a trivial point. It means that the survey approach adopted in this study has been vindicated to the extent of providing information about an aspect of political attitude and behavior that is apparently valid for the whole population. An approach which chose to study protesters alone would not have achieved this.

Reinforced by this information, it is now possible to proceed to a reappraisal of the results of this survey in the light of general theory as distinct from the theoretical appraisal of specific relationships. In this we shall return to our recurrent theme which compares the results of this study with the widespread scholarly assumption that Britain has a deferential political culture.

There could be many starting points for such a reappraisal. From a social psychological perspective, however, we seek a particular point of departure in the analysis which indicates that the focus of study is a *process of thought* rather than just a part of the political process. This is not at all easily expressed because there are vast grey areas of overlapping foci that confuse the distinction between mental and social processes and in many ways the practice of social psychology is in itself a scientific attempt to resolve this confusion. At the moment, we chart our course more by empirical examples than by the guiding light of theory. In this case the example is a fairly clear one. In stepping from the familiar forms of socio-political analysis of Chapter 4 into the analysis of more clearly personal and individual characteristics in Chapter 5 (i.e., the analysis of efficacy, conceptualization, and trust), we achieved the important shift in emphasis away from political sociology and into political social psychology.

It is at this point also that we require an act of theoretical imagination. While it is obvious even from the linear-additive model that only a multicausal explanation of protest potential will satisfy reasonable theoretical expectations, there is one irreducible factor that seems to lie at the core of a social psychological interpretation of protest potential. This factor is a sense of political competence. In political psychology, the term "competence" has been given a special meaning and identity by Almond and Verba's Civic Culture study. Basically, we mean by competence the same thing that Almond and Verba meant, but we shall propose a much more generalized and substantial concept then the single measure used by the Civic Culture study. But though we used the same measure of competence,[1] there is a conceptual discontinuity between the stimulus object used in the Almond and Verba study and the dependent variable of our study. Their question was: "Supposing a new bye-law [a Bill for a new law] were being considered by your local Council [was introduced into Parliament for discussion by MPs] and you considered this very unjust or harmful, what do you think you could do?"

While it is true that the progress of new legislation can often be the subject of protest movements, it is more obviously the business of *conventional* politics than it is of protest behavior. As our data suggest, specific acts of protest do not come to our respondents' minds—even to the minds of those who have a high protest potential—when they are asked to consider an attempt to influence the legislative process. But supposing we had asked: "Supposing your local Council wished to build a new road through your local park and you felt this was very unjust or harmful, what do you think you could do about it?" Would we have obtained the same distribution of responses? It seems reasonable to guess that the kind of personal competence that *is* relevant to protest potential would come through in response to that kind of hypothetical stimulus in a way that it would not do in response to any questions about laws and regulations, MPs and councillors.

Another characteristic of the Civic Culture concept of competence which narrows the range of the concept in a direction unhelpful to our purposes is that Almond and Verba link it, quite mistakenly in our view, to an essentially passive sense of self-confidence. According to Almond and Verba, Britain has a "deferent political culture" (p. 455). The competent citizen in Britain is one who feels himself able to participate in the democratic process but in a respectful manner. He will respectfully contact his MP, sign a petition (usually a "humble petition" at that), confer with his neighbours, and so on. The competent citizen may well voice a protest through the proper channels, but he would not step outside them. In all this he retains every expectation that his desires will be given full consideration by the authorities or even that they will be anticipated. When considered in the light of the protest potential scale and its correlates, this idea of competent citizenship seems suddenly rather unreal. At least it takes on distinctly middle-class, middle-aged, almost suburban shades of meaning that are very difficult to connote with the protest potential measured by our scale.

The concept of political competence that *is* appropriate to the understanding of protest potential is certainly one that reflects individual self-confidence but does so to a degree that removes the respectful, almost passive connotations that Almond and Verba found useful to describe their idea of the participant democratic citizen. The competence we wish to describe here has some distinctly brash overtones. We will come to grips with these overtones of meaning shortly, but let us first be certain that the core concept has been located accurately and point out its reflections in the pool of data that has been explored so far with this analysis.

The surest reflection of the influence of political competence that can be discerned in the data lies at the intersection of political efficacy and the respondent's level of political conceptualization. As in the Civic Culture, so too in our data: the competent democrat is an efficacious ideologue or an efficacious citizen who is at least able to interpret politics in articulate, issue-oriented terms. Interestingly, efficacy and conceptualization are only slightly correlated ($r = .14$). But the possession of both characteristics by a single individual advertises his political self-confidence in a most telling manner. The efficacious ideologue is a man or woman who understands the basic parameters of meaning that underlie the political process, makes judgements of the political parties on the basis of abstract conceptions, while at the same time retaining the belief that politicians (however unwillingly) will be responsive to the more insistent demands of the polity. Note that the term "ideologue" does not imply a specific ideology; efficacious ideologues are, in fact, slightly more likely to place themselves on the right rather than on the left of the left-right self-placement scale.

By no means all those enjoying this sense of political self-confidence will be ready to use unorthodox protest methods. Indeed, it is significant that a great many of them desist from protest but, rather pointedly, report that they have high levels of orthodox political participation. These people fit the Almond and Verba idea of the British participant democrat very well and it is of equal significance that, though eschewing protest themselves, they are very unwilling to support repressive measures against protesters. Their confidence in the democratic process is such that it includes the belief that, if things are done properly, no recourse to repression is necessary to meet dissent. But many other efficacious ideologues are prepared to protest. As we saw clearly in Chapter 5, they share an additional characteristic which separates them from their conventionally-inclined fellows and which does not at all resemble the stereotype of respectful citizenship. This additional factor is not the obvious one—youth. There are plenty of inefficacious low-conceptualizers among the young, and this is characteristic of the nonprotesters among young people. The key accelerating factor is political mistrust or cynicism.

The analysis in Chapter 5 substantiated Almond and Verba's very reasonable expectations that political competence is almost a necessary precondition of political participation in all its conventional aspects. Indeed, our far more direct measure of competence as the intersection of high efficacy and high political conceptualization predicts conventional participation rather more convincingly than much of the Civic Culture data. But the expectation that would commonly attach to this finding is that competence describes the essence of the sober, responsible citizen who *deferentially* performs his participatory civic duties when the opportunity arises and is certainly not the kind of personality that would be attracted to protest behavior. Our findings, however, dismiss that expectation. The moment that efficacious high-conceptualizers become cynical about the representative, legislative system of parliamentary democracy and begin to distrust the professional practitioners of the system, they manifest their preparedness to *add* protest to their range of behavioral options. While trust remains high, protest is usually disclaimed. But the possibility of protest becomes imminent among the competent citizens at really quite modest levels of cynicism. And among the competents, cynicism is much more common than trust. Thus many of Almond and Verba's participant citizens seem lately to have abandoned what deference they may ever have had.

Political mistrust or cynicism then, provides us with that key element of "brashness" or natural truculence that leads the young politically competent citizen to embrace protest. As measured in this survey, the political cynic believes that "people in politics" are habitual liars who run the country incompetently on behalf of a "few big interests" (usually that of the rich and powerful) except when the interests of their own party are concerned which come before all else. These beliefs are anyway sufficiently widespread to discount any general theory of deference but when they occur in the competent citizen they raise levels of political aggression almost unfailingly.

So we would place at the centre of a social psychological theory of protest potential what we have called the "three-levered trigger" of political aggression; the coalescence of political efficacy, capacity for conceptualization and distrust. This combination of cognitive skill and affective feeling states forms the core of the basic disposition of *disrespectful or aggressive political competence* that we hold to be the most important psychological component of protest potential.

Good evidence was produced that the three-way interaction that makes up this core competence occurred partly independently of political partisanship; quite sufficiently so at least to be accounted as the major nonpartisan influence on protest. What happens is that among left-wingers the interaction is dominated by the influence of cynicism and among the less numerous (though not less vociferous) potential protesters of the right, the influence of efficacy and high conceptualization is the dominant force. Also among the left cynics are a significant group of potential protesters whose cynicism is so great that the interpenetration of efficacy and trust (see Appendix) depresses their sense of efficacy to low levels even though, significantly, they have high conceptualization.

Once the implications of this underlying syndrome of aggressive self-confidence are understood and the concept is placed at the centre of the social psychology of protest, some of the other major findings of the survey assume a less idiosyncratic character than they may have appeared to have as the analysis took each in turn. Chapter 6 contained a painstaking series of tests of hypotheses drawn from a body of established theory which elaborates the nature of the causal relationships that may exist between subjective feelings of relative deprivation and political aggression. Contrary to commonly held theoretical expectations, we found that, while protesters do manifest a certain unease in that they are not sure they are getting all that they feel entitled to, this relationship was as much related to high expectations as it was to low achievement. It was certainly not related to actual need-deprivation in terms of hard cash. Also, despite their current uneasiness, young protesters were overwhelmingly convinced that their life was set upon an upward gradient of increasing material rewards and enlarged life satisfaction. But the self-anchoring scales that provided the base-line measurement of relative deprivation make no mention of how life satisfaction will or should be obtained. In the light of a theory of political competence, it becomes highly plausible to hold that our discontented young optimists place more emphasis upon their confidence in their own ability to *extract* improvements in life satisfaction for themselves than upon any passive expectation regarding improvements in the national economy, the distribution of wealth, or whatever.

It may be argued of course that the young optimistically self-confident protester's position in the life-cycle confounds the implications that may be drawn from this finding. The old, nonprotesters have every reason to expect a downturn in their life satisfaction but suffer obvious natural limits upon their protest potential. But even controlled for age, optimism still retained enough independent influence upon protest to suggest that it is in part another reflection of this same sense of brash self-confidence. This assertion does not necessarily detract from the modest success achieved in Chapter 6 in determining a "conditional-linkage" pathway between respondents' feelings of material relative deprivation (the belief that the government fails to redistribute wealth more equitably) and protest potential. This is itself an obvious and straightforward source of protest potential—especially when it is remembered that unofficial industrial action forms part of the protest scale. The key role played by political competence is that it is the core element upon which specific sources of grievance (which may be specifically political or even specifically partisan in character) may grow into political protest. This, it should be noted, is not at all the same thing as saying that somehow the antecedents of protest potential may be *reduced* to a personal feeling of aggressive political competence. Rather it seems that many of the specific explanations that have been determined in the analysis build upon this core notion.

This is true to some extent of even the most basic and obvious predictor of protest potential: the belief in the *effectiveness* of protest. There is an obviously straightforward relationship between a high protest potential and a high expectation that protest of the kinds supported is effective in pressing for changes. On the other hand, the expectation that protest is effective may plausibly be said to contain more than a little optimism. This is not to suggest that the optimistic self-confidence of protesters is naive, the prevalence of political cynicism among them precludes that conclusion. Protesters are people who expect reward but expect also to have to make a personal effort to obtain it.

The measure of overall dissatisfaction with government performance (the DGP index) seems to provide an additional linkage between the *cynicism* aspects of political competence and protest but is confused a little by partisan choice. Whereas *nonprotesters* who are dissatisfied with the government tend also to be left-wingers (or, more accurately, they tend more to be Labour supporters) *protesters* who are very dissatisfied with the government's performance are almost as likely to be right-wingers or centrists as they are to be leftists. This linkage seems to provide a special explanation of young working-class Tories' high protest potential and, as such, relates poorly to the other basic elements of political competence: high efficacy and high political conceptualization. These are not always the foremost characteristics of young working-class people. We have characterized the psychological antecedents of protest with a purposeful kind of brashness but the protest motivation of young working-class Tories seems tinged with more than a little surliness.

There are two very important aspects of the relationship between the development of postmaterialism and protest potential that serve our general thesis concerning political competence and the decline of deference. First, anyone who embraces a set of postmaterialist values, in either the public or personal value domain and especially in both, makes a fairly clear statement that he feels there is rather more to life than maintaining material and civil security (in the public domain) and providing those basic security needs of himself and his home (in the personal domain). Such a statement requires quite a high level of personal self-confidence, especially when expressed in the personal value domain. The postmaterialist aspects of political competence are not taken to excess by most protesters. The "new naturalism" described by Yankelovich ("New Values on Campus") in 1972 seems even in America to have been a short-lived phenomenon. Rather, postmaterialists seem self-confidently prepared to build upon the existing materialist base; they are personally quite willing to extract maximum benefit from the consumer society yet prepared also to work towards maximizing new goals which may make the material world more agreeable to live in. If, in their view, protest methods can serve these purposes, then protest there shall be. If this leads the postmaterialist protester into some apparently contradictory positions this, it seems, cannot be helped. It is merely a recognition that life, and especially political life, is complicated and that contradictions sometimes cannot be avoided.

Secondly, postmaterialism also reflects an overall sense of *optimism*, especially in the public value domain, that postmaterialist political goals are actually attainable. It may be that those expressing a preference for post-materialist goals have not thought too deeply about the wider or even the national implications of their demands for a change in value priorities. But there is no doubt that they are sufficiently optimistic to believe that the level of industrial production that contributes to present levels of material gratifi-cation (as they were experienced even in the uncertain and troubled days of later 1973 and early 1974) will continue to increase. It takes even greater optimism to believe they can increase when the continued security of the present sources of that wealth are subordinated to goals of greater social integration and freer participation in the decisions of the political commu-nity. Whether he knows it or not (and probably he does know it) the postmaterialist protester is prepared to take risks—or more likely he is prepared for the political community to take risks—of a kind that demand a high level of political self-confidence.

To summarize the argument so far: Some key aspects of Almond and Verba's Civic Culture theory have been reexamined in the light of the findings of this survey. The Civic Culture study described a participative citizen of a democratic political system of government. The two most important characteristics of the participant democrat are his high personal political competence and his well-tempered trust of the political system and its custodians. Less important theoretically, but considered to be of high explanatory value in the case of Britain, is an additional characteristic: an attitude of deference towards political authority which reinforces the important elements of trust. This contingent factor leads to a conceptualization of the politically competent citizen in Britain as a well-disciplined and respectful democrat who places high value upon proper channels of communication. Thus the Civic Culture study, and most of the similar work done subsequently, would lead to the expectation that political protest was not a salient feature of British political culture and what unorthodox protest does occur tends to be the work of political deviants.

The survey reported in the preceding pages contains little evidence to support these conclusions. If older people are disregarded on grounds of natural nonavailability, a serious commitment to the idea of protest, even illegal forms of protest, as a legitimate means of political redress is an unexpectedly widespread feature of the political culture in Britain. Especially among the young, protest potential was found to be the common property of people of all social characteristics and political persuasions and not merely of 'extremists' or 'militants' or any other fashionable *bete noir* of professional politicians and communicators. Rarely was the intention to protest accompanied by any systematic rejection of the conventional kinds of political behavior, rather it appears as a modern *extension* of the legitimate range of political options.

It was pointed out that Almond and Verba may have been misled into interpreting British political competence as a deferent competence not merely by traditional writings on the subject but also by the very nature of their measure of competence which is so worded as to inhibit the kinds of responses appropriate to political protest. The more sharply defined approach toward a core concept of political competence taken in our study, i.e., the intersection of high efficacy and high levels of political conceptualization, did not coexist easily with feelings of political trust. Certainly, there exists a positive correlation between trust and efficacy but this is due far more to widespread feelings of inefficacious cynicism than to the coalescence of feelings of efficacious trust. This finding itself casts doubt upon Britain's image as a deferent polity. The relatively small number of trusting efficacious high conceptualizers do indeed have the characteristics predicted by Almond and Verba. They have a high rate of conventional political participation which is unaccompanied by any recourse to protest behavior. But the remainder of those found to have a high level of political competence have also a very low opinion of politicians and among these people there is a very widespread commitment to the idea of political protest. Not, it should be emphasised once more, at the expense of conventional forms of political participation but in addition.

Overlaying and giving meaning and form to this basic relationship between aggressive political competence and protest potential are other influences which both reflect and reinforce this core psychological factor. Most important among these are:

(a) The politically motivating properties of the politicization of subjective dissatisfactions coupled with youthful optimism.
(b) The ideologically facilitating properties of a leftist political outlook. (This is important among the older respondents and the middle classes.)
(c) The psychologically and politically liberating properties of the development of postmaterialist values.
(d) The reinforcing power of the conviction that protest behavior is effective and repression by the authorities is ineffective.

These relationships are represented diagramatically in Figure 9.1.

This is not, of course, an empirically proven model. We drew encouragement from the results of the linear additive model, not proof. Now the influence of interaction must be considered, even if it cannot be simultaneously measured. The variables that have contributed their separate and sometimes combined effects to the explanation of protest are conceived in this diagram as contributing elements within six key *hypothetical constructs*. Within these hypothetical constructs are three interaction effects:

(1) As has been described in some detail, the core concept of political competence derives from the interaction of high political efficacy, high levels of political conceptualization, and low political trust.
(2) Whereas postmaterialism in the personal domain and postmaterialism in the public, political domain each have separate predictive power for high protest potential, possession of both characteristics accelerates protest potential by a degree much greater than that suggested by their multiple correlation.
(3) The separate relationships between relative deprivation, politicized dissatisfaction and protest potential are uncertain. But when arranged in the step-by-step accumulating function of a conditional linkage pathway, the arousal of protest through politicized dissatisfaction

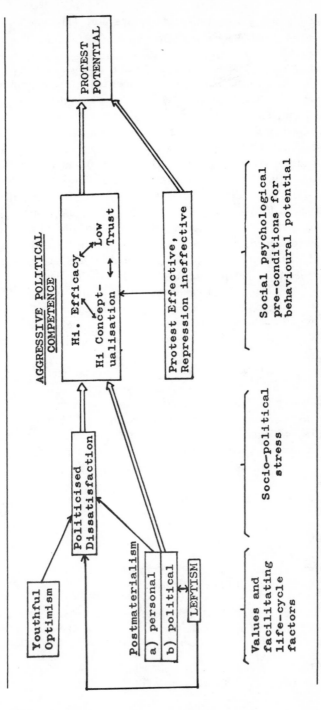

Figure 9.1: A SOCIAL PSYCHOLOGICAL MODEL OF POLITICAL PROTEST

may be quite clearly discerned through data which are not at all responsive to linear-additive treatment.

Better empirical support for the social psychological model of protest will wait upon further research. But some suggestions can be made regarding the use of the model in understanding unorthodox political behavior and its role in the process of political change. One temptation to be avoided is the urge to offer quantitative predictions about the levels of political protest in Britain. Some of the most reliable "predictors" of political behavior are nothing of the kind in the widest sense. For example, level of education is an excellent predictor of political involvement and voting frequency. Yet, as levels of education (quantitative levels, at least) increased, so the frequency of voting and involvement in political parties declined in the population. Another example, but at the individual level, is that people's level of subjective relative gratification (measured on Cantril scales) is an excellent "predictor" of their level of reported "happiness" (see Campbell et al. 1975). Yet, as people get older, their levels of relative gratification *rise* but their level of reported happiness *declines*. Nowhere in this thesis has any claim been made that this focus upon social psychological aspects of protest potential will "explain" all actual behavioral outcomes. Issues, opportunities, and the actions of authorities will all contribute their influence to determine people's political behavior in the future.

What has been achieved is a *description* of the present state of affairs in an area of the public political consciousness hitherto unexplored; a *test* in respect of predictions made from a very wide sweep of existing theory; and a *synthesis* of the information provided ("information" being the informed interpretation of the relationships between theoretical constructs and relevant data) into a new hypothetical configuration which is supported by empirical evidence. At the present level of development of the social sciences, to demand a "harder," more "scientific" outcome would be unrealistic. But it provides at least a basis for some brief speculative assessment of the wide social and political meaning of the phenomena we have observed and analyzed.

## Conclusions: Protest, Democratic Stability, and the Decline of the Civic Culture

Richard Rose (1975) writes: "Something has happened to government and to our belief in government in the past decade. Everywhere in the Western world, people who have looked to government to resolve their problems no longer look with confidence."

Rose goes on to describe a series of alternative scenarios wherein political authorities become increasingly overloaded with demands upon their increasingly scarce resources—political as well as material resources. The authorities are unable to satisfy these demands, nor can they diminish them by appeals to people to moderate their demands and expectations. We do not presume to have all or even most of the answers to the very difficult questions posed by Rose's article, but one crucial factor is obvious in the results of this study: There is in Britain a much lower level of political deference than was formerly believed and, as a direct consequence of this, doubt must be cast upon the implied passivity of the civic culture in Britain. Such a conclusion would account for the rise described by Rose in the pressures of political demand placed upon government (especially local government) by the polity. This rise in demand may be accompanied by a vigorous diversification of the ways in which demands may be made.

In their time, Almond and Verba, assessing the implications of the results of their own survey, were sufficiently certain of the success of the civic culture in creating a stable democracy in Britain, that they even felt it appropriate to warn that Britain may be carrying political deference to excess:

> It is possible that deference to political elites can go too far, and that the strongly hierarchical patterns in British politics . . . result from a balance weighted too heavily in the direction of the subject and deferential roles" (p. 494).

The results of this survey indicate that this statement has little credibility now even though it may have appealed to the conventional wisdom of the time. It was after all a statement made at the height of Macmillan's tenure of office and of Gaitskell's moderate opposition. But does this mean that Britain no longer has a stable democracy? If so, to what extent are the processes examined in this study actually contributing to increased instability?

The extent to which political protest as it is usually experienced in Britain is a threat to the existing political processes is in itself a subject of dispute. More extreme adherents of direct action methods will claim that protest behavior of the kinds implied in the protest potential scale contribute merely to a process of "repressive tolerance." Strikes, sit-ins, and demonstrations act as a form of safety valve to release the tensions and resentments against the alienative contradictions of the modern Capitalist State. From another point of view, Trevor Smith (in Benewick and Smith 1972, pp. 305-314) also locates the main causes of protest in the nature of the modern capitalist state and points to the development in the past few years of a huge bureaucratic machinery. This new style of central government is a process whereby "administration is substituted for politics," and this undermines the relevance of political argument to the relationship between community and authority. But Smith deprecates the widespread use of protest behavior as a remedy for this state of affairs on the grounds that it can so easily legitimize the increased use of selective repression by the authorities and can provoke open conflict between rival factions. Supporters of this view can point to the first clashes in 1968 between Catholic civil rights marchers and Protestant assailants matched by Catholic interference with the Apprentice Boys march in Londonderry,[2] which provided the starting point of a process that in five years destroyed the whole basis of political authority in Northern Ireland.

Among those, like April Carter, who see a more constructive role for protest and direct action within the framework of a formal liberal democracy, one argument that weighs most heavily is that formal or orthodox party politics is structurally incapable of handling adequately the increasing *range* of political cleavages and points of conflict that occur in a modern state. Carter goes further than the usual argument that direct action can be justified by liberal constitutional and democratic principles when the existing institutions of the state no longer embody these principles. She sees protest methods gradually assuming greater legitimacy as a means of general political opposition. It is a movement that *extends* the present range of behavioral options and permits effective opposition to new authority forces in modern society that are at the moment imperfectly controlled by the orthodox political process. This too is the evidence of this survey. A good example of these new interfaces between authority and community is the rise of huge property development companies that may cause, for good or evil, great changes in the structure of the community but are often answerable only to a small group of officials. Protest may augment conventional procedures which were not designed to cope with powerful new sources of authority.

In these speculative comments we have inched our way past the empirical boundaries of the data presented in this study. But we have not strayed out of reach. Even Almond and Verba were prepared to speculate that a decline in the level of trust would result in an increase in the numbers of those "available" for unorthodox activity (in the sense introduced by Kornhauser (1959) to describe a condition of estrangement from the normative activities of the mass of society):

> The role of social trust cannot be overemphasised. It is in a sense, a generalised resource that keeps a democratic polity functioning (p. 490).

The evidence of this survey is that political trust is at a much lower ebb than would seem healthy from Almond and Verba's view at least, for a democratic society; more particularly so since competence has remained high. But perhaps the British political community has proved to be, in a sense, more mature than given credit for. No riots have broken out, only the growth of a potent political attitude: politically competent cynicism.

Before the growth of trade unionism and the extension of the franchise, direct action and street protest were the *only* means of political redress available to common people, and it was an ugly process. While direct action will not necessarily strengthen parliamentary democracy, neither the political folk memory of Peterloo or the Gordon Riots nor even the modern disasters of Detroit, Watts and other riots should be permitted to prejudge the possible value of disorderly politics in the larger process of orderly political change. There are even some serious theorists who have an almost uncritical attitude towards protest. As Cohen puts it:

> The majority must rule but it must not silence; critical dissent by those who find adopted laws or policies unwise or unjust must continue vigorously without fear of reprisal. The protest of minorities, on every conceivable subject in the political sphere, is vital for the health of every democracy ... vigorous dissent must be protected and even encouraged ... genuine democracy demands dissent, thrives on protest (p. 13).

On the other hand, it would be unwise to say that this aspect of "genuine democracy" is without risk. Things can get out of hand and too easily lead to more extreme forms of dissent. This permits dissenting minorities to dictate to the majority, a situation which many hold to be as equally undemocratic as the reverse. Many of our respondents fear this and even though they are quite prepared to support and even engage in quite vigorous forms of protest like demonstrations, boycotts and strikes, along with those who will not protest they too grant to the authorities the right to curtail unruly elements. This basic dilemma of liberal democracy has been well expressed by Oscar Gass who says:

> I know that democracy is a technique for reaching agreement, but it in turn rests upon a measure of agreement. It is of course formally true that, if only you agree upon the technique for getting decisions, you don't have to agree upon the outcome. But that is merely like saying that people can ride on the same bus even when they want to get off at different places. The places must not be *too* different—or else they will have to set a value on riding beyond that of getting to their destination (p. 574).

One of the main points of this survey is that, whereas protest may at times seem an uncontrolled vehicle for political redress and certainly was so in the past, it now attracts large numbers of politically competent people. To extend Gass' analogy, we may be acquiring more vehicles for political action but they still travel familiar routes to known destinations. The risks are still there, of course, but probably we have little choice. There appears to be a movement of British political life away from a quiet and respectful participatory democracy towards a noisy and disrespectful participatory democracy. This ought still to leave a participatory democracy and one that people may find ultimately more satisfying than the present arrangements.


# NOTES

1. Almond and Verba also introduced an element of efficacy by asking people, in addition to their belief in what they might do to oppose a new law, whether or not the authorities might listen to their objections.

2. A procession of course, not actually a political demonstration even though it was perceived as such by many Catholics.

# APPENDIX ONE

# THE SAMPLE

The theory of probability sampling and the estimation of sampling error are the great strengths of survey research. The quality of a sample, however, cannot exceed the quality of the sampling frame from which it was drawn, i.e., the extent to which the list from which the sample is drawn is a complete listing of the target population it purports to describe. For this study, the target population was defined as: all residents of Great Britain excluding the Highlands of Scotland north of the Caledonian Canal, who have exceeded their 16th birthday on October 1, 1973. The sampling frame used was the electoral register. As a complete listing of the population the register has some obvious deficiencies. It is six months out of date when published and eighteen months obsolete before it is replaced. In this case the register was fourteen months out of date when interviewing started, but this was much less of a problem in our case because, as is explained below, we sampled *addresses* from the register, not individual electors. This still leaves us with the problem of dwellings left unoccupied and, in two cases, whole sampling points were demolished. The register's greatest deficiency is that it iists only those entitled to vote and in compiling the list, many people are missed, especially members of minority groups and and 17-year olds who, though rising 18, were not included because of misunderstanding about the rules regarding new electors.

Another practical boundary placed upon the quality of the sample is the amount of money available for interviewing. This dictates the degree of "clustering" that may be necessary. If the sample were spread evenly across the countryside, with very little concentration introduced by the sample design, it would be impossibly expensive to have interviewers go to respondents over very wide areas. (This too is why we ignore the Northern Highlands.)

With modern sampling techniques it is possible to end up with one's respondents neatly grouped in conveniently small areas and at the same time build in legitimate safeguards against selecting a bizarre sample at earlier stages of sampling. The technique is known as multistage sampling with stratification and clustering and is essentially the procedure whereby the effects of clustering (the increase of sampling error) are mitigated by judicious stratification.

All that is required of a sampling technique is that each member of the target population should have a known and nonzero chance of selection in the sample. Multistage sampling simplifies the task of selection by dividing the sample into "primary sampling units" according to (though not necessarily) some naturally occurring division. A fraction of PSUs are then sampled, having a chance of selection proportionate to the number of individuals they represent. At this stage, the sampling among PSUs may be stratified according to relevant demographic factors like region, urban/rural, or any other relevant factor. Then secondary sampling units may be sampled within each PSU and then individuals within each SSU. The logic of this procedure will become self-evident in the following description of the sampling method executed for this study:

The primary sampling units were *parliamentary constituencies*. They were listed separately within each of the registrar-general's eleven *standard regions* (stratification factor 1.) and then, within each region, divided into *borough* constituencies and *county* constituencies (SF2) and then further divided into six groups according to whether they were safe, average, or marginal (majorities of > 6000, 3000-6000, < 3000) Conservative or Labour seats (SF3). Having imposed this stratified order, computer procedures list the whole electorate as integers and from this list a simple interval sample of individual electors was then taken from a random starting-point to select 120 constituencies,

$$\text{(selection fraction} = \frac{120}{\text{total electorate}} = \frac{120}{39,798,899}$$

$$= \frac{1}{331,658} \text{ )}$$

This selects constituencies with a probability of selection proportionate to the size of their electorates.

Within each borough—or urban—constituency, two secondary sampling points (clusters) were randomly selected by use of tables of random numbers with a range greater than the number of electors, and names drawn by advancing through the register at every twentieth name. Eight names were drawn from one sampling point and nine from the other. In county—or rural—constituencies, where the spread of addresses is much greater, one sampling point was randomly selected and 17 names at 20-name intervals were drawn from the register. The names selected were not always the person interviewed. Someone from his or her *household*[1] was interviewed; this was done to include non-electors and to allow each household a chance of selection proportionate to its size, or at least proportionate to the number of electors it contained which of course slightly underrepresents households with a greater-than-average number of 16-17-year olds.

At this stage a refinement was introduced. For reasons explained in the text, we required to boost the numbers of young middle-class, well-educated, people in the sample. The rather crude but effective solution to this problem was to list the proportion of the economically active population of each selected constituency who fell into the registrar-general's "professional, managerial, employer" category, as recorded by the 1966 10% sample census. Nationally, this proportion is about 12%. We selected those constituencies wherein this proportion exceeded 20% (in five constituencies boundary changes forced informed guess) and drew 34 names (households) instead of 17. This was done by continuing to select names sequentially from the one or, usually, two sampling points elected and proceeding not to a total of 8 or 9, but to two totals of 17. This procedure resulted in 26 "predominantly middle-class" constituencies being double sampled. The results of analyses conducted in this volume are, of course, *reweighted* to account for this, but the number of cases in the "young middle-class" cells are increased to statistically satisfactory levels.

The method of selection adopted to find the actual *respondent within the household* was that prescribed by Kish. This technique (see Kish 1948) has been tested over 30 years of research in the United States and has proved very accurate. Each member of the household (in our case, those 16 and over) are listed, men first, then women, and assigned a number. One of eight selection tables is randomly applied according to a predetermined proportion and the respondent then determined by the number of persons in the household. "A household" was defined by a group sharing a meal-table. Households have been selected with a probability proportionate to the number of electors listed on the register. But individuals are subsequently selected with a probability proportionate to the numbers in the household. Thus this probability will differ from the number of electors if there are several nonvoters listed by the interviewers. This depresses the probability of an individual's selection if the number of electors is above average (and vice versa) but this was considered unimportant compared with the advantages of adding nonelectors to the sample.

This method is superior to other techniques for determining a sample containing nonelectors but does have one disadvantage. Because the interviewer has to stand on the doorstep listing household members, this procedure allows suspicion to develop in the minds of the reticent (i.e., about 75% of people who answer the door). Thus it must have undoubtably depressed the response rate. It is much easier for an interviewer to have a name ready and go straight for her target without asking a rather strange series of questions and juggling with figures before the confused gaze of her host. This procedure was very carefully rehearsed with interviewers and all the information used for selection was checked by the field supervisors and coded into the data set to be rechecked by computer. Only twenty-two misapplied selections found their way into the data set (1.2%) and were taken out. This was the first time the interviewers had used this technique and the degree of accuracy achieved must be credited to their impressive persistence.

The final response rate thus achieved was 1802 interviews from a possible 2345, or 77%, which is very good but not quite excellent. This proportion ranged from 72% in London up to 84% in Yorkshire and the Northeast.

## The Student Sample

There exists no adequate sampling frame for a national probability sample of students in Britain. Most colleges permit students to embargo the release of their addresses to outside enquirers and many do so. Students tend anyway to be highly mobile and what addresses are available soon take on a fictional quality. Accordingly, quota sampling techniques were employed. Interviewers went on campus armed with a sampling grid which directed them to fill a quota according to some of the known parameters of the student population. For example, 75% of students are men and 25% women; they are evenly divided between Arts and Science studies and evenly stratified into first, second, and third years of study. This technique can provide a good sample but is open to selection bias. That is to say, interviewers will select among students who are available and who will cooperate with them. Such students may not be wholly representative of the student body. Yet careful study of the sample obtained did not suggest the presence of any gross biasing factor. The institutions represented in the survey are as follows:

| Universities | Polytechnics |
|---|---|
| Bristol | Bristol |
| Manchester | Manchester |
| Newcastle | Newcastle |
| Birmingham | Birmingham |
| Warwick | Lanchester, Coventry |
| Oxford | Oxford |
| Kings, London | Wolverhampton |
| L.S.E. | City |

| | |
|---|---|
| Imperial, London | Thames |
| Brunel | North London |
| Reading | North East London |
| Aston | |
| Edinburgh | |
| Heriot Watt | |

The total of students interviewed was 289.

# NOTE

1. This need not include everyone at that address. In multihousehold addresses, the household listed was that of the first respondent encountered, defined as the group of people who share his or her domestic and catering arrangements.

# APPENDIX TWO

## THE INTERVIEWERS

As part of the briefing exercise, our interviewers were asked to complete the questionnaire for themselves. They were then asked to send their completed schedules directly to the investigator and not to their employer. Of the 104 interviewers employed on the survey, 63 returned their questionnaires in this way. Ironically, their response rate was 16% lower than the figure they obtained from the sample.

It should be noted that this does not represent an attempt to examine interviewer effects in the sample. That would be a rather different research proposition involving the use of cross-matched interviewers to hold constant the effects of factors like regional differences. We were merely curious to learn what our interviewers were like and what they thought about the questions they asked on our behalf.

Typically, interviewers are women (only one male interviewer was employed) and "young middle-aged" (average age is 31). All of them are, or have been married, and nearly all have children, 58% have school-age or younger children. Most (80%) regard themselves as "middle-class" and do so with some justification. Eighty-seven percent own or are buying their own houses and enjoy a family income much higher than average (a mean of 8.8 on the 1-12 scale compared with 6.7 for the population as a whole). Many of them (about 60%) claim to have come from family backgrounds they can describe as at least "fairly well off"—sufficiently so to send 37% of them to private school. Most of the remainder went to grammar school but only 3% went on to university. Sixty percent have some kind of educational qualifications.

With that kind of social profile, it is a routine matter to predict that many will have Conservative political sympathies. Yet, we were not quite prepared for the fact that only 6% have ever contemplated a vote for the Labour party whereas 78% are committed to the Tories, 10% to the Liberals, and 6% to no party at all. The word "committed" is used advisedly. 71% are interested in politics compared with 45% nationally and nine of them are members of the Conservative and Unionist party. *All* of them voted in the 1970 general election and fully 68% in the local council elections in 1973, twice the national average turnout for local elections. Particularly revealing is their distribution on the left-right self-placement scale:

| Left | 1 | 2 | 3 | 4 | 5 | 6 | 7 | 8 | 9 | 10 | Right |
|------|---|---|---|---|---|---|---|---|---|----|-------|
|  | % | % | % | % | % | % | % | % | % | % |  |
| Sample | 6 | 3 | 9 | 9 | 18 | 22 | 11 | 12 | 4 | 6 | $\bar{x} = 5.7$ |
| Interviewers | — | — | 2 | 2 | 7 | 23 | 18 | 30 | 13 | 6 | $\bar{x} = 7.2$ |

Predictably then, our interviewers go on to disclose much stronger than average sympathy scales for the Tories, and company directors, averagely high score for the police, small businessmen, and the church, average scores for colored immigrants, much lower than average scores for Labour, the unions and (surprisingly?) for the Women's Liberation movement, and express overt hostility towards student protesters and revolutionary groups.

Despite this, and in common with some of the middle-class Conservatives who have a high rate of orthodox political participation, their attitudes towards protest are distinctly ambivalent. Table A2.1 sets out their levels of endorsement of each of the protest and repression scale items, and we can see clearly that they have much *higher* than average levels of support for lawful forms of protest and even slightly higher for "blocking traffic with a street demonstration." Like other people, they reject slogan painting, damage, or violence, and their only marked deviation in a negative direction is their hostility toward strikes. Thus they confirm their support for political activism but at the same time, retain a strong belief that the police and the courts should have a free hand with "demonstrators" (they probably think of "demonstrators" as leftists anyway) but are much *less* likely to support the use of troops or government bans. They are, in summary, active, laissez-faire, Conservative democrats in the traditional sense. Whatever else their views may have done to influence the results of this study, they are unlikely to have introduced a leftist bias.

Table A2.1: Comparison of Interviewers' and Sample Responses to Protest and Repression Items

| | % Approving | | % Believe Effective | | % Might Do | |
|---|---|---|---|---|---|---|
| | Inter-viewers | Sample | Inter-viewers | Sample | Inter-viewers | Sample |
| *Protest* | | | | | | |
| Petitions | 100 | 86 | 100 | 63 | 92 | 77 |
| Demonstrations | 82 | 69 | 53 | 60 | 56 | 57 |
| Boycotts | 53 | 37 | 59 | 48 | 69 | 49 |
| Rent strikes | 16 | 24 | 21 | 27 | 21 | 33 |
| Strikes | 5 | 13 | 42 | 42 | 5 | 28 |
| Blockades | 18 | 15 | 32 | 31 | 17 | 24 |
| Occupations | 8 | 15 | 18 | 29 | 8 | 20 |
| Slogans | 0 | 1 | 3 | 6 | 2 | 7 |
| Damages | 0 | 1 | 2 | 10 | 0 | 3 |
| Violence | 0 | 2 | 2 | 11 | 1 | 5 |
| *Repression* | | | | | | |
| Courts punish | 90 | 76 | 79 | 67 | | |
| Police use force | 77 | 68 | 89 | 73 | | |
| Troops break strike | 17 | 41 | 74 | 55 | | |
| Government ban | 14 | 24 | 38 | 33 | | |

# APPENDIX THREE

## TECHNICAL DETAILS OF SCALE CONSTRUCTION
## AND RELIABILITIES OF SCALES
## NOT DEALT WITH IN TEXT

### The Protest Potential Scale (PPS)

The PPS is basically a cumulative Guttman-type scale with some second-order refinements. Guttman scaling (see Guttman 1950) is the most controversial of the techniques of attitude measurement in common usage and its choice in this case will require some justification at both the theoretical and technical levels.

Some scholars in the field have rejected the Guttman model altogether. Thus Scott's magisterial dismissal in the Handbook of Social Psychology:

> The cumulative scaling procedure is mentioned here only because it has been widely used; it is not recommended for attitude measurement" (in Lindsay and Aronson 1969, p. 224).

It is easy to see why the cumulative model has attracted so much scepticism. The principle from which it springs is almost embarrassingly simple when compared with more modern multidimensional scaling techniques. Guttman scaling demands that a sequence of questions should represent a series of "bench marks" along a *single* attitudinal continuum, each item representing a unique order of difficulty. The example most often quoted is the Borgardus social distance scale (see Bogardus 1925) in which respondents indicate to a series of questions whether they would admit a stimulus group (blacks, Catholic, or whomever) to progressively more intimate social relationship, e.g., to one's country, district, club, or family. The cumulative nature of the scoring procedure first *orders* each item by its magnitude of difficulty (i.e., the number of positive responses it attracts). There are only five response patterns (or "scale-types") that fit the cumulative model:

Would you admit (x) to your:

| Country | District | Club | Family | Scale score = |
|---------|----------|------|--------|---------------|
| No | No | No | No | 0 |
| Yes | No | No | No | 1 |
| Yes | Yes | No | No | 2 |
| Yes | Yes | Yes | No | 3 |
| Yes | Yes | Yes | Yes | 4 |

Any deviation from this pattern is counted as an error and is corrected. These may be single errors (i.e., uniquely determined scores),

| | | | | |
|---|---|---|---|---|
| eg: | Yes | No | Yes | Yes |
| which becomes: | Yes | Yes | Yes | Yes |

Or there may be uncertain patterns,

| | | | | |
|---|---|---|---|---|
| eg: | Yes | No | Yes | No |
| which may be: | Yes | Yes | Yes | No |
| or: | Yes | No | No | No |

or there may even be multiple errors,

| | | | | |
|---|---|---|---|---|
| eg: | No | No | Yes | Yes |

The number of such "corrections" made to create a perfect scale score for every respondent are then added up. The total number of errors are then ivided by the total number of responses (N respondents x n items) and the result subtracted from 1. The resulting "coefficient of reliability" is an index of the extent to which observed scores fit the cumulative model and will vary from 0.0 to 1.0 and an arbitrary criterion of .90 is usually taken to indicate a minimum satisfactory score. This sounds very stringent but is in fact rather easy to obtain; coefficients of up to .89 have to be generated from random data (see White and Sultz 1957), and the result is highly dependent upon the marginal popularities of the items. Highly skewed items will artificially inflate rep. by minimizing the range of the errors it is possible to make.

The whole procedure militates against the growing acceptance of a model of attitude structure that emphasizes multidimensional complexity. The process of striving after a neatly well-spread set of items will eliminate items on the basis of their popularities ("adjacent" items generate a lot of "errors" between them) and not according to their usefulness in describing the underlying attitude the whole scale is supposed to describe. And, as Scott says, this neat analytical result is achieved only at the cost of sacrificing discriminatory power:

Given the usual contribution to item responses of "random" and item-specific variance, a wide distribution of item magnitudes will not contribute maximally to the detection of intersubject differences in the focal attribute" (Lindsay and Aronson 1969, p. 224).

In addition to the above technical criticism it is also true that many of the so-called Guttman scales that appear in the literature do not have even the fundamental face validation of traversing a clear psychological or behavioral distance between the positive and negative poles of a single dimension. Anyone who chooses to use Guttman scaling must have some very good reasons, and must answer all the above criticisms.

The single dimension it is proposed to measure is people's readiness to engage in examples of unorthodox political behavior. The conceptual background is discussed fully in the text, and it will suffice to say here that, unlike so many other cumulative scales, the psychological distance implied by the refusal to step beyond signing a petition and the acceptance of the use of occupations and illegal demonstrations indeed traverses a psychologically and behaviorally significant distance between positive and negative affect. Also, the items marking the progression along this dimension are highly concrete and discrete stimulus objects—this is important in establishing unequivocal threshold points and is superior even to the Bogardus approach which takes a *single* stimulus object and merely increases the strength of the stimulus at each stage. Thus the conceptualization of the scale items is very well suited to the theory of Guttman scaling in a way that few other applications can be. The question underlying the scale is, "How far are you prepared to go?" and this is exactly the principle of cumulative scoring.

What about the limitations imposed by unidimensionality? This criticism, though valid in itself, forgets about the possibility of a dual or even a multiple conception of dimensionality in attitude scale construction which is in fact present in other forms of scaling where a single "attitude towards the object" score is determined upon. There may be a number of semiindependent *input* dimensions, but the process of data reduction implied by scaling results in a single *output* dimension. So it can be with Guttman scaling. Our pretest work determined that three "input" dimensions were important, conscious behavioral intentions (would do?), positive or negative affect (approve?), and utility (effective?). If each item is endowed with a score adjusted for differential weighting of the input dimension, then we have an unidimensional output dimension derived from more than a single attribute. For this main study, we judged that the effectiveness dimension stood sufficiently far away from the other two dimensions, and was of sufficient substantive interest in its own right, to merit separate treatment in the analysis and determined upon a dual input dimension combining the approval and behavioral intention scores.

The substantive meaning of the interdimensional relationships are dealt with in the text. It remains here to examine and specify the method of combination. First, inspection of the marginal distributions of the ten examples of unorthodox political behavior in Table 2.1 indicated at once that three items, "painting slogans on walls," "damaging property," and "personal violence" were unsuitable for scaling procedures of *any* kind since more than 90% of respondents rejected them out of hand. The "approval" and "behavioral intention" scores for the remaining seven items were then included in a simple principal axis factor analysis and the results are included in Table A3.1. A single factor is described having an eigenvalue greater than one which explains 32% of the total variance. The second "factor" is in fact a "difficulty factor" reflecting merely the *relative* item magnitude. All the items, for both the approval and intention scores, load consistently on the first factor. This is true even of "signing a petition" whose presence in a scale of unorthodox political behavior might be queried on a priori grounds. Thus we start with firm evidence of unidimensionality.

For each item, the approval and intention scores were combined to result in dichotomous scores suitable for scaleogram analysis. For reasons discussed in the text, the combination of scores was effected in this way:

| | Approval | | | | |
|---|---|---|---|---|---|
| Intentions | Strongly Approve | Approve | Dis- approve | Disapprove Strongly | Missing Data |
| Have done | 1 | 1 | 1 | 1 | MD |
| Would do | 1 | 1 | 1 | 1 | MD |
| Might do | 1 | 1 | 0 | 0 | MD |
| Never do | 0 | 0 | 0 | 0 | MD |
| Missing data | MD | MD | MD | MD | MD |

In the case of "lawful demonstrations," for example, the following division of the data occurred:

| | Approve | | Disapprove |
|---|---|---|---|
| Have done | 101 | (1) | 4 |
| Would do | 429 | | 28 |
| Might do | 335 | | 84 |
| Never do | 282 | (0) | 395 |

Table A3.1: Principal Axis Factor Analysis of Protest Items

| Item | "Dimension" | Factor I | Factor II | Commu-nalities |
|------|-------------|----------|-----------|----------------|
| (1) Signing petitions | Approval | .436 | .301 | .343 |
| | Behavioral intentions | .527 | .335 | .390 |
| (2) Lawful demonstrations | A. | .536 | .268 | .409 |
| | B.I. | .695 | .347 | .672 |
| (3) Boycotts | A. | .520 | .039 | .347 |
| | B.I. | .636 | .258 | .427 |
| (4) Rent strikes | A. | .469 | −.292 | .342 |
| | B.I. | .570 | −.102 | .346 |
| (5) Unofficial strikes | A. | .427 | −.424 | .394 |
| | B.I. | .558 | −.179 | .363 |
| (6) Occupying buildings | A. | .584 | −.321 | .452 |
| | B.I. | .660 | −.145 | .550 |
| (7) Blocking traffic | A. | .535 | −.196 | .329 |
| | B.I. | .626 | −.022 | .462 |
| Percentage of total variance explained: | | 32% | 6% | n = 1,389 |
| | Eigenvalue = | 4.41 | 0.93 | |

It should be noted that only 6% of the positive responses are found in the "disapprove-but-would-do" condition.

It will be seen from the factor loadings, and from the magnitude of each item that rent strikes and unofficial strikes occupy very similar positions on the positive-to-negative dimension and so are occupying buildings and blocking traffic. Scott says:

> Two equally popular items will either contribute a substantial number of errors or be mutually redundant. ... Such an item may be eliminated in the cause of scale analysis, or it may be dichotomised at a different point ... or it may be combined with one or more other items to produce a single artificial "items" (see Stouffer et al. 1952)" (ibid., p. 223).

In this case we take up Scott's latter recommendation and combine the two item pairs. This left us with five items and these were submitted to a computer scaleogram program, the "GSCORE" programme in OSIRIS. Options were selected that,

(a) eliminated all *cases* having more than two missing data responses out of five. There were 114 such cases;

(b) recoded *all* remaining missing data to *negative* scores;
(c) allowed the *maximum* error-range;
(d) corrected error scores by the MEDIAN method which, in the case of ambiguous scores [e.g., 1, 1, 0, 1, 0 which may be 1, 1, 1, 1, 0 *or* 1, 1, 0, 0, 0 will be scored '3' being the median value of the range of possible scores '2' and '4']. There were 245 such cases.

| | 0 | 1 | 2 | 3 | 4 (Rent/ Unofficial Strikes) | 5 |
|---|---|---|---|---|---|---|
| | (No Protest) | (Peti- tions) | (Demon- strations) | (Boy- cotts) | | (Occupations/ Blockades) |
| n = 1,671 | 357 | 352 | 345 | 250 | 173 | 194 |
| | 21% | 21% | 21% | 15% | 10% | 12% |

Number of errors = 510

Coefficient of reproducibility (rep.) = $\left| -\left(\dfrac{510}{1670 \times 5}\right)\right| = 0.939$

As we said earlier, rep. is a poor statistic and several additional steps were undertaken to obtain better measures of statistical reliability:

(1) Comparison with the simple additive model. The fourteen items contributing to the original scale were summed, using their original 1-4 distributions. The result was found to correlate with the PP scale at r = 0.45. The value of this relationship is of course depressed by the numbers of people who gave high approval score but get low PP scale scores because of their low will to participate.

(2) Comparison with the weighted additive model. The original fourteen scores were standardized and weighted by the loading each obtained on the principal factor reported in Table A3.1. The factor-scale correlated with the PP scale at r = 0.84. So, despite the effect of "approve-but-not-do" scores, the undimensionality derived from the factor analysis fits the simpler Guttman model very well.

(3) Estimation of the coefficient of scaleability (cf., Menzel 1953). The calculation was as follows:

$$\text{MREP (Minimum marginal reproducibility)} = \frac{M_{ij}}{N \times n} \quad \text{where } M = \textit{highest}$$

marginal response to each item, N = respondents, and n = items.

Percentage improvement in scaleability = Rep − MRep.

$$\theta\text{Scale} = \frac{\% \text{ improvement}}{1 - \text{MRep}}$$

$$\text{MRep} = \frac{1256 + 884 + 1098 + 1211 + 1328}{1671 \times 5} = 0.69$$

Percentage improvement = 0.939 − 0.690 = 24.9%

$$\theta\text{Scale} = \frac{0.249}{1 - 0.690} = \frac{0.249}{0.310} = \underline{0.80}$$

This result compares with an arbitrary figure of 0.6 which is regarded as adequate.

(4) Estimation of the index of consistency (Green 1956). This test (IC) compares REP with the REP that would be expected under conditions of statistical independence between items.

IC is calculated as follows:

$$\frac{er' + er''}{N \times n} = \frac{\text{REP I}}{}$$

$$\text{IC} = \frac{\text{REP} - \text{REP I}}{1 - \text{REP I}} \quad \begin{array}{lll} \text{where } er' & = & \text{errors of 1st magnitude} \\ \text{and } er'' & = & \text{errors of 2nd magnitude} \\ N & = & \text{respondents} \\ n & = & \text{items} \end{array}$$

| Items No. | Positive Marginals | er' | |
|-----------|--------------------|-----|-----|
| 1 & 2 | 1256,884 | $\dfrac{884\,(1671 - 1256)}{1671}$ | = 219.6 |
| 2 & 3 | 884,573 | $\dfrac{573\,(1671 - 884)}{n}$ | = 269.8 |
| 3 & 4 | 573,460 | $\dfrac{460\,(1671 - 460)}{n}$ | = 302.2 |
| 4 & 5 | 460,343 | $\dfrac{343\,(1671 - 460)}{n}$ | = 248.5 |
| | | er' | = 1040.1 |

| Items No. | Pos. M. | er'' |
|---|---|---|

1 & 2:  3 & 4      1256,884,  573,460

$$\frac{460 \times 573 \ (1671-1256) \ (1671-884)}{1671^3}$$

$$= \ 18.4$$

2 & 3:  4 & 5      884,573,  460,343

$$\frac{343 \times 460 \ (1671-573) \ (1671-884)}{1671^3}$$

$$= \ 29.2$$

$$er'' \ = \ 47.6$$

$$1 - REP \ I = \frac{(1040.4 + 47.6)}{1671 \times 5} = 1 - 0.8689 = 0.1311$$

$$IC = \frac{0.939 - 0.8689}{0.1311} = \ 0.534$$

This result compares with a figure of "about 0.50" which is considered acceptable. In view of the foregoing conceptual modifications to the Guttman model and the satisfactory outcome of these stringent tests of reliability, the PP-Scale was judged adequate for use.

## The Repression Potential Scale (RPS)

The RPS is a four item Guttman scale based on a single "approval" input dimension of:

(1) Courts giving severe sentences to demonstrators who disregard the police
(2) Police using force against demonstrators
(3) Government using troops to break strikes
(4) Government banning all political demonstrations.

The four-point approve-disapprove score for each item was dichotomized at its midpoint and these scores submitted to GSCORE. Options selected were the same as for the PPS except that only one missing data code was allowed and this eliminated 119 respondents. The following cumulative distribution was obtained:

| 0 (No Action) | 1 (Courts) | 2 (Police) | 3 (Troops) | 4 (Government Ban) | (n = 1,666) |
|---|---|---|---|---|---|
| 190 | 246 | 486 | 452 | 292 | |
| 12% | 15% | 29% | 27% | 17% | |

Number of errors = 350        $Rep = \left| - \frac{350}{1666 \times 4} \right. = 0.947$

Correlation between GSCORE & simple additive index = 0.84

Correlation between GSCORE & factor score        = 0.79

Coefficient of scaleability = 0.87

Index of consistency = 0.49

## The Orthodox Participation Scale (OPS)

The OPS is a seven-item Guttman scale based on a single input dimension of the self-reported *frequency* of participation in the following; listed in order of item-popularity

(1) Reading about politics in the newspapers
(2) Discussing politics with friends
(3) Working with others to help solve community problems
(4) Contact public officials or politicians
(5) Persuade friends to vote as self
(6) Attend political meetings or rallies
(7) Work for a political candidate.

Response categories were "often," "sometimes," "seldom," "never," and distributions were dichotomized between "sometimes" and "seldom" except for item 7 when "seldom" was allowed as a positive response because elections are held only seldom. These scores were submitted to the GSCORE programme with options selected as for the PPS. The following cumulative distribution was obtained:

| 0 (No Action) | 1 (Read) | 2 (Dis- cuss) | 3 Com- munity) | 4 (Con- tact) | 5 (Per- suade) | 6 (Attend) | 7 (Work) | (n = 1720) |
|---|---|---|---|---|---|---|---|---|
| 25% | 18% | 26% | 7% | 6% | 6% | 5% | 8% | |

Number of errors = 602          REP = 0.95

Correlation between GSCORE and simple additive index = 0.81
Correlation between GSCORE and factor scale = 0.86
Coefficient of scaleability = .74
Index of consistency = .39

## The Effectiveness of Protest Scale

For each of the items included in the protest potential scale, respondents were asked to estimate how effective they thought such action may be "in pressing for changes" on a four-point scale thus: "very effective," "somewhat effective," "not very effective," or "not at all effective." The distributions of responses given to these items are shown in Table 2.1. For reasons discussed in the text, these effectiveness scores did not conform to the unidimensional and cumulative pattern appropriate to Guttman-scale construction (coeffi-

Table A3.2: Correlations Between Effectiveness Scores for Protest Items

|  | Petitions | Demonstrations | Boycotts | Strikes | Rent Strikes | Blockades | Occupations |
|---|---|---|---|---|---|---|---|
| Petitions | — | | | | | | |
| Demonstrations | .38 | — | | | | | |
| Boycotts | .25 | .29 | — | | | | |
| Strikes | .06 | .19 | .34 | — | | | |
| Rent strikes | .13 | .22 | .25 | .33 | — | | |
| Blockades | .14 | .23 | .23 | .33 | .32 | — | |
| Occupations | .12 | .18 | .29 | .42 | .32 | .50 | — |

cient of reproducibility = .84, scalability = .34). However, the analysis required that a single effectiveness score should be derived from the item ratings and so other models of scaling were considered and the obvious first choice was to construct an additive Likert-type scale (Likert 1932).

The justification for Likert scaling is derived from measures of the internal consistency of the responses given to the test items, and these may be derived in turn from the matrix of correlations generated between items, as indicated in Table A3.2.

In Table A3.2 we can see that, as a result of ordering the items by their item magnitudes (i.e., their rank-order) most of the high correlations are thrown onto the diagonal. This reflects a residual approximation toward the Guttman model in which we would expect to find adjacent items closely correlated and nonadjacent items neutrally correlated.

Early methods for determining the reliability of Likert scales concentrated upon the item-scale correlation (i.e., the correlation between an item and the sum of all the other items), but this tended to overlook the internal consistency of the item pool. Other techniques tended to concentrate on the "split-half" reliability solution whereby the items were randomly divided into two groups, and the sum of the two correlated and corrected for the effects of halving. This procedure would be repeated to gain an impression of consistency, but this tended to minimize item reliabilities. These problems were resolved by Cronbach (1951), who developed an index of consistency called alpha ($\alpha$), which can be shown to be the average of all possible split-half correlations. McKennel has provided a method of estimating alpha through a convenient approximation formula:

$$\alpha = \frac{n r_{ij}}{1 + (N-1) r_{ij}}$$

where n = number of items, and
$r_{ij}$ = the average interitem correlation

In the case of the effectiveness scores the average interitem correlation is .26, which gives the following value for alpha:

$$= \frac{7 \times 0.26}{1 + (7-1)\, 0.26} = \frac{1.82}{2.56} = 0.71$$

According to Cronbach and well substantiated by McKennel and the work of the government social survey, a value of .60 is considered useable and .70 is considered good. Thus we may accept the items as forming a summative scale.

The alpha coefficient may also be used to determine item reliabilities by taking the average item-item correlation. The lowest item reliability in the scale is that for "petitions," but it is still 0.61, and the highest is for "blockades" at 0.76, indicating a reasonable homogeneity of the item pool.

## The Effectiveness of Repression Scale

The arguments for creating a summative Likert-type scale for this index are identical to the preceding argument concerning the effectiveness of protest scale, only more emphatic. Respondents' estimates, as discussed in the text, of the effectiveness of four kinds of government action to combat protest and strikes do not at all conform to the cumulative Guttman model (coefficient of reproducibility = 0.51), and this is also reflected in the non-diagonality of the interitem correlation matrix, as follows:

|  |  | 1 | 2 | 3 |
|---|---|---|---|---|
| (1) | Courts giving severe sentences | — | | |
| (2) | Police use force | .43 | — | |
| (3) | Troops break strikes | .23 | .33 | — |
| (4) | Government bans all demonstrations | .31 | .27 | .37 |

$$r_{ij} = .323, \; n = 4 \quad \alpha = \frac{4 \times 0.323}{1 + (3 \times 0.323)} = .66$$

With fewer items, the value of the average interitem coefficient becomes more critical, and here a value for $\bar{r}_{ij}$ of .323 yields a fairly marginal alpha of .66, but the evenness of the interitem values tends to favor the use of a summative scale.

## The Dissatisfaction with Government Index

Respondents were asked to indicate their satisfaction with the performance of the government in ten key areas of responsibility, according to whether they felt that the government's handling of this problem had been "very good," "good," "bad," or "very bad." The analysis required that a single index of satisfaction with government performance should be provided. Table A3.3 displays the correlation matrix generated by the item-satisfaction scores. Following earlier procedures, we find all associations are positive and that the average interitem correlation is .257, yielding an alpha coefficient of:

$$\alpha = \frac{10 \times 0.257}{1 + (9 \times 0.257)} = \frac{2.57}{3.31} = \underline{.78}$$

which is highly satisfactory. The lowest item alpha is for the colored immigrants item, at $\alpha = .69$.

But with a larger number of items, it is difficult to be certain that there may not be some clustering in the matrix, which would indicate the presence of significant subscales. That is to say, in addition to the general underlying dimension of satisfaction-dissatisfaction with the government, there may be special groupings of areas of dissatisfaction. For example, perhaps the tendency to be dissatisfied with "equality of wealth" will cluster with "equal rights for colored immigrants" and "equal rights for women" in a subscale having to do with an underlying attitude favorable towards *equality*. This is certainly the kind of result that was expected.

To test for this possibility, the ten items were factor analyzed through a principal axis solution and rotated to varimax criteria. The results are presented in Table A3.4.

**Table A3.3: Intercorrelation Matrix for Dissatisfaction with Government Items**

| Respondent's satisfaction with | A | B | C | D | E | F | G | H | I | J |
|---|---|---|---|---|---|---|---|---|---|---|
| (A) Looking after old people | — | | | | | | | | | |
| (B) Guaranteeing equal rights for men and women | .31 | — | | | | | | | | |
| (C) Seeing to it that everyone who wants a job can have one | .39 | .28 | — | | | | | | | |
| (D) Providing good education | .31 | .20 | .34 | — | | | | | | |
| (E) Providing good medical care | .28 | .21 | .35 | .48 | — | | | | | |
| (F) Providing adequate housing | .35 | .24 | .39 | .35 | .30 | — | | | | |
| (G) Fighting pollution | .25 | .17 | .25 | .22 | .21 | .37 | — | | | |
| (H) Guaranteeing neighborhoods safe from crime | .19 | .10 | .20 | .20 | .21 | .31 | .32 | — | | |
| (I) Providing equal rights for colored immigrants | .16 | .18 | .16 | .15 | .16 | .22 | .19 | .22 | — | |
| (J) Trying to even out differences in wealth between people | .30 | .27 | .32 | .20 | .18 | .41 | .26 | .24 | .20 | — |

Table A3.4.

|      |                         | (Unrotated Principal Axis) | | (Rotated to Varimax Criteria) | |
|------|-------------------------|-------------|-------------|-------------|-------------|
|      |                         | Factor 1 | Factor 2 | Factor 1 | Factor 2 |
| (1)  | Care of old             | .559 | −.000 | .427 | .360 |
| (2)  | Sex equality            | .417 | .023 | .339 | .249 |
| (3)  | Housing                 | .663 | .150 | .604 | .311 |
| (4)  | Pollution               | .483 | .186 | .489 | .168 |
| (5)  | Fight crime             | .422 | .161 | .427 | .148 |
| (6)  | Race equality           | .340 | .129 | .343 | .120 |
| (7)  | Economic equality       | .524 | .251 | .563 | .145 |
| (8)  | Full employment         | .599 | −.065 | .416 | .435 |
| (9)  | Education               | .570 | −.362 | .203 | .644 |
| (10) | Health                  | .546 | −.367 | .181 | .632 |
|      | Percentage of variance = | 33.7% | 10.8% | 86.2% | 13.8% |

These results indicate, surprisingly, that no subscales are present in the data. Two factors are found, it is true, but after rotation the first factor accounts for nearly all of the common variance between them and the second "factor" does not merit serious consideration. Nothing "different" is measured by the two items that make up the second factor: education and housing. What occurred in the analysis is almost certainly this: A principal axis solution searches first for a "consensual factor" (i.e., something most people tend to agree about, and in this case the analysis finds this consensual element in every item (more in the unrotated loadings). It then searches for a second factor among the remaining variance and, in practice, this tends to be a "disensual factor" (i.e., something people tend to disagree about). Now, whereas there is a slight "leftish" component in general dissatisfaction with the (then) Conservative government, there are a number of (probably Tory) respondents who still register dissatisfaction with education ("they did not do away with comprehensives," perhaps), and also there was dissatisfaction with the very fast inflation in house prices, which was eroding Harold Macmillan's dream of a "property-owning democracy." These two areas of middle-class Tory dissatisfaction were not related (by *Tories*) to other areas of dissatisfaction. Hence the unusually high correlation between the two items (.47—the only correlation above .41) and which provided the analysis with a two-item basis for a very weak second factor and the analysis seized upon it. But there is no case to be made for treating these two items separately and a summative scale to measure dissatisfaction with government performance is clearly the best strategy.

The variable was also required for analysis in categorical form and the total range of 10 to 40 was divided into the range:

| 10 – 21 | 22 – 25 | 26 – 30 | 31 – 40 |
|---------|---------|---------|---------|
| 42% | 24% | 19% | 15% |
| "satisfied" | "partly satisfied" | "dissatis- fied" | "very dis- satisfied" |

A skewed distribution was created deliberately to keep faith with the wide distribution of satisfaction with government performance in many areas of responsibility and to emphasize degrees of *dis*satisfaction which was thought a theoretically appropriate strategy to the prediction of protest potential.

## The Efficacy and Political Trust Scales

These scales are dealt with under the same heading because there exists a conceptual problem that affects both measures together. Some of the substantive aspects of this problem are dealt with in the text (see especially Chapter 5). Briefly, the problem concerns the unidimensionality of the efficacy scale and its relationship to political trust. There is one school of thought that insists that within the feeling of personal efficacy there exists an element of "perceived system responsiveness" that has more to do with political *trust* than with the supposed *basic* feeling of *personal* efficacy. This basic definition is that efficacy is an attitude towards political authority that implies the belief that, through *personal* influence, the individual may contribute, even in a modest way, to the political decision-making processes of government. The problem to which we refer revolves around the dilemma that some people, often politically sophisticated people, feel that they are personally the kind of person that can influence the course of events, but that the present incumbents of office are unwilling to listen even to efficacious citizens like themselves. Hence the intervention of the concept of political trust, causing a discontinuity in efficacy. For the moment though, the reliabilities of the two scales may be examined separately and the existence of a shared subscale tested subsequently.

### THE EFFICACY SCALE
(see Robinson et al. 1969, pp. 626-647)

The politically efficacious citizen is one who *disagrees* with the following statements:

(a) "People like me have no say in what the government does."
(b) "Voting is the only way people like me can have any influence on the way the government runs things."
(c) "Sometimes politics and government seem so complicated that a person like me cannot really understand what is going on."

**Table A3.5.**

|  |  | a | b | c | d | e |
|---|---|---|---|---|---|---|
| (a) | No say in Government | — | | | | |
| (b) | Voting only way | .26 | — | | | |
| (c) | Politics too complicated | .29 | .22 | — | | |
| (d) | Officials don't care | .37 | .20 | .37 | — | |
| (e) | MPs lose touch | .32 | .16 | .27 | .54 | — |
| (f) | Parties not interested | .34 | .16 | .29 | .58 | .67 |

$$\bar{r}ij = .34, \ n = 6, \ \alpha = \frac{6 \times 0.34}{1 + (5 \times 0.34)} = \frac{2.04}{2.70} = \underline{.76}$$

(d) "I don't think public officials care much about what people like me think."

(e) "Generally speaking, those we elect as MPs to Westminster lose touch with people pretty quickly."

(f) "Parties are only interested in their votes, not in their opinions." (for distributions see Table 5.4.)

Early use of this scale by its inventors (Campbell et al., *The American Voter*, 1960) in the United States showed that the scale conformed (surprisingly) to Guttman-scale criteria. This is certainly not the case in this British sample (coefficient of reproducibility = .81). The correlation matrix generated by those items is presented in Table A3.5.

An average intercorrelation of .34 yielded an alpha of .76, which is very encouraging. But this figure is inflated by what appears to be a close clustering of the three latter items in the scale and, suspiciously, it is these three items that are most suspected of contamination by the concept of trust. The weakest item in the scale is "voting is the only way," which has a reputation among political scientists for confusing respondents because the question implies that the act of voting *does* influence "the way the government runs things," which, from one point of view, the *cynical* efficacious citizen will beg leave to doubt. Here the notion of trust may intervene rather differently. Yet even this item has an item alpha of .64, and the impression remains that a normal summative scale of efficacy is a sound strategy. Let us turn for a moment then, to the trust scale itself.

### THE POLITICAL TRUST SCALE

The concept of political trust is less ambiguous but multifaceted. (The distinction between intrinsic trust and pragmatic trust is discussed in the text.) Four items were deployed in this study to measure trust and focus the respondent's attention upon the professional practitioners of politics in

Britain: Two items were adapted from the ISR political trust scale (see Robinson et al. 1969):

(a) "Generally speaking, would you say that this country is run for a few big interests concerned only for themselves or that it is run for the benefit of all the people?"

(b) "How much do you *trust* the Government in Westminster to do what is right?"

And two more items were devised by the author for use in this study which focus more clearly upon the intrinsic aspects of trust (i.e., personal probity of politicians) rather than the pragmatic aspects emphasised by the ISR items. These are:

(c) "When people in politics speak on television, or to newspapers, or in Parliament, how much, in your opinion, do they tell the truth?"

(d) "How much do you trust a British Government of either party to place the needs of this country *above* the interests of their own political party?"

The first item was scored dichotomously at first, giving a score of 1 to the trusting and of 4 to the cynical ("few big interests") in order to keep the weighted range similar to the other three items which were scored on a four-point scale: "Just about always," "most of the time," "only some of the time," "almost never." In addition, those 16% of the sample who said "don't know" to the first item (compared with only 3 - 5% on the other three items) were given a neutral score of 2.5 in order to minimize the amount of missing data for the entire scale. The distributions of the items are given in Table 5.5 The interitem correlations are given in Table A3.6.

The coefficients are almost uniformly high and the alpha value of 0.74 is highly satisfactory especially for a four-item scale. There seems little doubt that the idea of a dimension of political trust and cynicism has a coherent appeal for the majority of the sample.

Table A3.6.

|     |                                 | a   | b   | c   |
| --- | ------------------------------- | --- | --- | --- |
| (a) | Few big interests/all the people |     |     | —   |
| (b) | Trust to do what is right       | .41 | —   |     |
| (c) | Politicians tell truth          | .26 | .50 | —   |
| (d) | Country above party             | .36 | .51 | .47 |

$$\bar{r}_{ij} = .42, n = 4, \alpha = \frac{4 \times 0.42}{1 + (3 \times 0.42)} = 0.74$$

## Efficacy and Trust

The argument outlined earlier suggests two specific hypotheses:

(1) Items (d) (e) and (f) of the efficacy scale are so conditioned by an undertow of "perceived system responsiveness" that the scale should be divided into two, three-item scales; the first called *personal efficacy* (i.e., "some say in Government" + "voting not only way" + "politics not too complicated") and the second called *system responsiveness* (i.e., "officials do care" + "MPs keep in touch" + "parties are interested in opinions").

(2) That hypothesis one is not true and the 6-item scale is reliable and that, consequently, it is advisable to regard efficacy as a single dimension but a dualist concept which is, in practice, indivisible.

An appropriate test of these hypotheses is to introduce the unequivocal trust scale and create a single 10-item pool which may be factor-analyzed. The correlation matrix of this item pool is set out in Table A3.7 in such a way as to show the interscale relationships. The two most obvious "clusters" in Table A3.7 are system responsiveness and trust, and the average interitem correlation between the items of the two scales is .31, and, taken together, the system responsiveness/trust scale has an alpha of .86, which is even better than the system responsiveness/efficacy scale. When the three additive scales are calculated in accord with hypothesis one, the following interscale correlations are observed:

|                        | E   | SR  | T |
|------------------------|-----|-----|---|
| Personal Efficacy:     | -   |     |   |
| System Responsiveness: | .47 | -   |   |
| Political Trust:       | .17 | .48 | - |

This seems to settle the argument in favor of hypothesis one: we should have three scales because system responsiveness is strung, as it were, halfway between the two other scales. But this would prove nonsensical in the analysis because if we attempted to use all three scales together—just as the analysis in Chapter 5 would demand, the personal efficacy and trust scales, being relatively poorly related, would partial out completely the effect of system responsiveness upon any predicted variable. Hence the best strategy would be to combine the S-R scale with one or other and since, traditionally, it is part of the efficacy scale, there it should remain and hypothesis two should be upheld as the best strategy. So what seemed a simple matter of empirical determination has proved to be a conundrum. Having no other alternative, an appeal for settlement of the problems was made to factor analysis.

Table A3.7: Inter-item Correlations of Efficacy and Trust Items

|     |                       | A   | B   | C   | D   | E   | F   | G   | H   | I   | J   |
|-----|-----------------------|-----|-----|-----|-----|-----|-----|-----|-----|-----|-----|
| (a) | No say in government   | —   |     |     |     |     |     |     |     |     |     |
| (b) | Voting only way        | .26 | —   |     |     |     |     |     |     |     |     |
| (c) | Politics too complex   | .26 | .21 | —   |     |     |     |     |     |     |     |
| (d) | Officials don't care   | .37 | .20 | .38 | —   |     |     |     |     |     |     |
| (e) | MPs lose touch         | .37 | .17 | .27 | .53 | —   |     |     |     |     |     |
| (f) | Parties not interested | .32 | .16 | .29 | .57 | .65 | —   |     |     |     |     |
| (g) | Few big interests      | .14 | .05 | .07 | .28 | .27 | .31 | —   |     |     |     |
| (h) | Do not trust government| .19 | .00 | .11 | .33 | .31 | .35 | .41 | —   |     |     |
| (i) | MPs tell lies          | .13 | .03 | .11 | .28 | .26 | .32 | .26 | .51 | —   |     |
| (j) | Party above country    | .18 | .01 | .10 | .32 | .30 | .36 | .36 | .51 | .47 | —   |

Two (*not* three) factors emerged from the principal axis analysis of the ten-item pool and when rotated to varimax criteria gave the configuration in Table A3.8.

The results confirm that we have a classic example of conceptual inter-penetration between two scales. The most "contaminated" item concerns "parties are only interested in votes, not opinions" which loads equally only what are otherwise fairly clearly defined efficacy and trust scales but that trust continues to penetrate the efficacy scale through the two other "system responsiveness" items, generating the correlation of .40 between the two scales that was noted in the text. Hence, the decision was taken to retain the efficacy and trust scales as they are and to incorporate the conceptual interpenetrations between them into the substantive interpretations and influences made. This solution at least has the merit of consistency with the considerable literature on the subject. The only other possible solution, to

Table A3.8.

|     |                        | Factor I | Factor II |
|-----|------------------------|----------|-----------|
| (a) | No say in government    | .140     | .481      |
| (b) | Voting only way         | −.056    | .363      |
| (c) | Politics too complex    | .058     | .470      |
| (d) | Officials don't care    | .348     | .670      |
| (e) | MPs lose touch          | .348     | .640      |
| (f) | Parties not interested  | .416     | .643      |
| (g) | Few big interests       | .478     | .168      |
| (h) | Not trust government    | .748     | .068      |
| (i) | MPs tell lies           | .620     | .106      |
| (j) | Party over country      | .687     | .125      |

eliminate the ambiguous items and use only the personal efficacy and trust items, is not feasible because the three personal efficacy items (a, b, and c) return an alpha coefficient of only 0.49. It seems, in fact, that the notion of system responsiveness, despite its association with political trust, is actually indispensable to the proper interpretation of efficacy as traditionally measured by political scientists even though it is conceptually distinct. Clearly, further research is required on this subject:

Both variables were required for categorical analysis, and we divided as follows:

**Efficacy**

Low                                                                                    High

| 6 – 10 | 11 – 12 | 13 – 15 | 16 – 20 |
|--------|---------|---------|---------|
| 17% | 27% | 25% | 17% |

**Trust**

High                                                                                    Low

| 4 – 8.5 | 9 – 11.5 | 12 – 13.5 | 14 – 16 |
|---------|----------|-----------|---------|
| 24% | 32% | 28% | 16% |

# BIBLIOGRAPHY

Aaron, R. *Les Desillusions du Progres*. Paris: Calmann-Levy, 1969.

Aberbach, J.D. and Walker, J.L. "Political trust and racial ideology." *American Political Science Review*, 1969, No. 63, pp. 83-99.

Abrams, M. and Hall, J. *Life Satisfaction of the British People*. Paper given at OECD, Paris, May 1972.

Abrams, M. "The British middle class Socialist." *Encounter*, March 1975, pp. 7-15.

Abrams, P. and Little, A. "The young activist in British politics." *British Journal of Sociology*, Vol. XVI, 1965, No. 3.

Allerbeck, K.R. "Alternative explanations of participation in student movements." Paper presented to 7th World I.P.S.A Conference, Munich, September 1970, pp. 13-14.

Ali, T. *The Coming British Revolution*. London: Jonathan Cape, 1972.

Allport, G.W. "The composition of political attitudes." *American Journal of Sociology*, Vol. 35, 1929, pp. 220-238.

Almond, G.A. and Verba, S. *The Civic Culture*. Boston: Little, Brown, 1965.

Amery, L.S. *Thoughts on the Constitution*. London: Oxford University Press, 1953.

Apter, D.E. (ed.). *Ideology and Discontent*. New York: Free Press, 1964.

Bagehot, W. *The English Constitution*. London: Chapman & Hall, 1867.

Bendix, R. "Social stratification and political power" in Bendix R. and Lipset, S.M. (eds.), *Class Status and Power*. London: Routledge & Kegan Paul, 1967.

Benewick, R. *Political Violence and Public Order*. London: Penguin, 1969.

Benewick, R. and Smith, T.A. (eds.). *Direct Action and Democratic Politics*. London: Allen & Unwin, 1972.

Berkowitz, L. "The expression and reduction of hostility." *Psychological Bulletin*, 55, 1958, pp. 257-287.

———. "The study of urban violence: Some implications of laboratory studies of frustration and aggression." *American Behavioral Scientist*, Vol. 11, No. 4, 1968, pp. 14-17.

———. "Frustrations, comparisons, and other sources of emotional arousal as contributors to social unrest." *Journal of Social Issues*, Vol. 28, No. 1, 1972, pp. 77-91.

Blondel, J. *Voters, Parties and Leaders*. Middlesex, Eng.: Penguin, 1963.

Blumenthal, M.D., Kahn, R.L., Andrews, F.M. and Head, K.B. *Justifying Violence*. Ann Arbor, Mich.: University of Michigan, 1972.

Bogardus, E.S. "Measuring social distances." *Journal of Applied Psychology*, Vol. 9, 1925, pp. 299-308.

Bondurant, J. *The Conquest of Violence: The Gandhian Philosophy of Conflict*. Berkeley: University of California Press, 1965.

Bowen, D.R., Bowen, E.R., Gawiser, S.R. and Masotti, L.H. "Deprivation, mobility and orientation toward protest of the urban poor." *American Behavioral Scientist*, Vol. 11, No. 4, 1968, pp. 20-24.

Butler, D.E. and Stokes, D. *Political Change in Britain*. New York, St. Martin's, 1971.

Bwy, D. "Dimensions of social conflict in Latin America." *American Behavioral Scientist*, vol. 11, No. 4, 1968, pp. 39-50.

Calton-Hall, W.G. *Political Crime*. London: Allen & Unwin, 1923.

Campbell, A. et al. *The American Voter*. New York: John Wiley, 1960.

Campbell, A. "A la recherche d'un modele en psychologie electorale comparative." *Revue France Sociologie*, vol. VII, 1966.

Campbell, A. and Schumann, H. "Racial attitudes in fifteen American cities," in Supplemental Studies for the National Advisory Committee on Civil Disorders. Washington, D.C.: Government Printing Office, July 1968, pp. 11-67.

Campbell, A., Converse, P. and Rodgers, W.L. *The Perceived Quality of Life*. New York: Basic Books, 1976.

Cantor, N.F. *The Age of Protest*. New York: Howthorn, 1969.

Carr, L. and Roberts, S.O. "Correlates of civil-rights participation." *Journal of Social Psychology*, Vol. 67, 1965, pp. 259-267.

Carter, A. *Direct Action and Liberal Democracy*. London: Routledge & Kegan Paul, 1973.

Cavanna, H. "Protest in France," in Crick, B. and Robson, W.A., *Protest and Discontent*. Middlesex, Eng.: Penguin, 1970.

Centers, R. *The Psychology of Social Class*. Princeton, N.J.: Princeton University Press, 1949.

Chomsky, N. *Problems of Knowledge and Freedom*. New York: Random House, 1971.

Citrin, J. and Elkins, D.J. *Political Disaffection among British University Students*. Institute of International Studies, Research Series, No. 23, Berkeley, 1975.

Clutterbuck, R. *Protest and the Urban Guerrilla*. London: Cassell, 1973.

Cohen, C. *Civil Disobedience*. New York: Columbia University Press, 1971.

Converse, P.E. "The nature of belief systems in mass publics," in Apter, D.E. *Ideology and Discontent*. New York: Free Press, 1964.

Cox, B. *Civil Liberties in Britain*. Middlesex, Eng.: Penguin, 1975.

Crawford, T. and Naditch, M. "Relative deprivation, powerlessness and militancy: The psychology of social protest." *Psychiatry*, Vol. 33, No. 2, 1970, pp. 208-223.

Crick, B. and Robson, W.A. (eds.). *Protest and Discontent*. Middlesex, Eng.: Penguin, 1970.

Critchley, T.A. *The Conquest of Violence*. New York, Schocken, 1970.

Cronbach, L.J. "Coefficient alpha and the internal structure of tests." *Psychometrika*, Vol. 16, 1951, pp. 297-334.

Dahl, R.A. *Polyarchy: Participation and Opposition*. London: Yale University Press, 1973.

Davies, J.C. "Towards a theory of revolution." *American Sociological Review*, No. 27, 1962, pp. 5-19.

–––. (ed.). *When Men Revolt and Why*. New York: Free Press, 1971.

De Fleur, M.L. and Westie, F.R. "Verbal attitudes and overt acts: An experiment on the saliency of attitudes." *American Sociological Review*, Vol. 23, 1958, pp. 667-673.

Di Palma, G. *Apathy and Participation*. New York: Free Press, 1970.

Dollard, J., Doob, L.W., Miller, N.E., Mowrer, O.H. and Sears, R.R. *Frustration and Aggression*. New Haven, Conn.: Yale University Press, 1939.

Dowse, R.E. and Hughes, J.A. *Political Sociology*. New York: John Wiley, 1972, pp. 299-300.

Driver, C. *The Disarmers*. London: Hodder & Stoughton, 1964.

Easton, D. *A Systems Analysis of Political Life*. New York: John Wiley, 1965.

Eckstein, H. "The British political system," in Beer, S.H. and Ulam, A. *Patterns of Government*. New York, 1965.

———. "A theory of stable democracy," in Feierabend, Feierabend and Gurr (eds.). *Anger, Violence and Politics*. Englewood Cliffs, N.J.: Prentice-Hall, 1972.

Eisinger, P.K. "Racial differences in protest participation in an American city." Paper presented at the European Consortium for Political Research Workshop on "Political behavior, dissatisfaction, and protest," Mannheim, April 1973.

Eysenck, H.J. *The Psychology of Politics*. London: Routledge & Kegan Paul. 1963.

Feierabend, I.K., Feierabend, R.L. and Gurr T.R. (eds.). *Anger, Violence and Politics*. Englewood Cliffs, N.J. Prentice-Hall, 1972.

Feierabend, I.K., Feierabend, R.L. and Nesvold, B.A. "Social change and political violence: Cross-national patterns," in Graham and Gurr (eds.), pp. 632-687.

Finifter, A.W. "Dimensions of political alienation." *American Political Science Review*, No. 64, 1970, pp. 389-410.

Flacks, R. *Youth and Social Change*. Chicago: Rand McNally, 1971.

Fogelson, R.M. *Violence as Protest*. New York: Doubleday, 1971.

Fothogill, J.E. and Wilcock, L.T. "Interviewers and interviewing." *Incorporated Statistician*, Vol. 5 (Supplement), 1955, pp. 37-56.

Free, L.A. "Gauging thresholds of frustration." American Political Science Association Meeting, Sept. 1967.

Gamson, W.A. "Political trust and its ramifications," in Gilbert Abcarian and John W. Soule (eds.). *Social Psychology and Political Behavior: Problems and Prospects*. Columbus, Ohio, Charles E. Merrill, 1971, pp. 40-55.

———. *Power and Discontent*. Homewood, Ill.: Dorsey, 1968.

Gass, O. "Socialism and democracy." *Commentary*, Vol. 29, 1960, p. 574.

Geschwender, J. "Social structure and the Negro revolt: An examination of some hypotheses." *Social Forces*, No. 43, 1964, pp. 248-56.

Goffman, B. and Muller, E.N. "The strange case of relative gratification and potential for political violence: The V-curve hypothesis." *American Political Science Review*, Vol. 67, 1973, pp. 514-539.

Goldthorpe, J. and Lockwood D. *The Affluent Worker*. London: Cambridge University Press, 1968.

Green, B.F. "A method of scalogram analysis using summary statistics." *Psychometrika*, Vol. 21, 1956, pp. 79-88.

Gurr, T.R. *Why Men Rebel*. Princeton, N.J.: Princeton University Press, 1970.

Guttman, L. "The basis for scaleogram analysis," in Stouffer, S.A. et al. *Measurement and Prediction*. Princeton, N.J.: Princeton University Press, 1950.

Hain, P. *Don't Play with Apartheid*. London: Allen & Unwin, 1971.

———. *Radical Regeneration: Protest, Direct Action and Community Politics*. London: Quartet, 1975.

Halloran, J.D., Elliott, P., and Murdock, G. *Demonstrations and Communication: A Case Study*. Middlesex, Eng.: Penguin, 1970.

Heberle, R. *From Democracy to Nazism*. Baton Rouge, 1945.

Hobsbawm, E.J. *Primitive Rebels*. New York: Praeger, 1959.

Humphry, D. *Police Power and Black People*. London: Panther Books, 1972.

Huntington, S.P. "Postindustrial politics: How benign will it be?" *Comparative Politics*, Vol. 6, No. 2, Dec. 1973, p. 163.

Hyman, H.H. and Sheatsley, P.B. "the Authoritarian personality—a methodological critique," in Christie, R. and Jahoda, M. (eds.). *Studies in the Scope and Method of the Authoritarian Personality*. Free Press, Glencoe, Ill.: Free Press, 1954.

Hyman, H.H. et al. *Interviewing in Social Research*. Chicago: University of Chicago Press, 1954.

Hyman, H.H. and Singer, P.B. (eds.). *Readings in Reference Group Theory and Research*. New York: Macmillan, 1968.

Hyman, H.H. "Surveys in the study of political psychology," in Knutson, J. (ed.). *The Handbook of Political Psychology*. San Francisco: Jossey-Bass, 1973.

Inglehart, R. "The silent revolution in Europe: Intergenerational change in post-industrial societies." *American Political Science Review*, Vol. 65, No. 47, 1971, pp. 991-1017.

Kaase, M. *Political Ideology, Dissatisfaction and Protest*. Mannheim: Institut für Sozialwissenschaften an der Universität Mannheim, Sept. 1972.

Katz, D. "Functional approach to the study of attitudes." *Public Opinion Quarterly*. Vol. 24, 1960, pp. 163-204.

–––. "Survey methods in psychological research," in Gloch, C.Y. (ed.). *Survey Research in the Social Sciences*. New York: Russell Sage, 1967.

Kavanagh, D. "The deferential English: A comparative critique." *Government & Opposition*, Vol. VI, No. 4, 1971, pp. 331-360.

Keniston, K. *Young Radicals*. New York: Harcourt, Brace & World, 1968.

Klein, A. (Ed.). *Dissent, Power, and Confrontation*. New York: McGraw-Hill, 1971.

Kish, L. "A procedure for objective respondent selection within the household." *American Statistical Association Journal*. Sept. 1948, pp. 380-387.

Klingemann, H. and Inglehart, R. "Party identification, ideological preference and the left-right dimension among Western publics," in Budge, Ian and Crewe, Ivor (eds.). *Party Identification and Beyond*. New York: John Wiley, 1975.

Knutson, J.N. (ed.). *Handbook of Political Psychology*. San Francisco: Jossey-Bass, 1973.

Kornhauser, W. *The Politics of Mass Society*. Glencoe, Ill.: Free Press, 1959.

Lane, R.E. *Political Ideology*. Glencoe, Ill.: Free Press, 1962.

–––. *Political Thinking and Consciousness*. Chicago: Markham, 1969.

Leiden, C. and Schmitt, K.M. (eds.). *The Politics of Violence: Revolution in the Modern World*. Englewood Cliffs, N.J.: Prentice-Hall, 1968.

Lenin, V.I. *State and Revolution*. New York: International Publishers, 1932.

Lerner, D. *The Passing of Traditional Society*. New York: Free Press, 1958.

Lewin, K. *The Principles of Topological Psychology*. New York: McGraw-Hill, 1936.

Likert, R. "A technique for measuring attitudes." *Archives of Psychology*, No. 140, 1932.

Lindzey, G. and Aronson, E. *The Handbook of Social Psychology* (2nd.Ed.). Reading, Mass.: Addison-Wesley, 1962.

Linn, L.S. "Verbal attitudes and overt behavior: A study in racial discrimination." *Social Forces*, Vol. 44, 1965, pp. 353-364.

Lipset, S.M. *Student Politics*. New York: Basic Books, 1967.

–––. "Some social requisites of democracy." *American Political Science Review*. Vol. 55, 1959, pp. 69-105.

Lipsky, M. "Protest as a political resource." *American Political Science Review*, No. 62, 1968, pp. 1144-1158.

Lorenz, K. *On Aggression*. New York: Harcourt, Brace & World, 1966.

Lupsha, P.A. "An exploration of political violence: Some psychological theories versus indignation." *American Journal of Sociology*, Vol. II, No. 1, Fall 1971, pp. 89-104.

Macfarlane, L.J. *Political Disobedience*, London: Macmillan, 1971.

Madjwick, P.J. *The Politics of Rural Wales*. London: Hutchinson Educational, 1973.

Marsh, A. "Explorations in unorthodox political behaviour: A scale to measure 'protest potential.' " *European Journal of Political Research,* No. 2, 1974, pp. 107-129.

–––. "The 'silent revolution,' value priorities and the quality of life in Britain." *American Political Science Review,* Vol. LXIX, No. 1, March 1975, pp. 21-30.

Maslow, A.H. "A theory of human motivation." *Psychological Review,* No. 50, 1943, pp. 370-396.

–––. *Motivation and Personality.* New York: Harper & Row, 1954.

Masotti, L.H. and Bowen, D.R. (eds.). *Riots and Rebellion: Civil Violence in the Urban Community.* Beverly Hills: Sage Publications, 1968.

McClosky, H. "Survey research in political science," in Glock, C.Y. *Survey Research in the Social Sciences.* New York: Russel Sage, 1967.

McKennel, A.C. *Use of Coefficient Alpha in Constructing Attitude and Similar Scales.* Government Social Survey, Paper No. M.139 (undated).

McKenzie, R.T. and Silver, A. *Angels in Marble.* London: Heinemann, 1968.

McPhail, C. "Civil disorder participation: A critical examination of recent research." *American Sociological Review,* No. 36, 1971, pp. 1058-1073.

Merton, R.K. *Social Theory and Social Structure.* New York: Free Press, 1957.

Michener, H.A. and Zeller, R.A. "A test of Gamson's theory of political trust orientation." *Journal of Applied Social Psychology,* Vol. II, No. 2, 1972, pp. 138-156.

Milbrath, L.W. *Political Participation,* Chicago: Chicago University Press, 1965.

Miller, A. "Political Issues and Trust in Government: 1964-1970." *American Political Science Review,* No. 3, Sept. 1974, pp. 951-972.

Moorhouse, H.F. and Chamberlain, C.W. "Lower-class attitudes to property: Aspects of the counter ideology." *Sociology,* No. 8, Sept. 1974, pp. 387-405.

Morgan, J.M. and Sonquist, J.A. "Problems in the analysis of survey data, and a proposal." *American Statistical Association Journal,* June 1963, pp. 415-434.

Muller, E.N. "A non-alienation theory of political protest." (mimeograph), University of Mannheim, 1969.

–––. "A test of a partial theory of potential for political violence." *American Political Science Review,* No. 66, 1972, pp. 928-959.

–––. *Behavioural Correlates of Political Support.* Paper delivered to the Conference on Alienation and System Support, Iowa City, January 1975.

Nieburg, H.L. *Political Violence: The Behavioural Process.* New York: St. Martin's, 1969.

Nordlinger, E.A. *The Working-Class Tories.* London: MacGibbon and Kee, 1967.

O'Conner, R.I. "Political activism and moral reasoning: Political and apolitical students in Great Britain and France." *British Journal of Politics.*

Orwell, G. *Down and Out in Paris and London.* London: Gollancz, 1933.

Paige, J.M. "Political orientation and riot participation." *American Sociological Review,* No. 36, 1971, pp. 810-820.

Parkin, F. *Middle Class Radicalism.* New York: Praeger, 1968.

Pettigrew, T.F. "Racially separate or together." *Journal of Social Issues,* Vol. 25, No. 1, 1969, pp. 43-69.

Priestley, H. *Voice of Protest,* London: Leslie Frewin, 1968.

Priestly, J.B. *English Journey.* London, 1934.

Ransford, E.H. "Isolation, powerlessness and violence: A study of attitudes and participation in the Watts riot." *American Journal of Sociology,* No. 73, 1968, pp. 581-591.

Robinson, J., Krusk, J. and Head, K.B. *Measures of Political Attitudes.* Ann Arbor, Mich.: Institute for Social Research, 1969.

Rokeach, M. *The Nature of Human Values,* New York: Free Press, 1973.

Rose, E.J.B. et al. *Colour and Citizenship.* London: Oxford University Press, 1968.

Rose, R. (ed.). *Studies in British Politics*. London: Macmillan, 1966.

——— and Mossawir, H. "Voting and elections." *Political Studies*, Vol. XV, No. 2, 1967.

Rose, R. *Governing without Consensus*. London: Faber and Faber, 1973.

———. *Politics in England Today*. London: Faber and Faber, 1974.

———. "Risorse dei governi e sovraccarico di domande." *Rivista Italiana de Scienze Politica*, Vol. 2, 1975, pp. 235-276.

Rosenbaum, J.H. and Sederberg, P.C. "Vigilantism." *Comparative Politics*, Vol. 6, No. 4, July 1974, pp. 541-570.

Rosenbaum, W.A. *Political Culture*. London: Thomas Nelson, 1975.

Runciman, W.G. *Relative Deprivation and Social Justice*. Berkeley: University of California Press, 1966.

Särlvik, B. "The Swedish party system in a developmental perspective," in Rose, R. (ed.). *Electoral Behavior: A Comparative Handbook*. New York: Free Press, 1974.

Schwartz, D.C. *Political Alienation and Political Behavior*. Chicago: Aldine, 1973.

Scraton, W.W. *The President's Commission on Campus Violence: Report*. Washington, D.C.: Government Printing Office, 1970.

Sears, D. "Political behaviour," in Lindzey an Aronson (1969).

Seeman, M. "On the meaning of alienation." *American Sociological Review*, Vol. XXIV, No. 6, Dec. 1959, pp. 783-791.

Skolnick, J.H. *The Politics of Protest*. New York, Ballantine, 1969.

Spilerman, S. "The causes of racial disturbances: tests of an explanation." *American Sociological Review*, No. 36, 1971, pp. 427-442.

Stouffer, S.A., et al. *The American Soldier*. Princeton, N.J.: Princeton University Press, 1949.

Tanter, R. and Midlarsky, M. "A theory of revolution." *Journal of Conflict Resolution*, Vol. XI, No. 3, Sept. 1967.

Taylor, C.L. and Hudson, M.C. *World Handbook of Political and Social Indicators*, 2nd Edition. New Haven, Conn.: Yale University Press, 1972.

Taylor, I. and Taylor, L. *The Politics of Deviance*. Middlesex, Eng.: Penguin, 1973.

Thayer, G. *The British Political Fringe*. London: Anthony Blond, 1965.

Tittle, C.R. and Hill, R.J. "Attitude measurement and the prediction of behaviour: An evaluation of conditions and measurement techniques." *Sociometry*, Vol. 30, 1967, pp. 199-213.

Toch, H. *The Social Psychology of Social Movements*. Indianapolis: Bobbs-Merrill, 1965.

Touraine, A. *The Post-Industrial Society*. London: Wildwood House, 1974.

Turner, R.H. "The public perception of protest." *American Sociological Review*, Vol. 34, No. 6, 1969, pp. 815-29.

Van den Haag, E. *Political Violence and Civil Disobedience*. New York: Harper and Row, 1972.

Von Eschen, D., Kirk, J. and Pinard, M. "The conditions of direct action in democratic society." *Western Political Quarterly*, June 1969, pp. 309-325.

———. "The organisational substructure of disorderly politics." *Social Forces*, Vol. 49, No. 4, June 1971, pp. 529-544.

Weigel, R.H., Vernon, T.A.D., and Tognacci, L.N. "Specificity of the attitude as a determinant of attitude-behaviour congruence." *Journal of Personality and Social Psychology*, Vol. 30, No. 6, Dec. 1974, pp. 724-728.

Weiss, P. *The Marat/Sade*. New York: John Calder, 1965.

Weissburg, M.C. "Commentary on DeFleur and Westie's 'Attitude as a Scientific Concept.'" *Social Forces*, Vol. 43, 1964-65, pp. 422-5.

White, B.W. and Saltz, E. "The measurement of reproducibility." *Psychological Bulletin*, Vol. 54, No. 1, Jan. 1957, pp. 81-99.

Wicker, A. "Attitudes versus actions: The relationship of verbal and overt behaviour responses to attitude objects." *Journal of Social Issues*, No. 25, 1969, pp. 41-78.

Wilson, G.D. and Patterson, J.R. "A new measure of conservatism." *British Journal of Social and Clinical Psychology*, Vol. 7, 1968, pp. 264-269.

Wilson, J.Q. "The strategy of protest: Problems of Negro civic action." *Journal of Conflict Resolution*, Vol. V, No. 3, Sept. 1961, pp. 291-303.

Yankelovich, D. *The Changing Values on Campus*. New York: Washington Square Press, 1972.

# ABOUT THE AUTHOR

ALAN MARSH is a Senior Social Survey Officer with the Office of Population Censuses and Surveys in London. He received his B.A. from the School of African and Asian Studies, University of Sussex, 1969, and his Ph.D. in Social Psychology from the London School of Economics and Political Science in 1976. In the period 1974-1975 Dr. Marsh was a Ford Foundation West European Scholar at the University of Michigan. He has published widely in the field of race relations.